WAR FROM

Crises in World Politics

A Series of the Centre of International Studies, and the
Centre for Rising Powers, University of Cambridge
Edited by Professor Brendan Simms and Dr Amrita Narlikar

EMILE SIMPSON

War from the Ground Up

Twenty-First-Century Combat as Politics

OXFORD
UNIVERSITY PRESS

OXFORD
UNIVERSITY PRESS

Oxford University Press is a department of the
University of Oxford. It furthers the University's objective
of excellence in research, scholarship, and education
by publishing worldwide.

Oxford New York
Auckland Cape Town Dar es Salaam Hong Kong Karachi
Kuala Lumpur Madrid Melbourne Mexico City Nairobi
New Delhi Shanghai Taipei Toronto

With offices in
Argentina Austria Brazil Chile Czech Republic France Greece
Guatemala Hungary Italy Japan Poland Portugal Singapore
South Korea Switzerland Thailand Turkey Ukraine Vietnam

Oxford is a registered trade mark of Oxford University Press
in the UK and certain other countries.

Published in the United States of America by
Oxford University Press
198 Madison Avenue, New York, NY 10016

Library of Congress Cataloging-in-Publication Data is available
Emile Simpson
War from the Ground Up: Twenty-First-Century Combat as Politics
ISBN: 978-0-19933-353-0

Printed in India on acid-free paper

I dedicate this book to fallen brothers: Captain Martin Driver, Royal Anglian Regiment, and Lieutenant Neal Turkington, Royal Gurkha Rifles.

CONTENTS

ACKNOWLEDGEMENTS

I am grateful to the British Army for granting me a Defence Fellowship, and to the Royal Gurkha Rifles, for allowing me the time to undertake it; this gave me the opportunity to consolidate the range of experiences that form the basis of this book. I would like to thank the Oxford University Changing Character of War Programme for the stimulating collegiate environment that enriched both the text itself and the process of writing it. Thanks also to the Master and Fellows of Balliol College Oxford, in particular Martin Conway and Nicola Trott. Above all I am indebted to Prof. Hew Strachan, without whom this work would not have been possible, and whose insights encouraged me to see my own experiences in new ways. I owe especial thanks to all those who made the Fellowship possible and whose responses to the manuscript have been invaluable, namely Prof. Daniel Marston, Lt.Col. Gerald Strickland, Maj. Shaun Chandler, Prof. Brendan Simms, Brig. Richard Iron, Col. Jon Hazel, Col. Alex Alderson, Maj Bruce Radbourne, Maj. Nick King, Capt. Mike Martin, Andrea Baumann, Capt. Mike Stevens, John Jenkins. I extend great thanks to those whose conversations have shaped this book, in particular Ian Gordon, Will Clegg, Thomas Wide, Angus Henderson, Mark Hreczuck, Charles "Mitch" Conway, Scott Peelman, Paul Hollingshead, Dr. Conrad Crane, Dr. Robert Johnson, Nate Pulliam, Jerry Meyerle, Rowland Stout, Robert Hargrave, Stephen Carter, and Rhys Jones for help with the title. I would like to thank Michael Dwyer, Jon De Peyer, Brenda Stones, Dr. Sebastian Ballard for the maps, the publishing team at Hurst, and the Cambridge University Crises in World Politics Series for accepting the book. Thanks for their support to

ACKNOWLEDGEMENTS

my parents, James and Luisella. Thanks also to Maj. (retd.) Gerald Davies and the Gurkha Museum. Finally, I would like to thank the officers and soldiers of the 1st Battalion The Royal Gurkha Rifles with whom I served, especially Maj. Will Kefford, Maj. Charlie Crowe, Capt. Jit Bahadur Gharti, and C Company, to whom I owe a permanent debt of gratitude: *hami jasto kohi chaina. Jai Gurkha*!

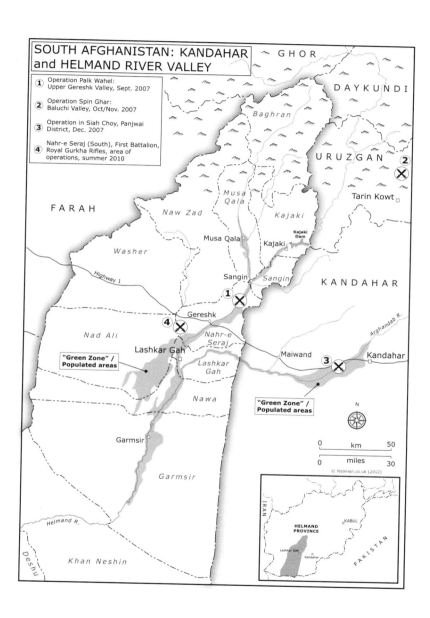

SOUTH AFGHANISTAN: KANDAHAR and HELMAND RIVER VALLEY

① Operation Palk Wahel:
Upper Gereshk Valley, Sept. 2007

② Operation Spin Ghar:
Baluchi Valley, Oct/Nov. 2007

③ Operation in Siah Choy, Panjwai
District, Dec. 2007

④ Nahr-e Seraj (South), First Battalion,
Royal Gurkha Rifles, area of
operations, summer 2010

G H O R

D A Y K U N D I

Baghran

U R U Z G A N ②⊗

Tarin Kowt

F A R A H

Naw Zad

Musa
Qala

Kajaki

Musa Qala

Kajaki
Dam

Kajaki

Washer

Highway 1

Sangin

Sangin

K A N D A H A R

①⊗

Gereshk

Arghandab R.

④⊗

Nahr-e
Seraj

Nad Ali

Lashkar Gah

Maiwand

③⊗

Kandahar

"Green Zone" /
Populated areas

Lashkar
Gah

Nawa

"Green Zone" /
Populated areas

N

0   km   50

0   miles   30

© Menman.co.uk (2012)

Garmsir

Garmsir

Helmand R.

Deshu

Khan Neshin

IRAN

KABUL

HELMAND
PROVINCE

Lashkar Gah

Kandahar

PAKISTAN

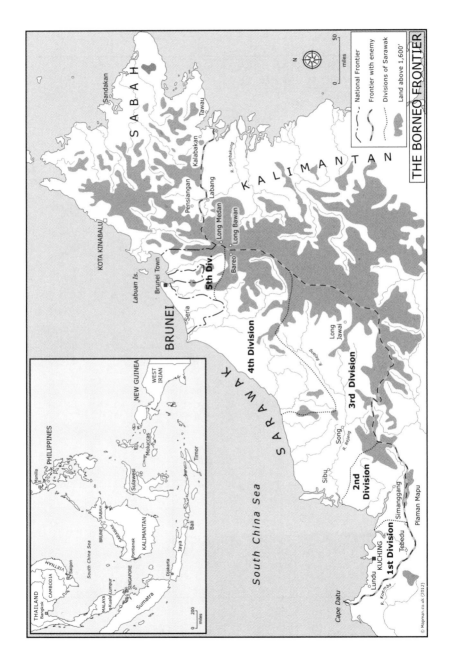

THE BORNEO FRONTIER

National Frontier
Frontier with enemy
Divisions of Sarawak
Land above 1,600'

N

0 ____ 50
miles

© Mapman.co.uk (2012)

SABAH

Sandakan

Tawau

KALIMANTAN

R. Sembakung

Kalabakan

Pensiangan

Labang

Long Medan

KOTA KINABALU

Long Bawan

Bareo

5th Div.

Labuan Is.

Brunei Town

BRUNEI

Seria

4th Division

Long Jawai

Baleh R.

3rd Division

Song

R. Rejang

Sibu

2nd
Division

S A R A W A K

South China Sea

Simanggang

Tebedu

1st Division

KUCHING

Lundu

R. Koemba

Plaman Mapu

Cape Datu

THAILAND
Bangkok

CAMBODIA

VIETNAM
Saigon

MALAYA
Kuala Lumpur

SINGAPORE

Sumatra

Djakarta

Jaya

Bali

South China Sea

Pontianak

BRUNEI
SARAWAK

KALIMANTAN

PHILIPPINES

Manila

Sulawesi

Moluccas

Timor

WEST
IRIAN

NEW GUINEA

0 ____ 200
miles

INTRODUCTION

War From The Ground Up presents a discussion of the concept of war in its contemporary context, specifically in terms of the conflict in Afghanistan. The tension that animates the argument throughout the book is the distinction between these practices: first, the use of armed force within a military domain that seeks to establish military conditions for a political solution, a practice traditionally associated with the concept of war; second, the use of armed force that directly seeks political, as opposed to specifically military, outcomes, which lies beyond the scope of war in its traditional paradigm.

These two practices are often not clear-cut in reality: they are not mutually exclusive in terms of a conflict's definition, as force can be used in alternative ways by different actors in the same conflict; neither can individual actors always be identified exclusively in terms of using one practice or the other, as the same actor can use force in both modes at different moments. However, my central proposition is that in order to clarify what is happening on the ground in contemporary armed conflict, there is a requirement to make the distinction between these two applications of armed force.

Conflicts that approximate to war in its traditional sense still exist, and will continue to do so. These are conflicts in which the military outcome does effectively force a political result. The military destruction of the Tamil Tigers in the Sri Lankan civil war is a recent example. However, the general tendency is a movement away from situations in which the armed forces set military conditions for a political solution: in many contemporary conflicts, while the activity of armed forces often

1

remains crucial to achieving a political result, military activity is not clearly distinguishable from political activity. The outcomes of contemporary conflicts are often better understood as constant evolutions of how power is configured, in relation to various audiences, and how that configuration is adjusted through the application of a variety of means, both violent and non-violent. This is distinct from the notion that war is the ultimate political act: decisive, finite, and primarily defined against one audience, the enemy. In correlation with this trend is the increasing departure from the traditional, sequential notion that diplomatic and military means set diplomatic and military conditions for one another through the lifetime of a conflict, but are essentially distinct both as means and conceptual boundaries, towards circumstances in which both are used simultaneously within conceptual domains that are not clearly military or political; neither war nor peace.

War From The Ground Up is not an academic account of the conflict in Afghanistan, nor is it a personal narrative. Yet in the three tours I have served in Afghanistan as a British infantry officer, it has struck me that this 'war' is really not what war is typically understood to be. This informs my analytical perspective, from the ground up, of the concept of war. This is a distinctive viewpoint: while most accounts of war look down at the battlefield from an academic perspective, or across it as a personal narrative, I draw instead on personal experience to look up from the battlefield and consider the concepts that put me there, and how those concepts played out on the ground.

The dynamics of the Afghan conflict as I have experienced them are encapsulated by the political posture displayed by an Afghan district governor I knew. He did not see most of the local insurgents as a problem. Was he actually on their side? No. He was from the provincial urban landowning class. Many of the local insurgents were the sons of their rural tenants. They did not represent a threat to his personal interests. He did, however, have a problem with other insurgents, namely the out-of-area Afghan fighters and foreign jihadists. Moreover, the governor was far more concerned about a group of the local police who were controlled by one of his political rivals. Against this background were powerful tribal and criminal dynamics which also cut across a polarised 'Afghan government versus Taliban' conception of the conflict. Such dynamics were not an anomaly. Most people in the Afghan conflict are really actors in their own right, and act according to their own interests, as opposed to that of a given side.

War is usually understood as a polarised contest. The concept of polarity is inherent in the idea that war is fought between sides. There are normally two sides in this concept of war. Even if the war involves several parties, they are typically separated and aligned as two sets of allies. This polarity is necessary for war as traditionally understood to perform its basic function as a political instrument: to provide a military outcome that sets conditions for a political solution. The distinction between one's own side and the enemy allows war to provide a see-saw-like, mutually exclusive outcome: defeat for one side is victory for the other. Even if the outcome of war is not absolute, the overall success or failure of a side in war is relative to an enemy.

The outcomes of many contemporary conflicts, however, are not exclusively defined against an enemy. In Afghanistan the defeat of the Taliban fades every year as a strategic priority relative to the stabilisation of the Afghan state, even if that means the endurance of a latent insurgency. Definition of the outcome of the Afghan conflict for the international coalition extends into the perceptions of audiences well beyond the insurgency. The Afghan people are deemed to be a central audience. Beyond Afghanistan the perception of the conflict's outcome within the Muslim world, and particularly in Pakistan, for instance, is a key factor. Moreover, the outcome in Afghanistan has global implications in terms of the credibility of the North Atlantic Treaty Organization (NATO), not least in terms of Chinese audiences.

This challenges the see-saw model of victory and defeat that is central to war as traditionally conceived. One can apply military pressure against the enemy in the Taliban, and more broadly to the insurgency. However, the defeat of insurgents in the military sense may assist in, but does not translate into, victory for the coalition because the interpretation of the conflict in terms of military metrics may well be a frame of reference to which most audiences do not subscribe. For example, the drone strikes in Pakistan are effective against the enemy in a military sense, but to argue that they contribute to a sense of coalition success among audiences other than the enemy is to ignore the widespread protests against them.

In war as traditionally conceived, military action is understood, and planned, in terms of its effect against the enemy. This is a fairly stable basis from which to determine a conflict's outcome, which is in the last analysis based on death and destruction, or its threat. However, when a conflict's outcome comes to be defined against audiences other than the enemy, strategy must adjust to the audience rather than assume that the application of force will be universally understood in terms of its effect against the enemy.

Thus in the traditional concept of war an audience other than the enemy (which is therefore beyond the range of armed force) is still considered to understand the conflict's outcome according to the military verdict of the battlefield between the sides actually fighting. When they do not, the military outcome does not provide a stable basis upon which to define a conflict's outcome. In such circumstances, should these audiences beyond the enemy matter to the strategist in terms of the conflict's outcome, strategy needs to consider military actions in terms of their likely political interpretations by these various audiences. This in turn leads to military action within war becoming highly politicised: the boundary between military and political activity is blurred. The use of force moves towards being simply an extension of policy the more it aims directly at political aims. This is distinct from the established idea, set out by Carl von Clausewitz (1780–1831), that the use of force in war is an extension of policy by other means. In the Clausewitzian sense, activity within the military domain ultimately seeks a political result, but via a specifically military outcome that sets conditions for it.

The blurring of military and political activity, common in contemporary conflict, can be elucidated by analogy to domestic politics in liberal democracies. In domestic politics, there is an animating tension between, say, two parties (like political parties and their various constituencies in liberal democracies, in the Afghan conflict the Afghan government and the insurgency can both be characterised as franchise movements which have an ideological core, beyond which people have subscribed to the franchise primarily to further their own interests). In the context of UK domestic politics, the other party may be an 'enemy' of sorts, but a party's success is only partly defined by popularity ratings relative to the other party.

Neither is the outcome a party has within a term in office defined in terms of 'victory' or 'defeat' (apart from in a general election, in which the result is, precisely, defined directly against the other 'enemy' party). Rather, the outcome that a party in government is recognised to have had is gauged: first, in relation to the audiences who are the objects of government policy; second, in terms of the effect it has, perhaps successful, perhaps not, along given policy lines. Both of these are subjective, and liable to evolve over time.

To produce and maintain its ambitions on given policy lines, the party needs to keep in balance an evolving constellation of political constituencies, deciding whose support to maintain, whose to win over, and whose to take risk on. This requires sustaining the loyalty of the 'home base' of more ideological supporters while simultaneously appealing to other audiences, many of whom will interpret political rhetoric foremost in relation to their own self-interest as opposed to strongly identifying with a political agenda. Success or failure will depend on how far a party can get this diverse set of audiences to subscribe to its political narrative.

Domestic politics take place in a fragmented, kaleidoscopic environment, in which sections of the electorate are thinking about their own interests, effectively competing vis-à-vis one another. While war is not usually understood through such a lens, the conflict in Afghanistan is precisely characterised by such a politically kaleidoscopic battlespace. The similarity between domestic politics and contemporary conflict is emphasised by the practice of counter-insurgency in Afghanistan: an approach that seeks to match actions and words so as to influence target audiences to subscribe to a given narrative. Moreover, just as in a general election, where parties need to configure their national narratives to find resonance in local issues, so too in many contemporary conflicts do big ideas need to be attuned to local circumstances.

The analogy with domestic politics in liberal democracies indicates how politically nuanced approaches, even down to the tactical level, are required to have effect in highly politicised, kaleidoscopic conflict environments. This approach contrasts with the default association of the application of armed forces in violent combat with a polarised conception of conflict as 'war'. The indiscriminate association of an aggressive and violent enemy with the traditional concept of war can frustrate more politically nuanced approaches. Hence a politician planning to have political effect may consult a geographical map to plan his or her campaign based on the distribution of voters. Yet the implication is that a political estimate has preceded decisions about where physically to allocate resources.

The military, however, tends by instinct to gravitate towards locations of violence to find and take on the enemy. In counter-insurgency, to intervene in a fight without first having anticipated the political risks and opportunities of such an action is in most cases (outside self-defence situations) to misunderstand the nature of such highly politicised conflict. The outcome of an action is usually better gauged by the chat at the bazaar the next day, and its equivalent higher up the political food chain, than body counts. The control of political space is as important, if not more important, than controlling physical space.

Strategic confusion can result when conflicts characterised by competition between many actors in a fragmented political environment are shoehorned into a traditional concept of war, with its two polarised sides. This fragmented competition may involve organised violence on a large scale, but is fundamentally different from war in the traditional sense: in many contemporary conflicts armed force seeks to have a direct political effect on audiences rather than setting conditions for a political solution through military effect against the enemy. In Afghanistan, activity (both violent and non-violent) by coalition forces and insurgents is frequently considered primarily in terms of the effect it will have on the local political situation, rather than thinking about the problem strictly in terms of the defeat of an enemy.

Whereas political considerations in war as traditionally conceived usually take place at the highest levels of military and civilian command, political considerations now drive operations even at the lowest level of command: the military dimension of war is pierced by political considerations at the tactical level. The fact that the military now tends to speak about 'battlespaces' rather than 'battlefields' acknowledges the expansion of the traditional, apolitical, military domain beyond the physical clash of armed forces to include its political, social and economic context even at the local level.

This trend is exaggerated when, as in Afghanistan, liberal powers and their armed forces conduct many actions through non-violent means, often termed 'non-kinetic' in military jargon. These have significantly expanded in the first decade of this century, not least due to the possibilities of the Internet and the proliferation of mobile phones, but also any number of other information media.

The 'information revolution' is as much a feature of the poorest countries in the world as the richest. This was brought home to me in an operation in rural Kandahar Province, South Afghanistan, in December 2007, when I caught up with a team of Afghan soldiers who were hunched over a mobile phone they had confiscated from a peasant in a remote mud compound, only to find them avidly debating the latest features of this new model, which was more advanced than the one I owned in the UK. This was not surreal, it was normal. The information revolution that is currently going on irreversibly accelerates and expands the information dimension of modern conflict right down to the tactical level.

In terms of the role of the information domain in contemporary conflict more broadly, as David Kilcullen has argued, successful insurgents, and now successful counter-insurgents, seek to persuade an audience in such a way that the political message delivered is an end in itself; this effectively reverses the role of information in conventional warfare, which tends to be about the explanation of actions.[1] The composition of forces at the tactical level, where civilian diplomats and development advisers, among others, often pursue the same local political goals as their military counterparts, reflects this fusion of the violent and the non-violent. Figure 1 is taken from a UK manual on stabilisation operations, which tend to be defined as operations of a lower intensity than conventional war that aim to have a given political effect in failing states. The diagram illustrates how people's perceptions are the object of the commander's activity; it also shows that he has many means, violent and non-violent, at his disposal to achieve this.

In summary, contemporary conflict tends to exaggerate this distinction: first, the use of armed force for directly political outcomes, outside the traditional concept of war; second, the use of force within a traditional concept of war, in which the military seeks a distinctly military outcome which then sets conditions for a political solution.

To re-emphasise the point, this distinction is not always clear on the ground. Commanders (in the context of Afghanistan, both coalition and insurgent commanders) will differ in their approaches. Should a commander ignore the political dimension of the conflict, and focus exclusively on killing those whom he perceives to be his enemies, then he is not using force for a directly political outcome; in reality few commanders will do this, but some have come close. By contrast, others, including the vast majority of coalition commanders in Afghanistan today, will be very closely attuned to political effect, be they at the tactical level, or

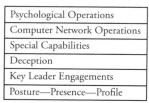

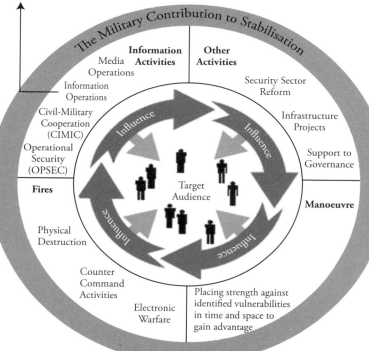

© Crown Copyright/MOD 2012

Figure 1: The Commander's Influence Tools: Aligning Actions, Words, and Images in Time and Space. From UK Joint Doctrine Publication 3–40: *Security and Stabilisation, The Military Contribution*, p. 3–15.

higher up, and consider all their actions, violent and non-violent, in these terms. What results is therefore a complex patchwork, which is why this distinction can be hard to perceive in actuality.

To develop this distinction requires an assessment of political and military activity not only in terms of the difference between political and military resources, but also in terms of what these activities seek to achieve: their aims.[2] In contemporary conflict resources remain a relatively stable axis of difference between military and political activity. Despite the use by armed forces of non-violent resources, whether organised violence has been applied or threatened, remains a central distinction between military and non-military activity (though this is increasingly complicated by activities such as cyber-threats). The difference between political and military aims, however, does not provide a clear distinction: how can military activity be distinct from political activity if, in seeking directly political rather than military outcomes, organised violence is a direct extension of policy?

When liberal democracies use force as a direct extension of political activity, the boundaries between war and peace become confused. There is no logical spatial, or chronological, limit to the 'War on Terror'. The 'War on Terror' as a phenomenon has been relabelled in various ways. One contemporary term is the 'Long War'. This is apt: the term implicitly makes an association between its objective, which, though ill-defined, can be understood partly in terms of a continuous effort to shape worldwide political perceptions according to the West's security interests, and its consequent lack of a clear end point, as perceptions continuously evolve.

What liberal powers do by blurring the conceptual boundaries between war and peace is often to militarise in a polarised manner pre-established patterns of political activity, which might otherwise not be part of the wider conflict. Robert Haddick wrote in 2008 that 'the Long War, characterised by tribal and ethnic conflicts, is a reality'.[3] That is indeed the case, but tribal and ethnic conflicts have been a reality for thousands of years; they pre-dated the Long War.

To frame political tensions, which have long existed, as part of a larger 'war' is a deliberate policy choice. That is, those tribal and ethnic conflicts were generally not a security problem for liberal powers until they were incorporated into a broader conception of a global conflict. The linkage of local and regional conflicts into a global conflict is not necessarily wrong in itself; there is a requirement to explain how conflicts, disputes and insurrections in different parts of the world affect one another. However, the consequence has been, and will continue to be, that liberal powers are pressured to take sides and invest military credibility in conflicts that may have no clear military solution within the terms of war as traditionally understood.

This interplay is clear on the ground in Afghanistan, where pre-existing patterns of political activity, be they tribal, narco, religious, sectarian, or many other possible factors, become issues which come to have a bearing on the political affiliations of Afghan audiences to either of the sides that compete for that affiliation in the Afghan conflict (usually understood as the government of Afghanistan and international coalition on the one hand, and the insurgency or the Taliban on the other). Yet in absorbing these pre-existing political tensions, the sides in the Afghan conflict themselves become less distinct, and become franchise movements, as a complex web of cross-cutting motivations compromise the neat polarised conception of conflict.

A book published by the Council for Emerging National Security Affairs (CENSA), a US think tank, in February 2011 was entitled *Hybrid Warfare and Transnational Threats: Perspectives for an Era of Persistent Conflict*.[4] Hybrid war is prominent in contemporary military thought, and I agree with many of its themes. Yet the conception of war as continuous conflict realised by the Long War subverts this traditional conception: that war is the ultimate form of decisiveness, which evidently requires an end point. The continuous conflict idea implicitly challenges the utility of war as a decisive political instrument.

This problem underlies the current debate as to the value of counter-insurgency as an approach to contemporary conflict. The Long War has been characterised as a 'global counter-insurgency'. This form of global counter-insurgency has been criticised on the basis that it is not as effective as conventional war, which Western militaries are better suited to fighting. The argument has sometimes been characterised as between 'crusaders', who advocate extending counter-insurgency-type thinking to defence policy beyond Afghanistan, and 'conservatives', who want the US to fight, and decisively win, conventional wars.[5]

The question might be framed as a choice: do liberal powers choose only to fight wars in their traditional form, typically by conventional means, and win them, or do they use military force outside the traditional conception of war, as a direct extension of political activity?

In operational terms, the latter option may be the more effective operational approach in politically fragmented, kaleidoscopic, conflict environments. Yet counter-insurgency can be expensive in blood and treasure.

INTRODUCTION

In strategic terms, preference for war in its traditional form might appear to be a more sensible option, as it presents a clear boundary between war and peace, which compartmentalises, and thus contains, violence in the world. Moreover, it usually allows Western military forces, when used, to win decisively in conventional military terms, rather than commit to conflicts which may lack a clear end point. However, there are evident problems with such a strategic approach. A policy decision only to fight wars with clear military solutions would mean to decline involvement in several situations in which enemies, especially non-state actors, refuse to engage in conventional battle against Western military forces. If there were legitimate Western security interests at stake, to refuse to fight anything but conventional battles might in reality mean not fighting at all, and thus to accept risk on those security concerns.

The use of armed force within a traditional conception of war on the one hand, and outside war, as 'armed politics' in a direct extension of policy, on the other, is an important distinction in the abstract. They are in theory fundamentally different modes of prosecuting conflict. However, because they are often hard to perceive on the ground, the failure to make such a distinction is understandable. The failure to distinguish, however, carries with it a risk of liberal powers potentially getting the worst of both parts: engagement in permanent conflicts in whose operational prosecution they are unskilled.

The reality may not be a choice between such stark alternatives. First, isolation of the alternatives implies that there is currently a choice. However, future conflicts may not provide the luxury of such choice; an enemy can force one to fight on his terms. That is a central tenet of hybrid war theory, and makes sense.[6] Counter-insurgency is likely to remain the more effective operational approach to deal with an enemy who wants to fight in an irregular manner. As this book argues, however, counter-insurgency is not a fixed but a highly flexible set of ideas, and does not necessarily need to be associated with expensive and drawn-out nation building. Counter-insurgency has often been a particularly resource efficient approach; yet the popularised historical record is partial because successful, resource efficient counter-insurgency campaigns have by their nature tended to be low profile precisely because they dealt with the issue discretely and with political sensitivity: how many people today have heard of the Dhofar campaign?

Second, the notion that future conflict in a world being so dramatically re-shaped by the information revolution can revert to traditional conventional war must be qualified. Short of absolute war, in which the primary goal is the annihilation of the enemy, the outcome of any more limited conflict will involve the perceptions of multiple strategic audiences who are unaligned to either side; how those audiences interpret the use of force politically will probably be essential to any military planning. This is likely to exclude the possibility that any future conventional war of a limited nature will take place in an apolitical military bubble whose outcome is defined exclusively against the enemy.

Third, contemporary conflict's conceptual boundaries are hard to define. The Sri Lankan civil war, for example, demonstrated a spectrum of means from low-intensity combat to high-intensity conventional battle on land and sea; only one side was a state actor (which evidently could not claim to represent the whole state), with the fighting being interspersed with periods of peace. The Chinese military aid to the Sri Lankan government in the final stage of the war, which tied into Chinese naval ambitions in the Indian Ocean, further complicates the categorisation of this conflict. Moreover, the conflict is not over in many ways. There remains a possibility of war crimes prosecutions in the future, should the political ground shift, and the governability of the Tamil population may well prove difficult in the longer term. Difficulty in categorising conflict, and making a distinction between war and peace, is frequent, not anomalous, in contemporary conflict.

These three caveats to the nature of this choice suggest that the distinction offered by such a choice does not impose a requirement to make a binary decision between two forms of conflict. Indeed to perform effectively in contemporary conflict, liberal powers do not need to make an absolute distinction between 'crusader' and 'conservative' positions.

To my mind, to have effect in a fragmented political environment, in which force is used as a direct extension of policy, counter-insurgency is usually a more effective operational approach than methods associated with conventional war. Counter-insurgency makes sense in theatres such as Afghanistan as an operational approach to achieve current policy goals. For a start, conventional war requires a clear enemy, which international coalitions do not have in Afghanistan or in the Long War. There is the option to use conventional force against insurgents, which has been used by Russia in Chechnya and by the Sri Lankan government against the Tamil Tigers. In both cases such methods were successful in a narrow sense. However, by engaging in such methods, which are typically associated with large-scale human rights violations, liberal powers compromise their own values.

The apparent choice between these two modes in which armed force can be applied is more usefully understood as a practical analytical tool, which operates in a dialectical manner. In terms of contemporary conflict, the analytical distinction between the use of force in war and in 'armed politics' outside war should in particular be made when liberal powers are tempted to elevate counter-insurgency from an operational approach within defined theatres to a global strategic approach. This is mistaken. The two are profoundly different propositions, even though they are already blurred to an extent in the Long War.

Counter-insurgency as the doctrinal basis of a national strategy is radically distinct from being the doctrinal basis of an operational approach. To conceptualise a national strategy as a type of global counter-insurgency is effectively to remove limitations on the conceptual expansion of the conflict, as an expanding multitude of different political issues are militarised in terms of their association with this concept. One consequence of the removal of limitation concerns the challenge to liberal democracies posed by Islamic fundamentalism. The liberal tradition, in the broad sense of the values that animate liberal democracies, is threatened by its use of a very broad and unstable concept of 'war' to deal with Islamic fundamentalist terrorism, an initially anomalous practice that seems now to have evolved into normality.

Moreover, there is today a particular urgency to investigate how to be effective in more limited, and typically more politicised, conflicts; for should strategists deem the use of force within more limited forms of armed conflict, and more moderate operational approaches such as counter-insurgency, to be ineffective, there may arise a temptation to apply military force in an unrestrained, absolute sense, because it 'works' more reliably in achieving a policy goal. That is, for the methods that decisively ended the Sri Lankan civil war to be understood as 'effective' is not only a profoundly dangerous attitude in terms of wider international stability, but represents the other side of the coin of failing effectively to prosecute armed conflicts using more limited and moderate operational approaches.

Finally, as the issue of how to define war rarely extends beyond specialist discussion, the public have not been much involved; yet the public's will and taxes must ultimately sustain strategic choices. The question of whether to commit to a 'generational war', to accept an 'era of persistent conflict', without a clear end-state, or, conversely, not to engage in countries in which there are genuine security concerns, should surely be an issue of public discussion, as the West seems to be sleepwalking into such a period of global generational conflict.

The first half of this book, Chapters 1 to 3, defines the problem and sets out the difficulty of employing a traditional paradigm of war in contemporary conflicts that tend to be characterised by fragmented, rather than polarised, political dynamics. Chapter 1 defines how war operates as a conceptual construct that seeks to connect armed force to political utility. Chapters 2 and 3 examine the evolution of war as a mechanism; in particular how war, as defined so influentially by Carl von Clausewitz, is today often misunderstood as a concept and has been misapplied in contemporary conflicts such as Afghanistan.

The second half of the book, Chapters 4 to 9, form three pairs that move on from the problems of the misapplication of the traditional paradigm of war to investigate possible solutions. Chapters 4 and 5 argue that strategy needs to be understood as a dialogue between the desire of policy and what is realistically achievable on the ground, rather than as a one-way relationship between policy and unquestioning tactical execution. This is necessary to construct a political context that enables any operational approach to be effective. Chapters 6 and 7 examine the construction of operational approaches, and argue for the utility of a pragmatic mindset in this context, using the Borneo Confrontation 1962–6 as an extended case study. Chapters 8 and 9 look at strategic narrative, the vital membrane that connects operational activity to its political context, a critical feature of contemporary conflict. They argue that the construction of strategic narrative resembles the art of persuasion, or rhetoric, as classically defined. The Conclusion considers contemporary strategic thought.

Strategy for liberal democracies involves all three parts of the state at war: the government, the people and the military. I have tried to write in a style that is not technical to acknowledge that all three need to be involved in strategy.

1

THE LANGUAGE OF WAR

Military activity has two possible connotations: the first is the actual use of organised violence, typically by armed forces; the second is the way in which this force is understood by an audience, particularly the enemy. Antulio J. Echevarria II has argued that 'while the US military remains eloquent in the vernacular of battle, it is still developing fluency in the language of war'.[1] If the 'vernacular of battle' is technical military proficiency, the language of war is what links the use of force to political meaning. The language of war in this sense is not war poetry or its equivalent; it describes the interpretive structure that 'war' provides to give meaning to the use of force, just as an actual language gives particular meaning to a given sound or script. This chapter argues that it is the language of war that gives wider meaning to the vernacular of battle; the strategist must harmonise them both for war to have utility as an instrument of policy.

War as an interpretive structure

The following passage is an account of the first moments of a battle fought by the Gurkha battlegroup I was part of in a mountain valley of Uruzgan Province, South Afghanistan in October 2007, during a two-week operation named *Spin Ghar* (White Mountain).[2] I wrote it up in 2008 after I returned to the UK, to document a personal experience before it was forgotten, with a view to it perhaps forming part of a regimental history later on. Re-reading it today, it is clear that this account has rough edges. However, I will reproduce it largely un-edited to attempt to transmit that experience, and show that for soldiers to be fixated with the enemy is normal, in the sense that when actually closing with the enemy in battle, any other way of understanding the situation goes against the emotional grain of the situation; for the protagonist to understand combat as anything other than an intensely polarised confrontation is in reality very difficult.

Figure 2: Detail of the narrow northern section of the Baluchi Valley, Uruzgan Province, South Afghanistan.

There is nothing more impressive than a company of Gurkhas in full assault order at night on the eve of battle. The three platoons and headquarters were arranged into five 'chalks', each sitting twenty metres apart on the tarmac runway, a surface which still felt hot after midnight. These were further divided into two 'sticks' of roughly fifteen men sitting behind one another; each of these would embark onto the designated side of their chalk's twin-bladed Chinook helicopter. My team (8 Platoon) had an air of confidence, aggression, and the residual apprehension which inevitably accompanies anticipation of close-quarter battle.

C Company was to lead the assault into the Baluchi Valley. This was an insurgent stronghold deep in the mountainous area of Uruzgan Province. There had been no international coalition troops here for over a year, since an Australian operation had successfully cleared the valley in a vicious fight, although the Taliban had since reoccupied it.

I had three hours sleep then woke up at 2300, had a shower, and got my combat gear on: desert combats; body armour; helmet; belt and pouches; twenty-two magazines worth of ammunition (one in my rifle, five in my belt, another emergency one in my rucksack, and fifteen in bandoliers which formed part of the platoon reserve); radio and spare batteries; night vision (helmet-mounted infra-red, weapon-mounted thermal sights); grenades (high explosive, smoke, red phosphorus); three litres of water; rations; bayonet; maps; and air photos of my platoon's first objective.

The platoon had rehearsed helicopter exit drills to the last detail. Every man understood the orders, and knew his part in the first phase of the operation to gain a foothold right in the enemy's command centre. What more was there to do at this stage?

The night was mild but dark, and the soldiers' faces, blackened with camouflage cream, glimmered in the half-light of the runway lights. I had a quick chat to Charlie Crowe, the company commander, who was walking around the company; he wanted everyone to be ready for a fight. This is the moment when at Sandhurst I would have imagined giving an inspiring pre-battle speech; in the event I delivered nothing of the sort. When I stood up to speak to the guys in the near dark I was looking at thirty professional soldiers whom I knew I could trust with my life and felt safe with. They were not superhuman, and many were quite young. Individually, some were probably braver than others, but as a platoon, each of them was a Gurkha soldier, not an individual. The self-perception of this status, and the ethos that underwrites it, or Gurkha *kaida*, meant that they would fight for one another, all get through it, and get through the enemy. In the end the platoon huddled together and my platoon sergeant, my three corporals (the section commanders) and I said a few brief words. I said something like 'All right lads, I have full confidence in you. Just do your job, pass on information, and make sure you account for your battle-buddy. We'll get in there and hammer them'. Anyone who has heard a group of Gurkhas acknowledge you with a resounding, short, and aggressive 'Yes, Saheb!' is filled with pride and confidence.

We had to wait two hours until 'Y-Hour' (take-off). I spent most of the time chatting to a group of my younger soldiers. Their chief topic of interest on that occasion was the secret method to chatting up 'European girls'. This continued in a series of ripostes, typical of banter with Gurkhas: 'Just tell them you're a Gurkha soldier'. 'But we are shorter than them, Saheb!' (Laughter from the rest of the section.) 'Well just impress them with exaggerated war stories'. 'But they will be afraid, Saheb'. And so it drifted on. The Chinook crew who came over to wish us good luck shook us back to the real world.

The rear ramp was down, and I sat behind the tail gunner. The seats were up for the assault landing, so all of my men sat facing each other on the metal deck. The rotor blades make conversation impossible except through headsets. I was given one as the chalk commander, so listened in to the chat between the pilots and the tail gunner. I watched the four other Chinooks and two Apache escort helicopter silhouettes fly in formation, all lights off, tearing across the *dasht* (desert) at low level, the lights of Kandahar city itself in the distance the only obvious reference point as we headed north towards the mountains. It was both amusing and nerve calming to have the pilots' game of hangman and I spy over the headset as the commentary which accompanied the visual spectacle.

Everyone re-focused as the aircraft climbed steeply then banked round a mountain range, and the air got a lot colder. I knew that 'L-Hour' (landing) was imminent. Would the small advance team be in position to secure the landing site? Would we be attacked on landing? What were the 'actions on' if we took casualties as soon as we stepped off the ship? All these questions raced through my head, but we had planned thoroughly and rehearsed all of these scenarios. In uncertainty, thorough knowledge of the plan is what one's immediate doubts fall back on. Hence the importance of the confidence we had in the plan and the Battalion Commanding Officer, Lieutenant Colonel Jonny Bourne, who had planned the operation meticulously with his staff. He would be landing thirty minutes after us with A Company and Battalion Tactical Headquarters.

The tail gunner gave us five minutes. We all shook each other. 'one minute!' Everyone stood up and held onto the rail as the pilot descended steeply. Sharp landing. Everyone buckles to absorb the impact, especially with the amount of weight we are carrying. Ramp fully down: go. Nothing is actually said, we all knew what we were doing. I jumped out, sank slightly into the soft ploughed field and looked up at the large mountain to my right as I ran. Good, that was East and I knew where I was from the air-photo engraved in my head. I ran forward 10 metres, made eye contact with my Corporal next to me, giving the signal to turn right. Another 10 metres, down on one knee, scanned the ground with my thermal sight for threats. The lads had piled out of the helicopter in seconds and the ship was already taking off by the time my Platoon Sergeant, Bel Gurung, had done the headcount—he gave me the 'all in' and we moved off. The grouped figures of the five chalks were visible in the other corners of the field as white heat signatures against a black background through my sight. The fainting 'chug chug chug' of the Chinook rotor blades gave way to total silence. We took off the plastic bin bags we had used to cover our weapons from the helicopter dust off.

I led the platoon to the designated rendezvous with the rest of the company. Everything was going to plan, and the worst scenario of contact on landing was now thankfully redundant. Out of the darkness came the guide: 'All right mate, how's it going? Basically, the Taliban's over there, and we're going to take you to the line of departure down this creek here, mate'. Things are far less stressful when you're actually on the ground and the 'Op' has started, and started well. A winding 300m in a stream to the start line and we would meet our intended H-Hour (start of the attack).

John Jeffcoat's Seven Platoon went in first on time at 0400. The sound of the bar mine used to blow the hole in the wall ripped through the night. Seven Platoon wrapped up their objective efficiently without firing a shot. They found a few men with AK-47s and ammunition whom they had taken well and truly by surprise. Quick chat with JJ on the radio net to gain situational awareness and confirmation that he was secure, and my lads moved to the next target. Now everyone was awake, we had to move fast. Confirm with lead Corporal that the imposing wall ahead of us is the right compound. Flank protection in position. Fire base in position. Assault teams in position. Engineers prep bar mine. Engineers plus two Gurkhas approach wall, bar mine in place. Get on the radio: 'Bar mine in twenty seconds'. Get down. Nothing, wait another minute to make sure it is not a delayed fuse. Dud. Engineers go up again, another bar mine. Bang. Feel the pressure of two bar mines go off from our position twenty metres away behind cover. Get up, use weapon-mounted torches to penetrate the dust that has been kicked up. This is the most dangerous part of the assault, and my job is to get the platoon forward. A neat compound clearance by two four-man 'bricks', over-watched by the roof team, who had clambered up as soon as the blast went off. Don't need to commit my reserve because there is no resistance. Compound clear. Rabindra's 9 Platoon echelon through us to take the next objective. My platoon is now the company reserve and we can settle a bit.

As dawn breaks there is a ghost town feel to the small hamlet that comprises 'Objective Churchill'. After a brief pause to re-balance the company, Charlie Crowe got his platoon commanders together and sent us out to clear the area. The insurgents had been playing their usual game of watching us and declining to fight at night, where our technology counted against them.

At around 8 a.m. my platoon was contacted from the right at a distance of 100 metres with a machine gun burst. One of my riflemen was hit just above his eye, probably by a ricochet. 'Man down!' Displaying routine bravery, one of my Lance Corporals, Bharat, ran out in the middle of this fire-fight to drag him into cover. My men dart for cover and fire back in the enemy's direction. Furious staccato shouting in Nepali-English mixture against a backdrop of automatic fire, ours and the enemy's: target indications from the riflemen who have spotted the *dushman*: '*najik ko ruck oooh bata, hoina, hoina...tyahan cha!* Moving left to right! *Aundai cha! Duita dushman, hoina tinjana*'. [Two/three enemy popping out intermittently by a tree.] Translated into fire control orders from the section commanders: '*dushman* half left *najik ko ruck* 100m *bata* section y-rapiiiiiid fire'. After pushing out flank protection, I leave the corporals to direct the shooting. I'm lying on my belt buckle with my radio operator getting an exact GPS grid for myself and telling Charlie where I think the enemy is and what they're doing. Casualty status from the Platoon Sergeant to tell me the casualty was safely back with the Company Sergeant Major. Sergeant Bel is invaluable; I know that he will square everything away so I can focus on the battle.

My platoon was not the only one in contact; in fact, we were at the periphery of the main battle. The insurgents were probing the company from several directions. The most intense fighting was going on to my flank, where there had been a serious casualty. JJ's 7 Platoon did very well and repelled the insurgents through sheer aggression, extracting the casualty under fire [two Military Crosses were subsequently awarded in relation to that action].

Charlie Crowe got on the radio net to give a reverse SITREP (situation report) and told us that we were now fighting a company defensive battle. The Apache helicopters circling overhead, and our snipers on the ground, were detecting and engaging insurgent teams in depth too. This was the opening of a three-day battle of frequent small skirmishes against a probing enemy.

Figure 3: Compound in Baluchi Valley immediately after fighting. Two Gurkhas on the roof scan the ground for the enemy.

How do we understand this event? On the one hand, we can see it through the concept of battle: one company did this, another company did that, and the enemy responded in a particular way. Within this military frame of reference, the outcome of the battle is an evolution of the military situation: success or failure is judged according to one's position relative to the enemy. If one asks a commander what is going on during a battle, the typical response will be a briefing, describing arrows on a map illustrating friendly and enemy forces. In this sense the concept of battle allocates a rational meaning to events. What could be seen as several men fighting somewhat chaotically is rationalised as the articulation of a military plan that gives meaning to the actions of individuals.

Yet battle is as much this rational phenomenon as a set of personal experiences for those involved. While this may be common sense, we typically distinguish personal experiences from the military outcome. Banter on the tarmac may be part of how a solider remembers the battle, but has nothing to do with its military outcome. Yet in the West's contemporary conflicts people's reception of events, including battles, through the lens of their personal experience does matter to the conflict's outcome.

In Afghanistan today the support of the people is vital to the outcome of the conflict for all sides. However, the peasants of the Baluchi Valley would not have seen the battle in terms of arrows on maps. For them it is not a 'company clearance of an objective as part of a wider battlegroup operation', which it was for us; they would not have known what that was. The discourse of battle we use to understand the phenomenon we are in makes little sense to them. From their homes they see snapshots of the battle between us and the Taliban and hear about other incidents from their friends. Their primary interest is the safety and property of themselves and their fellow villagers, usually far more so than the wider political struggle between the Taliban and the government.

In this case gaining the support of the people of the Baluchi Valley was not the primary objective of the operation. The objective was to clear out entrenched insurgent positions which were protecting their resupply route and to clear the way for an Australian reconstruction task force to hold the area. In a different part of the operation, Dutch troops were to clear the valley from the other end. This turned out to be problematic at the Dutch government level. There were thus several lenses available to view the operation, depending on one's point of view.

This has important ramifications for how we think about war and armed conflict more generally. If our strategy attempts to persuade people to subscribe to a particular political position (in Afghanistan essentially the rule of the Afghan government), we need to think about how those people will interpret our actions in political terms. To an extent, the concepts of battle, and war, do not need explaining; people are familiar with the concept of two sides fighting. However, to use this as an exclusive interpretive framework to judge success or failure in battle or war is a very narrow basis for understanding, as it does not incorporate the possibility of a personal response being the basis for a political viewpoint.

We may well have 'won' the battle in our own definition of the event, but members of the audience will have had their own political interpretation of the event, be it apathy, anger, satisfaction, or disappointment, that the insurgents have been cleared out, or something else: whatever it is, there will have been a political response as locals understand us on their terms. To borrow a term from social science, we 'cannot not communicate'.[3] Once we acknowledge that people's political views matter to our own definition of success or failure, an exclusively military definition of success or failure relative to the enemy in battle is insufficient.

At the political level it is perhaps too easy to assume that local actors understand the conflict in the same way. Conrad Crane, who edited the US Counterinsurgency Field Manual, has argued that this is, however, a common mistake that Westerners have tended to make in Iraq and Afghanistan. In both cases, local politicians at all levels of government simultaneously have a longer and shorter political viewpoint than does the coalition: while they will have to deal with the situation when the coalition leaves, they also need to survive the next political crisis.[4]

Time matters in interpretation of conflict. To use an analogy from the world of finance, that an investor making a long-term investment does not expect decisive short-term gains is the norm. However, war as a concept tends to associate the battlefield with brutal, finite outcomes whose results are immediately apparent (there are evidently exceptions, but the issue here is one of general public perceptions more than historical reality). The quick victories in the Gulf War, in 2001 in Afghanistan, and in 2003 in Iraq could legitimately promote such attitudes, since the Gulf War was a genuine war, and in their early stages these last two conflicts were genuinely wars too. One problem of extending the idea of war beyond the stage where that concept can legitimately be applied is that the association of battlefield activity with decisive outcomes is maintained. Yet in Iraq and Afghanistan the investment on the battle-field has often proved to be realised on a longer-term basis.

A good example of this was Operation Moshtarak, to secure key parts of Central Helmand that were held by insurgents in 2010, specifically in Marjah and Nad-Ali. The operation was also intended to have effect beyond Central Helmand, in presenting a clear defeat of the Taliban narrative to the Afghan people and wider international audiences. The initial clearance was successful. However, properly securing the area, gaining the people's confidence and establishing a basic level of govern-ance have taken longer. Only around two years later, in late 2011, did it become clear that the insurgency had been marginalised there to the point where the Afghan government could legitimately be said to con-trol those areas: a long-term success.

Counter-insurgency is a long-term investment. The effort has only been properly resourced in Afghanistan from 2009, and since then it has borne fruit. However, by applying a construction of war to the Afghan conflict, a counter-insurgent's successes are often masked because the bandwagon, which according to the traditional paradigm of war only really pays attention during periods of intense battlefield activity, has left by the time the gap between initial costliness and even-tual success is closed.

The way in which people's perceptions are influenced by the presence or absence of interpretive structures such as war is essential to under-standing contemporary conflict, but is sometimes neglected by strategy. To analyse the evolution of war as a military interpretive structure, we need to examine the relationship between war and strategy, and how this has evolved in the West's contemporary conflicts.

The function of war

What is war good for? War can provide an existential justification for its participants on an individual level, who may see their participation as an end in itself. Yet in terms of its political actors, typically states, war is usually understood as a political act. What defines 'political' has been contested. Policy can be defined narrowly as state policy; this suggests a degree of political calculation. Policy can, however, be defined more broadly. Carl von Clausewitz (1780–1831), for instance, understood policy as war's animating idea.

There is perhaps a temptation, particularly for liberal powers, to see war as an instrument of policy which is used 'rationally' for legitimate ends. Clausewitz's point is that all war has some kind of rationale ('policy') because it is a human phenomenon, but that rationale need not be 'rational' in the liberal sense. Indeed Clausewitz lived at the juncture of the Enlightenment, with its advocacy of reason, and Romanticism, with its penchant for emotional instinct. However one defines policy within the conception of war as a political instrument, the essential point is that war's justification, and thus its basic logic, lies beyond itself. This was famously summarised by Clausewitz: 'war...is a continuation of political intercourse, carried on with other means'.[5]

Two concepts are contained within the term 'means' in this dictum. The first concept is that war can be understood to be the phenomenon by which the clash of organised violence in time and space is identified. Clausewitz himself understood the essence of war to be the violent clash: 'essentially war is fighting'.[6] Ultimately wars are phenomena which are external to everyone; that is, wars go beyond the boundaries of any individual experience because they are defined by the aggregated activity of a multitude of people. However, what unifies individual experiences into 'war' is their association with the clash of organised violence. In this sense, while policy intentions of either side will shape war, war has its own independent existence, formed through reciprocal violent clash.

Even within a war, soldiers may feel well removed from 'the war', when pulled back from the line, where the violence is. There is a striking moment of self-realisation in *Quartered Safe Out Here* (1992) by George MacDonald Fraser, his autobiographical account of his experience as a soldier in the Burma campaign during the Second World War.[7] He is told by his Platoon Sergeant that he is the point man of his Platoon, which is at the head of the Battalion, which is itself the point Battalion of the point Division leading the 14th Army on its advance towards Rangoon; at this point the war seems far more immediate to Fraser than it would to a soldier marching in a column to the rear! Indeed for soldiers it is the experience of violence which tends to be the aspect of war most firmly imprinted on the mind.

Even for civilian leaders, who usually do not experience actual violence, the responsibility of the direction of violence through war invests war with a particular significance. While military preparations and diplomatic activity may anticipate a conflict, a war is typically understood to have 'started' when troops cross their line of departure in the expectation of combat. The opening stage of the Second World War for Britain illustrates the popular association of war and violence; it has come to be known as the 'Phoney War' because of the absence of serious violence.

The 'means' referred to in Clausewitz's dictum that war is an extension of policy by other means can therefore be understood in this first sense as the organised violence itself, typically the use of armed force.

The second sense in which the 'means' in Clausewitz's dictum can be understood is less obvious, but equally important. It relates to the notion that war itself as a phenomenon is a political instrument, not just the actual use of force within war. For example, British strategy in 1939–40 envisaged a long-haul strategy in which maritime economic blockade would play a central role, which was the policy adopted from the outset. To see the early period of Britain's part in the war as 'phoney' thus exemplifies both the fixation of associating war with violence on land and the analytical limitations of such a narrow conception of war.[8]

The limitations of a concept that only recognises war to be the actual use of organised violence—armed force—suggests a requirement for a broader analysis. War as an analytical unit can comprehend long periods of non-violence. The Napoleonic Wars, for example, actually involved relatively long periods of peace. At the time, it was uncertain if that peace would last, but it was not war. Retrospectively to impose the term 'Napoleonic Wars' suggests a broader analytical understanding, but that was not necessarily available at the time.

War's logic can to an extent operate in times of peace too, typically when there is a possibility of war if violence is threatened: arms races, for example, are driven by an anticipation of violence. Moreover, the political, social and economic dynamics that precede wars, and cause them, continue to operate in war; any analysis which only recognises periods of actual violence as 'war' will be limited in its conceptual boundaries. The proxy wars of the Cold War, for instance, cannot be understood outside the context of the possibility of an escalation to nuclear war.[9] War therefore needs to be understood as an analytical framework as much as an empirical phenomenon. Where to draw the line will vary in each case.

The second concept available in the 'means' of Clausewitz's dictum expanded the concept of war beyond the clash of organised violence to encompass its role as an analytical framework: 'war' itself was understood to be an instrument of policy distinct from the use of force within it. Clausewitz emphasised how war was a particular framework to resolve some kind of contested decision. For Clausewitz, war in this capacity was a type of trial.[10] Like a legal trial, war was a structure with a recognised form that provided a decision between opponents: 'by committing to this gigantic duel...both sides initiate a major decision'.[11]

To understand war as a means (an instrument) of policy in the context of Clausewitz's dictum therefore has two designations. The use of force is an instrument, but war itself is equally an instrument in terms of the analytical framework it provides for armed force to reach a decision—the war's outcome.

What reconciles these two 'instruments' within a single conception of war as an instrument of policy is the idea that force is simply another way to communicate meaning, another language. If force is a 'language', war is the interpreter who acts as a medium between the speaker and the listener. Clausewitz himself argued that force was simply another means to communicate a political intention; this supported his argument that war is a continuation of political intercourse by other means, not something entirely different. Thus political relations are not suspended when 'diplomatic notes are no longer exchanged', as war is 'just another expression of their [a people's] thoughts, another form of speech or writing'. Therefore 'the main lines along which military events progress, and to which they are restricted, are political lines that continue throughout the war into the subsequent peace'.[12]

Once seen as a form of language, force assumes the same properties as language in terms of the capacity to transmit meaning. The critical convergence of language and the use of force is that the 'meaning' of an action, including violent actions—like the meaning of the spoken or written word—is not self-contained. Meaning has to be interpreted by a human agent. The meaning of an action in war (the outcome of a battle, for example) may be mutually recognised, just as two people may well agree on the meaning of a text or a speech. Equally, two people may interpret differently the meaning of the same text, speech or action in accordance with their own prejudices. The same applies to the use of force.

The entire practice of deception, which is as old as war itself, is premised on the idea that force can be interpreted differently. William the Conqueror feigned a retreat at the Battle of Hastings which successfully lured King Harold's Anglo-Saxon army out of formation in pursuit of what they thought was a fleeing rabble, only to be defeated by a Norman counter-attack. In Afghanistan today there is huge competition between the insurgency and the Afghan government/coalition to present the meaning of actions in different ways. The 'outcomes' of skirmishes and battles in Afghanistan are rarely agreed upon.

As an infantry platoon commander in 2007, my first operation was the clearance of the Upper Gereshk Valley, Helmand, in a brigade-level operation. The insurgents were engaged, cleared out, and the mission was achieved. Yet the insurgents would also have claimed it as a victory because they had inflicted some casualties on us, and we did not stay to hold the ground we had cleared. The outcome of the operation in the longer term is debatable since several similar operations in the same area have been mounted since then.[13] Moreover, the 'meaning' of the battle for local people was most likely nothing to do with who 'won'. They would be far more concerned with the battle in terms of their own safety and property.

The importance of the visual deed and the instability of its interpretation in contemporary conflict extend to non-military actions too. For example, the video deliberately released online in April 2009 by a militant group linked to the Pakistani Taliban of a man whipping a young girl thirty-four times for being publicly seen with a married man was intended to gain approval for the implementation of Sharia law in the Swat Valley. The video actually provoked widespread criticism from the Pakistani public and increased support for their army's actions against militants.[14]

Once actions in war (both violent and non-violent) are seen as a form of language used to communicate meaning in the context of an argument, there is a possibility of being misunderstood. In order to use war successfully as an instrument of policy, one's actions in war ultimately need to be interpreted in accordance with the intent of one's policy. Thus strategy in relation to war seeks to link the meaning of tactical actions with the intent of policy to deliver the desired policy end-state. To do this, strategy seeks to invest actions in war with their desired meaning. Hence strategy has to harmonise both of the 'instruments' that are contained in the idea of war as an extension of policy by other means. Strategy does not merely need to orchestrate tactical actions (the use of force), but also construct the interpretive structure which gives them meaning and links them to the end of policy.

The imperative to have a stable interpretive structure in order to convert actions into a desired meaning can be illustrated through a theological analogy.[15] In this analogy the interpretation of the Biblical text (as a form of language) is taken to be analogous to the interpretation of tactical actions (as another form of language), typically the use of force, in armed conflict. The Catholic tradition has a certain view of the Bible's meaning. However, it does not place sole authority for the interpretation of the Bible in the Bible itself. That would open up the interpretation of the Bible to individual interpretation, which could be different from that of the Church. Therefore the Catholic Church requires Catholics to observe the authority of the Church in the interpretation of the Bible and in the determination of which texts make up the Biblical canon. The doctrine of the Catholic Church therefore serves as a structure to interpret the Bible.

The necessity of this interpretive structure for the Catholic tradition to preserve coherence of meaning has been exemplified in theological debates when Church authority has been ignored and scripture interpreted in an alternative way. The theological clashes and religious wars between Catholics and Protestants during the Reformation are just one prominent example of how politically significant interpretive differences can be.

In some branches of the Protestant tradition, which typically recognises only the authority of the Biblical text, the interpretive structure provided by the Church is removed. This opens up the possibility for widespread differences in interpretation, as individuals interpret meaning in accordance with their own beliefs and prejudices. The manifold theological differences between the Catholic and Protestant traditions exemplify this. One assumption that has justified the investiture of sole authority in the Biblical text itself is that the Bible has a 'literal' meaning which is self-contained. The multitude of branches within the Protestant tradition which claim a unique theological position based on a particular Biblical interpretation bears witness to the fact that there is no such thing as the literal interpretation of a text: a text interpreted literally is in fact a text read according to a personal interpretive structure.[16] Where people make up their own minds about the meaning of a text, rather than subscribe to a stable interpretive structure, the result is a fragmentation of meaning.

The meaning of any action, speech or text is not therefore self-contained; meaning is what is interpreted, and can vary in accordance with the pre-existing prejudices of the interpreter. This applies universally, not just in war. War as an abstract concept performs a similar function to Catholic Church doctrine in our theological analogy: it offers the strategist a template for the language of force to be interpreted in a way which invests it with military, and ultimately political, meaning.

War provides an interpretive hierarchy to give meaning to events within itself, typically a sequence of violent actions. A group of people killing each other in an apparently chaotic fight can provide all sorts of meanings for the participants and the onlookers. Yet war calls this event a battle. Battles are mechanisms which produce a meaning (an outcome) within the context of the wider war: a defeat, a victory, a stalemate. In accordance with the interpretive hierarchy of war, the significance of the outcome is relative to its impact on the wider war. In many cases the meaning of a battle is uncertain precisely because its effect on the outcome of the war as a whole is hard to gauge.

War, like a legal trial, or a boxing match, invests its internal actions with a particular meaning: actions in war, like the barrister's words in court, or punches in a boxing match, have a particular significance within that context. Clausewitz stressed that an action in war (such as the capture of a fortress, for example) has no value in itself. He used a metaphor from business: a single transaction only makes sense in terms of a businessman's overall balance; the advantages and disadvantages of a single action in war also only make sense in terms of the final balance.[17] The final balance is the outcome of the war, its verdict; this has a political meaning. War thus provides an interpretive mechanism that gives force political utility. This is political utility in the broad sense. Fear and the desire for self-preservation, for example, may not qualify as political motivations in a narrow sense, but are political in the broad sense of articulating the communities' intentions.

To summarise thus far, there are two symbiotic possibilities inherent in the proposition that war is an extension of policy by other means. The first is the use of organised violence to achieve an objective of policy. The second, often ignored, is the notion that war itself is an instrument in the sense that it provides an interpretive template which strategy uses to give a particular meaning to that organised violence. For strategy to be able to utilise war as an instrument of policy, it must be cognisant of both of these possibilities and harmonise them in accordance with the intention of policy.

The exploitation of interpretive difference: strategic asymmetry

We must make an important distinction between war in the abstract and war in reality. The instrument, or interpretive template, provided by war is different in theory and in practice. War in reality offers a fixed, universally recognised, interpretive template only in a narrow sense: ultimately, complete physical destruction of the enemy permanently remains a possibility in war. The physical imprint of force, namely its capacity to kill and destroy and literally force a behavioural change in the enemy, has always been a regular feature of human behaviour. This represents in a narrow sense a distinct and universally recognised military sphere: the historically enduring idea that if two sides fight, the winner and loser are distinguished in terms of who comes off best in physical terms.

However, in a broader sense, beyond physical destruction, war in practice does not provide a stable interpretive construct. While the physical imprint of violence may be permanent, the way in which that physical component of war is perceived in political terms is what gives force political utility. This is true in any conflict which ends with anything less than the total destruction of the enemy, as the 'defeat' of those who remain alive is by logic defined in terms that go beyond physical destruction: the meaning of defeat for the remaining enemy is a perceived state. For war's outcome to have purchase on people, they need to accept its meaning; if they do not, they may well see things differently. Beyond physical destruction, war does not therefore provide the strategist with an apolitical military domain whose rules are fixed, within which the use of force relative to the enemy is the only variable which influences the outcome of war.

A war's military outcome is not a stable concept beyond the narrow physical sense, as it requires the people upon whom that outcome is supposed to have meaning to interpret events in the same way as the strategist who seeks that outcome. Thus if one uses war as an instrument to achieve a political outcome, one must align actions with an understanding of how the recipient will interpret them. Put more formally, that understanding can be described as an interpretive framework that invests the actions that it bounds with a meaning that people accept. Thus strategy cannot think about the use of force as an instrument of policy which operates exclusively in a fixed military interpretive environment provided by war should people not see events through this lens (a circumstance frequent in contemporary conflict). Strategy must in reality configure the abstract template of war to provide an interpretive structure that has purchase on its audiences. In short, war is a malleable interpretive concept which needs be adjusted to invest force with the meaning desired by policy.

Strategy's ability to adjust war's interpretive concept, and mould it to its advantage, is premised on the assumption that war is a flexible, rather than a fixed, interpretive structure. That assumption is in turn premised on the fact that war is not a single, objectively definable, event.

War in practice is not a single phenomenon. A war's boundaries tend to be defined by fighting. The idea that there is, or was, 'a war' relates only to the idea that both sides acknowledge to be in the same fight in a geographical and chronological sense. Yet if war is a continuation of policy, the limits of 'a' war even in time and space can be contested. For some of the insurgents in the current conflict in Afghanistan, their war is part of a wider war against the West. For others, it is a war limited to Afghanistan. For the majority, it is about local issues.

The coalition shows the same lack of definition: some of the junior partners see their primary interests in terms of the diplomatic benefits of supporting the coalition; for others it is a wider regional conflict; for various constituencies of coalition domestic populations, the conflict is part of a thematic struggle in relation to fundamentalism, drugs, women's rights, or other factors and combinations; for others still, the conflict now has no clear aim other than to get out with some credibility. Some coalition partners are on a 'reconstruction mission' and resist the notion, for perfectly legitimate reasons, that they are involved in a war. The first reference by the German Chancellor to German forces being in a war was made only in September 2009, despite involvement in the same coalition command structure since 2001.[18] In reality, among insurgents and the coalition alike, the boundaries between these definitions, like 'the' war's own boundaries, are confused and evolve.

The coalition campaign in Afghanistan will focus on transition to Afghan security forces until, on current plans, the process is complete by 2015, even though a smaller coalition force will likely endure. This process will draw out any differences in the interpretive structures through which the government of Afghanistan and coalition forces understand the conflict. Geographically, there may well be areas on the periphery that the Afghan government are not overly concerned about securing, yet in which coalition forces have invested significant credibility, and lost many lives, to that end. The Afghan government is also likely to have a far more nuanced view of which entities, groups or individuals should be targeted on the basis of their affiliation to the insurgency. The powerful criminal patronage networks which operate in Afghanistan may be a coalition target, but unless they pose an existential threat to the Afghan state, they may well not bother the government, especially since these networks typically have strong government connections.

Many wars are not fought over the same political goal, which makes the notion that war provides a single 'decision' redundant. Hew Strachan argues in an article on 'Strategy and the Limitation of War' (2008) that in retrospect wars are often seen, mistakenly, as single units.[19] He uses the two World Wars as examples. The very term 'First World War' implies a single phenomenon. Yet individual states understood the function of that war in particular terms. Japan seized the German colony of Tsingtao in China. This foothold on the Shantung peninsula was the start point for subsequent Japanese imperialism in China and the Pacific. Turkey also joined the war for regional objectives. The Young Turks saw an opportunity for the Ottoman Empire to throw off the yoke of Great Power domination. Strachan argues that 'three Balkan states entered the war to advance local ambitions, not to promote the broader claims of the Great Powers, the values of German *Kultur*, the rule of law, or the rights of small nations'.[20] Indeed, through the eyes of small powers, Strachan states that the First World War started as a Balkan war, the third since 1912, and it continued as one beyond 1918. As a war of Turkish independence, it continued until 1922. Therefore 'to understand the First World War as a global war, we have first to disaggregate it into a series of regional conflicts'.[21] Strachan's argument illustrates the concept that war does not provide a single, universal, interpretive structure. Each actor fought its own 'war' for its own ends. This was primarily defined in terms of difference in political aims.

General Sir Rupert Smith identified this in his experience of coalition warfare in the late twentieth century: 'the glue that holds a coalition together is a common enemy, not a common desired political outcome'.[22] In the context of the 'Long War' and the war in Afghanistan, the idea of a common enemy to hold together coalitions is so powerful that it distorts strategy, as insurgencies which are actually composed of a multitude of different actors tend incorrectly to be categorised as homogeneous enemies. Conversely, it also distorts the Taliban leadership's political agenda, as their superficial coherence with the wider insurgency is based partly on the presence of an enemy against whom they can unite; yet if that enemy does leave, they may well fracture and lose power. The label of war, when used to package a historical, or an ongoing phenomenon, can ignore critical nuances; the term 'the First World War', like the 'war in Afghanistan' are labels that suggest a degree of coherence to the war's spatial and chronological boundaries which were, or are, in fact unique to each participant.

Yet the time and space argument does not extend to all wars; some wars were essentially a single phenomenon in a physical sense. The Falklands War of 1982, for example, was for the most part the same in time and space for both sides.[23] The time and space argument in itself is therefore insufficient to challenge the idea that war can provide a single, fixed, interpretive structure. In cases such as the Falklands, it is tempting to argue that war did, more or less, provide just that (although the tensions between Britain and Argentina over the Falklands at the time of writing this book in February 2012 indicate that even the well-defined period of actual fighting was only part of a broader and ongoing confrontation).

However, in any war, regardless of how close it comes to being understood as a single entity in time and space, 'war' cannot be a single interpretive structure because war does not have independent authority to adjudicate its own outcome.

'War' does not decide who wins and loses. The idea that 'war' provides a verdict implies that both sides have relinquished authority to decide the war's verdict to 'war' itself, as if 'war' is an independent judge who lies beyond human agency. That 'war' is such a judge is necessarily an (erroneously) implied proposition when military activity is incorrectly understood through the lens of a disconnected and self-referencing military domain, in which armed forces fight each other subject only to the verdict of 'war'. Clausewitz's comparison of war with a legal trial is ill-founded in the sense that in a court of law there is indeed an independent judge. The legal trial is a single, legally defined, interpretive structure into which both sides enter and receive an independent verdict. War is a contest, which may resemble a trial, but with a key difference: each side is its own judge. This can be taken to extremes, especially in a context in which international law is not upheld. Desperate measures in war are often proportional to perceived loss.

Clausewitz correctly described war as a 'clash of wills'. If the military verdict of the battlefield is mutually recognised, this is not because both sides have accepted the verdict of some abstract God of War: one side has forced its will over the other. War is a competition to impose meaning on people, as much emotional as rational, in which one's enemy is usually the key target audience. Defeat is not a 'verdict' handed out by an independent arbitrator of war; defeat is a perceived state which typically is violently forced (or successfully threatened) by one side upon the other. If a war is in progress, by logic neither side has yet given up: each side is still trying to impose its verdict, its judgement, on the other (or at least to mitigate the sentence of the other). Defeat occurs when one side accepts the verdict given by the other side, is destroyed, or becomes no longer relevant. The political compromises that have settled most wars are indicative of the difficulty of ever fully imposing a verdict on the other side.

The central deduction for strategic thought is that war is not a military 'boxing ring' that both sides enter into with a fixed set of rules (a single interpretive structure), from which a verdict is independently adjudicated purely on the basis of the fighting. War is a street fight. Each party fights for its own reasons, and by its own rules. Any 'verdict' from a street fight is entirely subjective beyond the physical impact, and possibly death; if one wants one's opponent to accept one's 'verdict', that meaning needs to be forced upon them. There may be a crowd watching, in which case to be seen to 'win', if one cares for their opinion, one's rules need broadly to align with theirs (we will deal with the issue of audiences in the next chapter).

The fact that each side plays by its own rules need not preclude a common interpretation of a particular action in war. Interpretation of international law may condition responses to the extent that they are similar. Moreover, several battles throughout history have been mutually acknowledged as a defeat for one and a victory for the other. For instance in the year 9 CE, three Roman legions under Publius Quinc-tilius Varus were totally destroyed in the Teutoburg Forest in Germania (near present-day Osnabrück). This was hailed as a major victory by the Germanic chief Arminius, who sent Varus' head to other Germanic chiefs to try to form an anti-Roman alliance. The Emperor Augustus clearly acknowledged the defeat, reportedly shouting from his palace walls, 'Quinctilius Varus, give me back my legions!' This definite identification of defeat was confirmed when Roman historians subsequently referred to the battle as the *clades Variana* (the Varian disaster).[24] However, one must not confuse a mutual acknowledgement of a battle's meaning with the idea that war in these cases provides a single interpretive structure.

What we have in such cases is not both sides submitting to the 'rules' of war in the abstract; instead both sides still have their own set of rules, but they are symmetrical. That is, when war does provide a common interpretive structure, it is because both sides are using an identical interpretive template of war. This can create an illusion that war is a single interpretive structure, but it is only an illusion. The exception to this is the concept of absolute war, which is rarely found in reality. In such a circumstance, where complete physical destruction of the enemy is the only goal, war is perhaps a universal cognitive concept (and nor should we lose sight of this possibility in an era of nuclear weapons).

In some situations the key variable is the extent to which the war is fought over the same issue. The more there is a disparity between the combatants' respective policy aims, the greater will be the degree of asymmetry in their application of the interpretive structure provided by war. However, strategy can also exploit asymmetry when the conflict is essentially fought over the same goal. In this latter case the emphasis will be primarily on having a flexible understanding of the military utility of armed force on the battlefield.

When symmetry is lost, what we have are asymmetric interpretive structures. The Vietnam War is perhaps the classic example of this in the twentieth century. In April 1975 in Hanoi, a week before the fall of Saigon, Colonel Harry Summers of the US army told his North Viet-namese counterpart Colonel Tu, 'You never beat us on the battlefield', to which Tu replied, 'That may be so, but it is also irrelevant'. The North Vietnamese may have not beaten the United States 'on the battlefield' in the sense of the physical destruction of the enemy, but a week later they did effectively beat the South Vietnamese by a conventional invasion, having outlasted the US political will to fight. Interviewed in 1996 Colonel Summers stated: 'We were caught up in this business of counter-insurgency, winning hearts and minds, the whole business of a social revolution rather than a war. North Vietnam was playing by the old rules. They saw it as the Second Indochina War'.[25]

This vignette exemplifies how war is a personalised interpretive structure for each actor (normally each 'side') in war, but can also vary within an organisation, such as the US military in the case of Vietnam. The interpretive structure each side possesses will depend on how the template of war in the abstract is applied to reality. In cases where the meaning of battle is mutually recognised, both sides have effectively applied the same template. However, one side can deliberately move away from an interpretive structure that is symmetrical to the enemy's in order to achieve an advantage. This emphasises how the application and adjustment of the interpretive template of war when used in reality is as much an instrument of war as the use of force within it.

As war's most conspicuous feature is combat, it is easy to become preoccupied with the notion that battles define the meaning of wars, normally in terms of victory and defeat. Colonel Tu's response encapsulates the argument that battles are only what define wars and their outcomes if, for the participants, battles define wars and their outcomes. This idea becomes progressively more important the further one moves away from the battlefield and towards the strategic level (that is, one would not want to forget that for the soldier on the battlefield, the brutal exchange of violence will always be the central feature of combat experience, and will remain very influential in how he personally gauges a battle's outcome).

Colonel Summers, in his interview, highlights the fact that modes of understanding war as a cognitive unit can vary, and that this has profound strategic significance. In his analysis of Vietnam, while both sides in a physical sense fought the same war, their interpretive concepts of the war differed significantly, and allocated different meanings to the same actions. This is what is communicated by Colonel Summers' metaphor of the United States and the Vietnamese having played by different rules.

Vietnam is an example to show that strategy has to comprehend war as an interpretive construct. While there were tensions in US strategy making, and several actors who saw things differently, mainstream US strategy during the period of US escalation in Vietnam assumed that war was an essentially stable interpretive construct. Indeed this assumption had not been significantly challenged in the Second World War or Korea, where many of the senior US officers in Vietnam had cut their teeth. General Westmoreland's emphasis on destruction of the enemy within a limited war context (a concept familiar in military theory associated with a traditional, Clausewitzian, paradigm of war) did not achieve sufficient purchase on the North Vietnamese political leadership during his tenure to give the apparent tactical victories political utility.

Strategy has the ability to define war itself as an interpretive template in its interests. This can be taken to extremes by the calculating political leader, who can totally invert the normal association between military victory and a successful political outcome. For example, in 1973 Egypt could be thought to have been militarily defeated by Israel in the Yom Kippur War. However, Anwar Sadat, from one perspective, very much achieved his intent, which was primarily a re-negotiation of the Suez Canal issue at the UN in his favour.

Asymmetric warfare has two connotations. It operates in a different sense within both of the instruments of war implied in the means of Clausewitz's dictum that war is an extension of policy by other means.

In terms of the first instrument, the use of force, asymmetry is common sense. It means that one gains an advantage by fighting differently: attacking with overwhelming force, using airpower against people on the ground, attacking at night, not wearing uniform, the use of roadside bombs. All tactical actions seek an asymmetric advantage over the opponent.

In terms of the second instrument, the interpretive structure provided by war itself, asymmetry means that the actors in war, normally 'sides', possess a different interpretive template of war. To return to the metaphor of war as a trial in which each side is its own judge, it may well be the case that both judges are using the same—symmetrical—criteria for judging the case; in this case there is an illusion that there is a single set of rules provided by war. Yet the discerning strategist may see that this is an illusion, and change his rules to his advantage. This is asymmetry in the strategic sense. By logic, once one side opts for strategic asymmetry, the other side is no longer symmetric either. Both sides are now in competition to construct more appealing strategic narratives of what the conflict is about. Strategy becomes increasingly similar to rhetoric, the art of persuasion (which is the subject of Chapters 8 and 9).

This chapter has sought to describe the language of war in terms of an additional, and often unrecognised, possibility in terms of how we understand the 'means' in Clausewitz's dictum of war being an extension of policy by other means. The actual use of armed force for political ends is the more obvious interpretation of the dictum. However, without harmonisation with the interpretive structure provided by war, the less obvious interpretation of the dictum, armed force may fail to have political utility because it is misunderstood.

The two means available in Clausewitz's dictum do not compete with one another; they are symbiotic. Force does possess a universal interpretive quality in the specific and extreme sense of physical destruction. Dead people cannot interpret anything. If force is used in this manner, typically in the context of unrestrained war, force does have a universally recognised literal sense. Although, even then, those still alive will interpret those deaths. The abuses that often accompany the absolute use of force may restrain an actor who looks beyond the fighting to its consequences. The International Criminal Court may, or may not, play an important role in this regard in the future.

The majority of conflicts, however, do not approach absolute states; their outcomes are defined in more subjective political terms. Because the utility of force in terms of its perceived outcomes is not wholly subject to literal interpretation, the strategist in war has to combine the physical and the perceived, the two possibilities of Clausewitz's dictum; their interaction is how the strategist achieves the goal of policy, which is the subject of the next chapter.

2

CLAUSEWITZIAN WAR
AND CONTEMPORARY CONFLICT

The notion that war involves armed opponents (one's own side and the enemy) is as old as war itself. For example, in *The Art of War* written by Sun Tzu in ancient China (possibly sixth century BCE), this idea is taken for granted. Polarity between two sides allows war to provide a see-saw-like outcome: defeat and victory are mutually exclusive; they are defined in inverse relation to one another.

In Afghanistan, in the earlier phase of the conflict, the coalition shoe-horned the actual political situation into a construction that was more polarised than was the case in reality. The overly binary conception within which military force was used antagonised the political situation. The 2006 International Security and Assistance Force (ISAF) deployment into Helmand Province, Southern Afghanistan, which was based on a British-led task force, exemplifies this.

One argument concerning the UK deployment into Helmand is about miscalculation: that the deployment was not the primary British governmental option in terms of the UK role in Afghanistan, but was a course that was not corrected when events unfolded to bring about such a move. The purpose of the deployment was then not clear, or at least, there were significantly different interpretations, creating a misalignment between policy and method. This argument, interesting though it is, lies outside the scope of this book. To offer a properly researched

Figure 4: This Louis XIV cannon bears the inscription '*ultima ratio regum*' (the final argument of kings), a powerful visual statement asserting that war in its traditional conception has been seen as the ultimate form of political decision.[1]

evaluation of this line of argument would require far more access to UK government and North Atlantic Treaty Organization (NATO) policy documents than is currently available. Hence I take the UK deployment as a start point, and examine some of the issues that shaped the early development of the campaign once it had started.

The factor I focus on is the extent to which the interpretive framework of Clausewitzian war, in which armed forces are supposed to set military conditions for a political solution, was dragged into a circumstance that was in actuality far closer to the use of force for directly political outcomes.

Helmand 2006

On 4 June 2006 one of the earliest major contacts of the British army in Helmand took place in the village of Alizai, just east of the town of Nowzad, in northern Helmand. A Gurkha platoon was ambushed while driving through the village on its way to form an outer cordon to arrest a suspected insurgent commander. The Gurkhas' role was part of a larger operation by the 3rd Battalion the Parachute Regiment, called Op Mutay. The arrest operation turned into an intense six-hour battle for the Gurkha and Para soldiers. Before the operation, the local Afghan police commander advised the Gurkha platoon commander to expect a fight in the village and refused to go on the operation himself.[2] The Alizais are a tribe of northern Helmand, and this village was one of theirs. The symbolism that the British army's first big fight should be here was perhaps obvious to the Afghan police commander at the time. Yet in 2006 the language of the British army in Helmand was of the Government of the Islamic Republic of Afghanistan, 'GIRoA', versus the Taliban.

This vignette exemplifies in microcosm a wider conceptual problem of the British campaign in 2006. A traditional, polarised view of the conflict was overly privileged, which encouraged the army and its political masters to understand those who offered armed opposition to the Afghan government primarily as a unified 'Taliban' movement. This had reciprocal consequences, and encouraged the polarisation against British forces of actors and groups who were not particularly ideologically committed to the Taliban.

In a formal submission of evidence to the British parliament's 2009 report on Afghanistan-Pakistan, Lord Malloch-Brown, a Foreign Office minister in Prime Minister Gordon Brown's government, stated: 'as with any good military action by this country over the centuries, we have stepped up our game and our commitment, and reinforced our effort to deal with an enemy who has been tougher than we initially thought would be the case. Please do not misunderstand me: it is not a surprise that we faced an insurgency in Helmand, which is the reason why we went there. We knew it was there, we wanted to take it on and it has been a hard fight'.[3] Apart from the fact that it has been a hard fight, this analysis is confused.

While there was certainly serious tribal and factional tension, there was not a significant pre-existing Taliban insurgency in Helmand. There had been sporadic but intense individual fights involving coalition forces across southern Afghanistan pre-2006. However, if there were a more genuine Taliban-led insurgency in the south, its focus was on Kandahar more than Helmand. The ferocious fighting in 2006 between the Canadians and insurgents in Panjwai District to the west of Kandahar city was arguably the Taliban leadership's focus in the south.

In Helmand, there was a spate of assassinations of people associated with the Afghan government in late 2005 and early 2006, but not widespread fighting. The British Secretary of Defence John Reid saw the mission in 2006 as a reconstruction mission. His statement at a Kabul press conference on 23 April 2006 about his aspiration that there might have been no shots fired has been taken out of context. The statement communicated his intention that British forces were not looking for a fight; this made sense at the time precisely because there was no large-scale insurgency in Helmand. This perspective is at odds with Lord Malloch-Brown's recollection of the facts. So where did the insurgency come from?

A large core of the 'Taliban' of 2006 used to be on the Afghan government 'side', in that they were the militia controlled by Sher Mohammed Akhundzada, the Provincial Governor from 2001 to 2005. Akhundzada stepped down as the Provincial Governor of Helmand in December 2005, largely due to British pressure in Kabul to have him removed, mainly because he was involved in narcotics and had abused his position in government to further his own interests: nine tons of opium had been found in his compound in June 2005. In a 2009 interview with the *Daily Telegraph*, Akhundzada stated what is common knowledge in Afghanistan, but has bizarrely not received much attention in the UK:

'When I was no longer governor the government stopped paying for the people who supported me', he said. 'I sent 3,000 of them off to the Taliban because I could not afford to support them but the Taliban was making payments'.[4]

Akhundzada's argument exploits the polarised model through which the coalition viewed the conflict. Thus he presents himself as the victim who is forced to support his men by having the 'Taliban' pay them. Akhundzada hides behind the idea of the 'Taliban' to conceal his real agenda, which was to keep himself in power. Many of the 'Taliban' in northern Helmand were his men, over whom he still exercised control. Akhundzada's actions in Helmand were consistent with his self-interest, in that his line has always been that only he can deliver security in the province; after he was sacked as governor, his subsequent actions could be interpreted as a message that he wanted to show that the coalition needed him because he was the only one who held real power. Akhundzada had been shamed and lost face: a key factor given his family's importance in the province, which was perhaps not sufficiently recognised at the time.

Akhundzada's actions following his dismissal are only to be considered a change of 'sides' if one erroneously imposes a polarised model of war on the conflict. Akhundzada and his men did not 'change sides'; they remained on their own side. Akhundzada was, and remains at the time of writing, very close to President Karzai. The two families became friends in exile in Pakistan in the 1990s, and have intermarried.[5] After Akhundzada was dismissed, his brother became the Deputy Provincial Governor and he himself became a Senator in Kabul. He has consistently undermined the Provincial Governor Gulab Mangal, at the time of writing, and has sought to have Kabul appoint district governors and police chiefs in Helmand who are loyal to him. The Governor of Kajaki District in northern Helmand, for example, is at the time of writing Mullah Sharafudin Akhundzada, his brother-in-law. As long as such nuances are viewed through a polarised model, we fail to understand the politically kaleidoscopic dynamics of the conflict.

The majority of insurgents in Helmand in 2006 were Afghan militias, including Akhundzada's Alizai militia in northern Helmand, who were fighting for their interests.[6] There was a strong interplay between their motivations and that of the Taliban leadership, which had been trying to re-assert itself in the south from 2002. However, this relationship is better understood in terms of subscription to a franchise movement rather than as a unified, ideologically driven Taliban insurgency.

The same would apply to the other major block of the 2006 Helmand insurgency, who were fighters from the Ishaqzai tribe around Sangin. They had been badly abused by the representatives of the Afghan government when Akhundzada was the Provincial Governor, specifically by the Provincial National Directorate of Security Chief Daud Mohammed Khan, who was from the rival Alikozai tribe.[7] Ironically the Alizai and Ishaqzais who joined the insurgency overcame their previous hostility to one another to fight a new common enemy in ISAF and the reconfigured Afghan Provincial Government. These insurgent factions used the Taliban as a franchise which they could tap into for support. In this sense their behaviour was entirely consistent and logical in Afghan political terms.

Despite the popular conception of the Taliban surging over the Pakistan border in 2006 into southern Afghanistan, the majority of fighters in Helmand in 2006 were Afghans, albeit with support from groups of foreign fighters, who were mainly from Pakistan. The real surge in foreign fighters in Helmand, fighting in formed groups, seems to have come later in 2007 when a group from South Waziristan based itself in an area south of Sangin for the best part of the year. This foreign group became very unpopular in Sangin, as they were far more ruthless in the application of sharia law than the local insurgents, which contributed to the unsuccessful Sangin uprising against the Taliban in 2007 led by the Alikozai tribe.

The political history of Helmand between 2001 and 2005 exemplifies how labels such as 'Taliban' and 'government' were used figuratively by local actors to benefit their interests in a kaleidoscopic political environment, manoeuvring vis-à-vis one another. Elements of the insurgency, and indeed elements of the Afghan National Security Forces, could be seen as holding patterns for factional interests until the next stage of their conflict with each other.

After 2001 local militia commanders had carved up Helmand between them as the coalition looked for allies to sweep up the remnants of the Taliban and al-Qaeda. Apart from Akhundzada, Malem Mir Wali brought his militia recruited mainly from the Barakzai tribe, which was based out of Gereshk, Helmand's second city, within the Afghan government security structure. He subsequently served as Member of Parliament for Helmand in Kabul. Other key posts went to militia commanders who had de facto control in the districts. Thus Daud Mohammed Khan, who controlled an Alikozai militia from Sangin, became the provincial head of the National Directorate of Security. Abdul Rahman Jan, who controlled a militia from the Noorzai tribe, became the Chief of Police.

Mike Martin, a British army officer, and Pashto speaker, with close knowledge of central Helmand, has argued in *A Brief History of Helmand* (2011) that the fact that these militia commanders were all on the government 'side' meant little. They continued to attack one another, and those outside the government patronage network, and dressed up this ongoing low-level violence as government versus 'Taliban'. Martin cites several clashes in the early days between Abdul Rahman Jan and Akhundzada, and between Malim Mir Wali and Akhundzada; subsequently Abdul Rahman Jan joined Akhundzada in attacking Malem Mir

Wali's men. Martin makes clear how all actors used their connections to the coalition to attack their rivals. At one point Malem Mir Wali and Gul Agha Sherzai, the Barakzai governor of Kandahar, almost managed to persuade the US military to strike Akhundzada himself. This was only vetoed with the intervention of the senior US general in Kabul.[8]

The background to this was another layer of tribal-factional conflict that involved the Barakzai tribe and Malim Mir Wali, the leader of a mainly Barakzai militia called the 93rd Division, an anachronistic legacy of the Soviet era. Daud Mohammed Khan had come into confrontation with Malim Mir Wali over the expansion of the former's power base in Sangin into the latter's in central Helmand. This tension linked into wider power balances in southern Afghanistan between Barakzai strongman Gul Agha Sherzai (who backed Mir Wali) and President Karzai's late half-brother Ahmed Wali Karzai (who backed Sher Mohammed Akhundzada and Daud Mohammed Khan), both powerful government figures who were competing for power in Kandahar city. This led to a series of clashes near Gereshk, the second city of Helmand, which ultimately resulted in the disarmament of the 93rd Division by the government and the marginalisation of Barakzai power in central Helmand.

These clashes were dressed up as part of the government against Taliban fight, as comments from Sher Mohammed Akhundzada's spokesman concerning Afghan army and police operations in September 2005 exemplify: 'anti-insurgency operations conducted in Gereshk District of the southern Helmand Province have led to the killing of a large number of miscreants and arrest of 60'.[9] Indeed the practice of arresting tribal enemies as 'Taliban', and the theft of one another's opium stocks as operations against 'drug smugglers', was commonplace.[10] Sarah Chayes' book, *The Punishment of Virtue* (2006), paints a similar picture of the kaleidoscopic dynamics in Kandahar city in the early years of the current Afghan conflict.[11]

In the context of Helmand, Martin makes clear that the biggest losers were groups who were 'not included in government patronage networks'. The Ishaqzai in Sangin, the Kharotei in Nad-e Ali and the Kakars in Garmsir, for example, were tribal groups not represented in the provincial government, and were rapaciously abused. These groups are today associated with the insurgency in Helmand. Their reasons for appealing to the Taliban were logical in terms of self-interest rather than as part of a wider 'Taliban' ideological agenda. Antonio Giustozzi has argued in *Koran, Kalashnikov and Laptop: The Neo-Taliban Insurgency in Afghanistan 2002–2007* (2008) that the extent to which 'Karzai's cronies' antagonised particular groups of people gave the Taliban a ready base of support.[12]In a Chatham House paper on Afghanistan of December 2010, Stephen Carter and Kate Clark argued that:

The human rights officer at the European Union told one author that they had documented illegal arrests, torture and other abuses carried out by government officials and police in the province [Helmand pre-2006]… Tribal enmity aggravated many of these injustices: Alizai circles around Governor Akhundzada marginalised and 'taxed' Achakzai communities, and officials have been accused of selectively eradicating poppy crops and punishing smugglers belonging to tribal rivals, and of packing state offices and security forces with their tribal supporters… The conflict in Helmand is to a large extent a drugs turf war … with figures on both the government and Taliban sides protecting their interests.[13]

The actual reasons for the violence of 2006 are complex. There was no doubt an element of cross-border pressure directed by the Taliban leadership from Pakistan, which increased in late 2005. However, tribal loyalties and the self-interest of the Afghan government power brokers cut across a neat insurgent-versus-government narrative.

Martin argues that after Daud Mohammed Khan, Abdul Rahman Jan and Akhundzada were successively removed from office by international pressure in 2005 and threatened (or actually disarmed) by the national disarmament process, there was a power vacuum, as they had been the de facto government forces. Critically, ejecting them from the Afghan government structure removed their incentive to support President Karzai. The deployment in 2006 thus tried to extend the rule of the by-then non-existent Provincial Afghan Government. This was particularly problematic in northern Helmand, the heartland of the Alizais who had a history of hostility to the British. When British troops legitimately fought back against those who attacked them, they antagonised what was a more complex political issue; this contributed to the formation of a more genuine and lethal insurgency.

General Sir Peter Wall, in evidence to the Defence Select Committee's July 2011 report, discusses the earlier part of the summer of 2006 in Helmand. He states that the 'crisis started to unfold' when:

the Taliban had the District Centres in Northern Helmand under pressure (…) There was, undoubtedly, pressure coming from the Akhundzada axis. If the

Government flag had fallen in any of these district centres and the Taliban flag had replaced it—it was totemic stuff like that, it was the battle of the flagpoles in some ways—the UK effort, in terms of its recognition of Afghan political motivation from the district level through the provincial level up to the national level ... would have been in political jeopardy.[14]

Hence General Wall acknowledges the importance of local political dynamics, but identifies that as the wider perception of the conflict was framed in terms of government versus Taliban, this constrained British actions. More specifically, the British had to intervene in northern Helmand, in the sense that Afghan government authority, as subjective a term as that may have been in 2006 in Helmand, could not be seen politically to have been displaced by that of the 'Taliban'. This was despite the 'Taliban' insurgents being in actuality for the most part local political factions, who had previously themselves effectively been the Afghan government forces. General Wall's evidence illustrates how of having understood the conflict through an overly polarised lens was a broad issue, engaging the perceptions of wider strategic audiences, as much as that of the military on the ground, who may have understood some of the basic local political factors at the time (as General Wall does), but were nonetheless trapped in a two-way narrative.

In Helmand in 2006, and indeed more widely in Afghanistan, the reciprocal escalation of violence, unconstrained by genuinely bilateral state structures which serve to channel and contain violence, has unnecessarily created enemies for the coalition and catalysed the insurgency in its earlier phases. This encouraged the growth of what David Kilcullen has termed 'accidental guerrillas'.[15]

The case of the Kharotei tribe in central Helmand's Nad-Ali district, which I base on Michael Martin's personal involvement in understanding these dynamics, exemplifies the problem of a polarised concept of conflict generating 'accidental guerrillas'. The Kharotei are one of a number of groups who moved to Nad-Ali from eastern Afghanistan as economic migrants during the 1950s and 1960s. There had been long-running tension over land rights there with other tribes, particularly the Noorzai. This tension was emphasised in the control of revenue from the opium crop, a hostility which pre-dated the 2001 Afghan conflict.

Nad-Ali was not a 'Taliban' area during the early part of the British operation in Helmand. In 2006 and 2007 British convoys could generally drive through it without attack. The local Afghan police in 2007 were dominated by the Noorzai tribe. They wanted the Kharotei opium crop, and fought them for it. This group of the Afghan police then claimed to be fighting the 'Taliban' and got support from British troops, who were indeed engaged by fighters of the Kharotei tribal militia. That move itself had been prefigured by the British forces' suspicions of the village where the Kharotei tribal leadership lived, called Shin Kalay. When British forces had first moved into Nad-Ali in 2008 and asked the district governor, a Noorzai, where the Taliban were based, he had pointed this village out, in line with his interests.[16] The Kharotei fighters then were accidental guerrillas; later they could probably be more genuinely defined as Taliban, as war's reciprocal violence accentuated emotional antagonism.

In summary, the political history of Helmand immediately before and during 2006 demonstrates that this was not a two way fight, but an extension of pre-existing, normal, kaleidoscopic political activity, albeit within a context in which the use of violence to further political ends was relatively normal too. To an extent local factional interests were able to exploit the coalition's initial naivety as to the actual political dynamics of Helmand in 2006 and tap into coalition resources to further their interests against other factions. However, the coalition was also achieving its aims in Helmand and in Afghanistan, which had more to do with global issues such as terrorism than purely the benefit of the Afghan people. So the extent to which local actors used the coalition to pursue their own ends needs to be seen in the context of the whole Afghan operation having aims beyond Afghanistan: there was give and take operating in both directions—between the coalition and local partners.

The category of people who are most ruthlessly exploited by subscription to a polarised conception of the conflict are often the foreign jihadists. They are typically, and somewhat tragically, Pakistani teenagers who are exploited by local Afghan insurgent commanders as 'martyrs' for cannon fodder. In my experience idealistic young foreign jihadists are often viciously bullied by older local insurgent commanders to perform attacks in which they will very likely die; their terrified pleadings and regrets at the last minute are frequently the response. I have tended to come across this reality, which presents a far more authentic voice than jihadist videos, when Afghan insurgent commanders have been known to banter to one another about their 'unwilling martyr', a standard, and grotesque, joke among them. Far from participating in what they thought was an ideological war, many young jihadists are in fact being exploited by local actors to pursue their own interests. Indeed, suicide bombers are sometimes sold between Afghan insurgent commanders.

Just as the polarised Afghan government-Taliban model is insufficient to comprehend the conflict in itself, so too is an exclusive retention of other models, for example the idea that it is not a war but a tribal conflict. Tribal motivations are important, but tend to be quickly discarded when they do not serve the actor's self-interest. The ruthless pragmatism that has characterised the political history of Helmand since the start of the Soviet war supports this.

There are definite axes of tension in the conflict, which can in themselves be polarised, such as the most important driver of the conflict: the Afghan government-insurgency antagonism. To deconstruct that to the point where it plays no role would be nonsense; it remains the most important tension. However, the point is that these central tensions exist within a far more complex web of affiliations, and to see everything through a single, if pre-eminent, axis of tension is myopic. The key tensions are simply powerful magnets, which can work to repel and attract actors in the political kaleidoscope; the only truly consistent themes are self-interest and survival, the latter meant in both a political and a literal sense.

The illegitimacy of the rigidly polarised narrative went for a long time undetected by the British parliament's official reports on Helmand, which did not understand that many of the 'Taliban' were already there before 2006, albeit as militias who had backed the Afghan government. Such narrow conceptual boundaries led to confusion. Lord Malloch-Brown elsewhere in his evidence to the Foreign Affairs Select Committee in 2009 asserts that 'the strength of the insurgent opposition we have faced in Helmand has surprised us; there is no way around that'.[17] Actually, there might well have been a way around that, which was to have understood the situation on its own terms, rather than to have imposed an artificial and simplistic polarity. The February 2011 House of Commons Foreign Affairs Committee Report presents a more realistic assessment. For instance, it recognises the insurgency as a franchise:

For the purposes of propaganda, the Taliban is keen for the insurgency to be regarded as a unified movement under the banner of the Islamic Emirate of Afghanistan, which is ostensibly controlled by Mullah Mohammed Omar and the Rahbari Shura (Supreme Council). In reality, the Afghan insurgency is a mix of Islamist factions, power-hungry warlords, criminals and tribal group-ings, all pursuing their own economic, political, criminal and social agendas and interests, from local feuds to establishing a pan-Islamic caliphate. Three major groups operate under the banner of the Islamic Emirate of Afghanistan: Mullah Omar's Taliban, the Haqqani Network and the Hizb-e-Islami faction led by Gulbuddin Hekmatyar. While the latter two sometimes co-operate with the Taliban leadership, they are considered autonomous factions.[18]

While it should be credited with a far better standard of analysis than what had gone before, this February 2011 parliamentary report received very little media attention in the UK. However, the wider debate does seem to be evolving towards a more sophisticated appreciation of the insurgency. An article by Anthony King in April 2011, for example, is cognisant of the actual political dynamics at play in Afghanistan, which are fragmented rather than binary:

The British see Helmand and the conflict in which they are involved in dualistic terms; the legitimate centralised state of Afghanistan represented in Helmand by the governor against the Taliban insurgency—the white state against the shadow state. The British are seeking to ensure that the balance of power is in favour of GIRoA. Yet, this binary perspective, although in line with conven-tional counter-insurgency thinking, seems to be simplistic in relation to Hel-mand. Indeed, it may fundamentally misrepresent the political conflict in Helmand… The battle for Helmand may perhaps surprisingly not primarily be between GIRoA and the Taliban, represented as the legitimate and shadow governments, but between Britain's projected and idealised model of GIRoA and actual, existing power structures and power-brokers in Helmand: Sher Mohammed Akhundzada and his patrimonial networks.[19]

The latest official version of the UK 2006 Helmand deployment at the time of writing is the July 2011 House of Commons Defence Com-mittee Fourth Report on *Operations in Afghanistan*.[20] Lack of intelli-gence about the situation in Helmand before the deployment is a theme that runs throughout the report. The report cites a military view that the assessment of the Taliban's intent in 2006 was correct, but not the assess-ment of their capability.[21]

This view, however, does not take into account the key nuance in terms of defining the insurgency's 'intent' that the 2011 Foreign Affairs Committee report recognised. The insurgency is a fragmented franchise organisation. Hence the Taliban senior leadership may well have a coherent intent. But can 'the Taliban' in the sense of the wider insur-gency have 'an intent' if they are a constellation of different groups?

No. Moreover, the argument that their capacity was underestimated is not correct. The scale of the insurgency increased with the British deployment, not before it; the subsequent resource mismatch followed from this. That in 2011 much of the report's oral evidence still held on to the highly problematic notion that 'the Taliban' could be characterised as a coherent enemy force in 2006 is perhaps indicative of how far ingrained is the basic conception that conflict is polarised, and how powerfully such a lens can distort, and erase the nuance, from the historical record.

In summary, there was not a significant 'Taliban' insurgency in the south in 2005. Partly this was because Kabul exercised so little visible presence there from 2002 to 2005 that there was little to rebel against. The violence that did take place was mainly a reaction against the behaviour of Akhundzada and his associates. In one sense this could legitimately be said to represent insurgent violence against the government, Akhundzada being the Provincial Governor; but to characterise this as a 'Taliban' insurgency is drastically to oversimplify the local political driving factors.

There was undoubtedly growing violence, but most of the violence that did occur was the product of factional interests sometimes dressed up as polarised conflict to exploit ISAF resources. The British deployment catalysed the insurgency because it shoehorned a kaleidoscopic political environment into an overly polarised model, which gave disparate groups a violent focus in a common enemy. Combined with political moves, such as the timing of Akhundzada's dismissal, this led to a reconfiguration whereby political interests that had supported the Afghan government turned against it. When local political actors moved away from the Afghan government franchise, this left only a rump of an Afghan government in Helmand whose rule was to be extended. The factions that had supported the Afghan government, but switched to the Taliban franchise, put pressure on the towns of northern Helmand, forcing a response. British soldiers on the ground were left holding the baby.[22]

This book is not primarily about Afghanistan. However, the Helmand case study illustrates how strategy must understand a problem on its own terms, not through dogmatically applied conceptual structures. In Afghanistan the coalition has moved away from a binary model of the conflict, and has since 2009 performed better; it now recognises the legitimacy of the franchise argument, but took a long time to do so—almost a decade of violence since 2001.

How did this happen? We need to trace the history of how war and strategy have been understood to understand the problem of how war is conceived in the present. The remainder of this chapter examines three cornerstones of war as traditionally understood in the Clausewitzian tradition: the principle of polarity; the physical and perceived components of war's outcome; and strategic audiences (those upon whom the strategist through war seeks to have an outcome) and their relationship to the state.

The principle of polarity and the role of the enemy

The enemy is traditionally what a 'military' outcome in war is defined against. War, according to Carl von Clausewitz, the most influential theorist of war in the Western tradition, was by necessity a polarised contest: 'war is the impact of opposing forces', which could be likened to a 'giant duel' made up of countless smaller duels.[23] This two-way polarity is depicted by Clausewitz in the first paragraph of *On War* by two men wrestling, which symbolised how war's function is 'an act of force to compel our enemy to do our will'.[24] The polarity between opponents is what makes war a contest which provides a decision, a resolution of the argument.[25]

Clausewitz categorised wars in accordance with how far they sought to achieve a decision. *Ganze Krieg*, which can be translated as absolute war, was not just the unrestrained use of violence; it was war that aimed at absolute political settlement through total destruction, or total submission, of the enemy.[26] Absolute war was 'saturated by the urge for a decision' in the sense that the absolute means of such a war were consistent with its absolute political aims. As wars moved away from the conceptual pole of *ganze Krieg* there was a corresponding reduction between the application of violence and the intended political outcome, until one reached the point where violence was merely threatened as part of normal political activity: 'the less a decision is actively sought by the belligerents, the more the war becomes a matter of mutual observation'.[27]

Clausewitz's analytical originality was to associate the forms of war between polarised opponents, attack and defence, with war's capacity to provide political meaning through a decision. For Clausewitz, war starts with defence, in that unresisted attack is not war.[28] So polarity is present from the outset as resistance is a prerequisite of war. War necessarily brings both forms into being, because attack and defence cannot exist without the other.[29]

Force can then be understood as a type of language. As in a verbal argument, the negative form (defence) is about prevention of the enemy's argument; the positive form (attack) is about the assertion of one's own argument. For example, in a purely defensive battle (a siege with no counter-attack, for instance) the defending commander seeks to delay the decision as far as possible: 'a defensive battle that remains undecided at sunset can be considered to be won'. In offensive battle 'the aim of the commander is to expedite the decision'.[30] The positive and negative forms are present at all levels of war, in battle, both sides alternate between attack and defence, right down to the lowest level where a soldier alternates between use of a sword and shield, or their modern equivalents.

Hence polarity provided a military scale to give meaning to actions in combat. The meaning of actions in combat for Clausewitz was a synthesis of both forms, as in a verbal argument in terms of landing blows and parrying the opponent's to produce a result: attack pushed the counter of war's outcome on this scale towards victory, and defence pushed against attack: 'polarity does not lie in the attack or the defence, but in the object both seek to achieve: the decision'.[31] The decision could be absolute: 'in battle each side aims at victory; that is a case of true polarity, since the victory of one side excludes the victory of the other'.[32] However, Clausewitz recognised that the outcome was usually relative: 'it is not possible in every war for the victor to overthrow his enemy completely'. However, according to the principle of polarity, war provided a single, mutually-recognised scale which determined the relative superiority that set military conditions for a political outcome: 'victory normally results from the superiority of one side; from a greater aggregate of physical and psychological strength ... every reduction in strength on one side can be regarded as an increase in the other'.[33]

In summary, Clausewitz interpreted the antagonistic polarity between opponents in terms of a dialectic expressed in the form of attack and defence which provided meaning to their clash in combat. That meaning was defined in terms of a see-saw-like military scale: whether an outcome (victory or defeat) was absolute or more limited, was, critically, defined against one's enemy. This concept gives a cognitive stability to what military actions mean in war.

Without polarity, force loses decisive political meaning. Sometimes it is necessary to accentuate an existing polarity to give force political utility. In the Bosnian conflict of the 1990s, for example, the UN forces failed to achieve any decisive outcome because their political masters took a morally relative point of view. The desire to avoid another such scenario was influential in Prime Minister Tony Blair's decisive stance on Kosovo in 1999.

However, the right and wrong of the Kosovan issue were not at all clear. There were in fact crimes being committed by both sides, by the Serbian para-military forces and the Kosovo Liberation Army (KLA). This was reported by a fact-finding mission led by the Organisation for Co-operation and Security in Europe prior to the NATO intervention. The criminal associations of the KLA, and its follow-on groups (it was officially disbanded in 1999), have since been widely documented. However, the NATO coalition presented the conflict in terms of a case of right versus wrong and achieved a decisive outcome against Serbia, at least in the short-term. In the longer term the legacy of the conflict is less clear-cut in political terms, not least in the on-going issue of the recognition of Kosovo.

In 1999 the NATO coalition was able to shape the battlefield in Kosovo in terms of its presentation of a clear case of right versus wrong; even though things were more morally complex on the ground: by taking a clear stance decisive action was possible. Yet this needs to be distinguished from the situation in Afghanistan. In Kosovo a polarity between two sides already existed; the shaping of the battlefield in political terms was to bring the international community, especially NATO countries, behind one side, allowing war's mechanism in the Clausewitzian sense to function. Yet in circumstances in which there is very little polarity to begin with, war's mechanism in the traditional Clausewitzian conception is compromised from the outset.

What pre-2001 polarity exists in the Afghan conflict is strongly associated with the tension between the Tajik-dominated Northern Alliance and the Pashtun-dominated Taliban. The difficulty here is that accentuating such polarity to define the enemy better can engender its own unwanted sectarian tensions. This is partly why the Afghan government try not to present themselves as the reincarnated Northern Alliance, and the Taliban distance themselves from the label of being a Pashtun nationalistic movement: it is the conflict itself that encourages tensions that both sides, wanting to avoid the break-up of Afghanistan on ethnic lines, resist.

The Kosovo example also illustrates that polarity is relative. Parties to a conflict may only be drawn together temporarily. Part of strategy's role is thus the orchestration and manipulation of polarity in relation to another party to present an enemy against whom a 'military' result can be defined. This is usually most obvious in the escalatory moves that anticipate armed conflict.

The physical and perceived components of war's political outcome

Polarity can give cognitive stability to what military action in war means, but how then does a military outcome translate into a political outcome? Power can be understood as a relationship. This idea resonates with how Clausewitz understood war as the clash of wills, in which one sought to impose one's will on the enemy. For Clausewitz, the 'decision' provided by the mechanism of war through the polarised dialectic of attack and defence had a physical and a perceived component.

The physical component of a war's outcome can be adjusted to give little room to be persuaded of an alternative view. As Admiral J. C. Wylie argued in *Military Strategy: A General Theory of Power Control* (1967): 'the ultimate determinant in war is the man on the scene with a gun'.[34] This can be taken to extremes in war. If the enemy is entirely destroyed, one's own side can dictate the interpretation of events into the historical record. There is no Carthaginian interpretation of the destruction of Carthage. Rome's victory was truly written by the victors. This theme comes across powerfully in the speech the Roman historian Tacitus attributes (fictitiously) to the tribal chief Calgacus, who describes Roman imperial practice in a speech defying the extension of Roman rule in Britain: 'to robbery, butchery, and rapine, they give the lying name of 'government'; they create a wasteland and call it peace'.[35]

The outcome of war at its end, in the Clausewitzian conception, connected a military outcome (the physical component, as defined by the use of force) into a political outcome which ideally served the ends of policy. In a very few cases the political outcome took the form of the utter destruction of the enemy in lieu of a political settlement, such as the total destruction of Carthage by Rome in the Third Punic War (149–146 BCE). However, in most instances the political settlement is a verdict subscribed to by the enemy: this may be imposed on the defeated party, who lies prostrate; in other cases the relative gains and losses in war give a military outcome which provides the basis of a negotiated or de facto political settlement. Hence beyond extreme cases in which a war's outcome is exclusively defined by the total destruction of the enemy, war's outcome includes a perceived component in terms of having forced the enemy to accept a certain behaviour.

Thus the purpose of force in war was for Clausewitz to make the enemy acquiesce in one's intent: 'war…cannot be considered to have ended so long as the enemy's will has not been broken'.[36] The strategist used war to impose a decision on the enemy; that decision, the war's outcome, was as much what was perceived to be real as what was real. This is encapsulated by none other than Russell Crowe as General Maximus in the film *Gladiator* when, taunted by the enemy commander across the battlefield, one of his officers states: 'People should know when they are conquered'; Maximus answers: 'Would you, Quintus? Would I?'[37]

The problem Clausewitz identified was that perception is often not durable; it can evolve. The enemy's 'will' could return: 'the hardships of that situation [defeat] must not of course be transient—at least not in appearance. Otherwise the enemy would not give in but wait for things to improve'.[38] For instance, the rhetoric of the 'undefeated army' in inter-war Germany compromised the notion of German 'defeat' upon which the stipulations of the Great War peace treaties were predicated. Field Marshal Viscount Slim deals with this problem in *Defeat into Victory* (1956), his classic account of the Burma campaign.[39] He ordered all the Japanese officers ceremonially to snap their own swords at the surrender parades so that there could be no myth of the undefeated army. The stability of strategic effect—the output which war's mechanism offers—corresponds to how durable is the perception of defeat.

Defeat for Clausewitz was a perceived state, a construct. As perceptions can change, defeat is not a stable concept, and therefore neither is victory. For instance, a battle may destroy part of the enemy force, but it is how that event is interpreted by the enemy that invests the battle with significance in terms of the wider war: the enemy may perceive himself to be defeated or, alternatively, carry on. Clausewitz argued that there was a 'culminating point' of attack which is the furthest extent to which one can go before one's position becomes over-extended and indefensible.[40] That is where attack must turn to defence. If one goes too far, what might initially have been interpreted to have been a success may come to be seen as failure.

The unstable nature of victory is evident in history. For example, the Roman Emperor Trajan conquered vast swathes of territory, such as the new province of Mesopotamia; many of these 'gains' subsequently had to be abandoned by his successor Hadrian, as they were not realistically sustainable. In retrospect Trajan's victories seemed more like failures for the Roman Empire. The idea of the culminating point makes just as much sense in political as military terms in contemporary conflict: coalition policy goals in Afghanistan, whose ambitions inflated after the success of the initial Taliban defeat, have had to be scaled back to allow the coalition to succeed in the goals it sets itself.

This applies as much to wars as to battles. In 1529 Sultan Suleiman failed to take Vienna after an unsuccessful siege. A major Ottoman campaign had failed. Yet he returned to his capital Constantinople in celebration, as if he had won a major victory through the campaign's moderate extension of Ottoman territory in the Balkans. By adjusting his strategic narrative he was received as a victor, and has been remembered as 'Suleiman the Magnificent'. Ironically this is an appellation used by Westerners, who tend to identify with those who defeated him at Vienna; the Ottomans themselves called him the 'lawgiver'. Ultimately victory is what is interpreted as such.

So is defeat. Wolfgang Schivelbusch has argued in *The Culture of Defeat* that defeat is a malleable concept.[41] He focuses primarily on three cases of defeat: the Confederacy after the US Civil War; France after the Franco-Prussian War; and Germany after the First World War. In each instance post-war narratives were suggested, and gained considerable purchase, by the ostensibly 'defeated' who rejected that claim.

Even at the lowest level of war victory and defeat are often subjective constructs. For example, there was a small skirmish on 27 September 2007 near the village of Hyderabad in the Upper Gereshk Valley, Helmand Province, Afghanistan. 8 Platoon of C Company, First Battalion Royal Gurkha Rifles (1 RGR), was engaged by insurgents on the banks of the River Helmand. Objectively, one could describe the events in terms of its physical reality. Gurkha soldiers and insurgent fighters moved in a certain way. Bullets, rocket-propelled grenades and mortar-fire were exchanged, which travelled on certain trajectories. Commands were given. There were casualties. However, no person ever has access to that complete and objective understanding. The underlying physical reality is understood though subjective, perceived interpretation.

I remember the event mainly in terms of staying low and moving fast, as the army's expression goes, in a field of high corn which was above head height, speaking to my company commander on the radio, and trying to reposition my three sections (eight-man combat teams) based on my fragmentary understanding of what was going on. Even after the skirmish, when experiences were compared with the rest of the platoon, the event, like all combat, remained a subjective collection of experiences as remembered by members of the group. Rifleman Padam Shrees, for example, spent twenty minutes pinned down in a field at the forward point of the platoon, returning fire despite being highly exposed. Corporal Basanta, commanding the forward section, was at the most vicious point of the action, with great courage directing his section to suppress the various enemy firing points to the front while under sustained rocket-propelled grenade (RPG) and machine-gun fire themselves.[42]

The platoon sergeant, Bel Gurung, assisted by Lance Corporal Chaman's section, was focused on dealing with two of our casualties, both riflemen: one with RPG fragment in his leg; the other, the platoon radio operator, with a small piece of shrapnel in his neck. The two four-man fire teams of Corporal Tara's section were bounding past one another and firing in turn up an irrigation stream at 90 degrees to the forward section, trying to set up some depth to our platoon position to block the insurgents who were trying to outflank us.

All the participants in this skirmish would only see it from a particular and fragmentary perspective. Even if the insurgents' recollections of the event were incorporated, or indeed those of the local villagers (some of whom may well have been insurgents themselves), the interpretation of the event would remain subjective, both in terms of what happened and who 'won'.

However, this was a small and short skirmish, which makes it possible to gather together the various perspectives, at least on one's own side, and paint a relatively coherent picture of what happened. The problem of subjective interpretations correlates to the size of the picture. When a battlespace is an entire country, and there are multiple, overlapping sets of target audiences, the instability of any assertion of 'what happened' really starts to become problematic.

This subjectivity makes narratives malleable, just as Suleiman the Magnificent understood. In July 2010 Major Shaun Chandler was commanding A Company 1 RGR in central Helmand. He knew the insurgents were telling villagers that we were cowards because we did not fight man to man, but used aircraft and artillery. Major Chandler shaped perceptions by very rarely using helicopter support, never using aircraft, and never using artillery. He repeatedly outmanoeuvred the insurgents using basic infantry tactics and snipers. At one point he invited the insurgents, through the villagers, to a 'fair' fight in a field at a given time in which he would only bring twelve men, and not use air support or artillery. He showed up on time, the villagers showed up to watch, but the insurgents refused to fight. After thirty minutes Major Chandler walked into the middle of the field by himself and looked around, making a visual statement to the villagers. This lost the insurgents a lot of credibility in the village as the events were perceived by all parties—us, the villagers and the insurgents—as a defeat for the insurgents' narrative.[43]

In the language of strategic thought today, Clausewitz's emphasis on the perceived quality of a war's decision is expressed in terms of the 'strategic narrative'. War has an underlying physical reality (the events), and the interpretation of that reality (the version). Strategic narrative is essentially an aspirational version of events which associates the two. If one's strategic narrative is to defeat the enemy in order to impose a given political outcome on him, one is victorious, or has 'succeeded' in today's parlance, once that is understood to have happened. In this sense, success or failure in war are perceived states in the minds of one's intended audience. War can be understood as a competition between strategic narratives, a theme fully considered in Chapters 8 and 9.

Strategic audiences: the objects of war's outcome

Clausewitz understood that the perceived component of a war's 'decision' was subjective because the interpretation of the physical component could vary depending on the interpreter. It may therefore appear paradoxical that Clausewitz both recognised the conceptual instability of war's outcome—its decision—but equally stressed that war's function was a mechanism to provide a decision. This paradox is largely resolved by two concepts that Clausewitz implicitly presupposed in all war. The first, described above, was the polarisation of war on a single axis, which produced two 'sides'. This narrowed the possible conceptualisation of war's outcome in terms of a see-saw of victory and defeat. The second was the idea that, even though war's outcome was an interpreted state, its interpreters—the strategic audiences—were primarily the sides themselves. To return to the metaphor of war as a trial, this is the idea that each side is its own judge and seeks to impose its verdict on the other.

For Clausewitz, although he did not use the term, the definition of 'strategic audiences' in war was very straightforward: the first division was between one's own side and the enemy, according to the principle of polarity; the second division was between the army, people and government within each side (assuming, as Clausewitz did, that the sides were state actors). In today's terms these would be seen as 'strategic audiences', that is, the groups of people whom strategy seeks to convince of its narrative. Ultimately they are the arbiters of war's outcome: their perceptions are the strategist's objective, in terms of influencing them, or of making them irrelevant, in accordance with the intent of policy.

Thus in war one seeks to defeat an enemy. The enemy loses when he is defeated. This can be either because he accepts himself that he is defeated, or because even if he does not accept it, he is now irrelevant to one's definition of victory. For example, the remnants of the Malayan Communist Party only surrendered in 1989. However, for most people, including Britain, the Malayan Emergency had been 'won' by 1960. The Malayan Communist Party in this sense could interpret the outcome however it wanted; it was no longer relevant to British policy, and thus no longer a strategic audience.

What is central in Clausewitz's conception of war is the idea that the strategic audiences of war were contained within the 'state' of either side. They won or lost the war with their state. This is really the essence of *inter-state* war as a mechanism of war, as opposed to just the description of two states fighting. The element 'inter' communicates the notion that the issue is between these two polarised constituencies, and does not primarily involve other 'audiences'. The mechanism by which war provided an outcome was for Clausewitz brutally simple. Rendered in today's parlance, strategy sought to impose its strategic narrative on the enemy through force, or its threat. The enemy came to subscribe to one's narrative, died, or became no longer relevant.

Yet success in war was not just about the defeat of the enemy; it was also necessary to unify the strategic audiences who were within one's own side behind one's strategic narrative. Strategy had to maintain unity between the strategic audiences who were within one's state: government, army and people. Since war was for Clausewitz a 'clash of wills', all three of these elements contributed to the coherence and strength of a given side's will. Clausewitz discussed cases where the government resists the people's 'passion' for war because it is not a good idea in rational terms. He also discussed cases in which the people's passion has to be artificially stoked to get support for the government plan.[44] Clausewitz repeatedly stresses the 'moral' component in terms of the army. The army is not a robotic tool; soldiers are human; the inference for strategy today is that the army is an audience in itself.

When strategy fails to unify the strategic audiences who are within one's own side, the state cannot act as a 'judge' to provide a coherent verdict of war's outcome. During the Vietnam War there were massive differences in perceptions of success between the US administration on the one hand and large tranches of domestic public opinion; this is not to mention disillusion among sections of lower ranks of the military on the ground later on in the conflict. That is, if victory, or success, is only interpreted as such by one element of the state, it is compromised as a legitimate analysis.

The flexibility of the Clausewitzian paradigm of war

This chapter started in Afghanistan, as an example of a contemporary conflict in which the implicit application of the conceptual structure of war in the Clausewitzian paradigm was inappropriate. The temptation is to indicate the redundancy of Clausewitzian thought to contemporary conflict. That would be incorrect. Clausewitz's analysis was not intended to describe circumstances in which armed force was used as a direct extension of political activity outside of war.

An astute evaluation of the conceptual framework of a conflict outside traditional war was presented by US army General Raymond Odierno, who had extensive command experience in Iraq 2006–10, including as overall coalition commander. When asked at a press conference in March 2010 if the war in Iraq was effectively over, he replied: 'war is a very different concept… I call [Iraq] more of an operation, not a war'.[45]

The traditional, Clausewitzian, paradigm of war assumes that there is mutual understanding of war as an interpretive unit. This provides mutual recognition of the military outcome. Strategy can then focus on the application of military force itself (combat), which Clausewitz argued was the 'only means of war'.[46] Yet Clausewitz realised that war's interpretive structure would be revised if the military outcome were *not* mutually observed. This occurred when a more effective form of war made the previous one redundant.

For Clausewitz, who wrote *On War* between 1816 and 1830, after Napoleon's defeat in 1815, a more limited form of war would only have a function 'so long as it is tacitly understood that the opponent follows suit. But is it possible to tell how long this condition will be observed? The French Revolution surprised us in the false security of our ancient skills, and drove us from Châlons to Moscow'. The function of war in the Napoleonic paradigm made war's previous function redundant; to enter into war with Napoleon with a mindset of limited political goals, and a corresponding limitation of the use of force, was not possible.[47] The relevance of this observation today would be that the evolution of the use of force directly for political purposes, outside of war, on a large scale, is quite possibly irreversible: armed actors imitate what is effective in each other's practice, especially in response to the information revolution.

In Clausewitz's analysis, in the eighteenth century war was mutually understood by European powers in terms that did not make it 'absolute': the enemy was out-manoeuvred rather than totally destroyed; this emphasised the perceived over the physical component of defeat.[48] Yet in his own lifetime Clausewitz saw warfare expand beyond its eighteenth-century limitations to approach its absolute state: 'we might doubt whether our notion of its [war's] absolute nature had any reality, if we had not seen real warfare make its appearance in this absolute completeness right in our own times'.[49] The social forces of the French Revolution of 1789 led to a French force which in 1793 'beggared all imagination' because 'suddenly war became the business of the people, all thirty million of them'. The massive perception shift in the scale of war that he directly experienced in his own lifetime is essential to understand what Clausewitz attempted intellectually to come to terms with in *On War*. In 1792 at the Battle of Valmy, towards the start of the Revolutionary Wars, 64,000 men on one side fought against 30,000 on the other in a battle lasting one day. By 1813 at the Battle of Leipzig, 365,000 men fought 195,000 in a battle lasting three days.[50]

The numbers were only one aspect of a massive evolution in how people understood war's basic form. What Clausewitz terms 'strategic manoeuvre' did not work against Napoleon's asymmetric approach that emphasised physical, as opposed to perceived, superiority. Napoleon's emphasis on seeking victory in physical terms through the pursuit of decisive battle was taken to extremes by employment within an unrestrained political context. This approach was characterised by the concept of exploitation: the ruthless pursuit of the enemy to his total submission. War was now a fight for state survival, not a political game: 'the sole aim of war was to overthrow the opponent'.[51]

The concept of failure to identify a transformation in war informed Clausewitz's analysis of Prussia's crushing defeat at the Battle of Jena by Napoleon in 1806. Prussia entered still thinking in the eighteenth-century mode; this was the mode that saw war's objectives in terms of 'a couple of fortresses and a medium-sized province'. Yet Napoleon, 'the God of War himself', thought of war in terms of far greater objectives: 'would Prussia...have risked war with France if she had suspected that the first shot would set off a mine that would blow her to the skies?'[52] In Clausewitz's view, Prussia's strategists had not understood the significance of the novelty and asymmetry of Napoleon's concept of war:

In the eighteenth century...war was an affair of governments alone... At the onset of the nineteenth century, peoples themselves were in the scale on either side... Such a transformation might have led to new ways of thinking about it. In 1805, 1806, and 1809 they might have recognised that total ruin was a possibility—indeed it stared them right in the face... They did not however change their attitudes sufficiently... They failed because the transformations of war had not yet been fully revealed by history.[53]

The functionality of war in terms of its provision of a military decision has been constantly revised. The point Clausewitz makes is that military victory meant a very different thing at the time of his birth than after the Napoleonic Wars. The deliberate subversion of the interpretive unit provided by war can be understood in terms of asymmetric warfare in the strategic sense: Napoleon deliberately, and brutally, ignored the conventions of eighteenth-century warfare to gain an advantage. The interpretive evolution of war can therefore occur within the Clausewitzian paradigm, indeed it is normal.

Clausewitz's analysis of war's mechanism is flexible and does not resist change; it accounts for it. For Clausewitz war retained utility through reconfiguration, and evolved frequently. Napoleon may have changed the rules of war, but he still thought of victory in terms of the defeat of the enemy. In this paradigm military action sets conditions for a political solution, but two circumstances are presupposed: first is the principle of polarity; second is the notion that strategic audiences in war are primarily contained within the states at war. In short, war in its traditional form can work as a mechanism to deliver a political decision when there is an enemy, and one defines the outcome against him. Asymmetry within that paradigm drives war's evolution in terms of military innovation and the ends that policy seeks in war; war, however, remains distinct from peace.

Strategic asymmetry is therefore not what is distinctive about contemporary conflict. Clausewitz's paradigm of war accepts that it is a normal feature of war's evolution. The distinctive feature of contemporary conflict is the absence, or more typically the compromise, of the two prerequisites that bound the circumstance of war, and thus allow war's mechanism to function as a political instrument. Afghanistan is one example of the consequence of confusing Clausewitzian war with armed politics outside war. The next chapter deals with the subversion of the Clausewitzian paradigm of war that occurs when it is used to incorporate strategic audiences beyond the enemy.

3

GLOBALISATION
AND CONTEMPORARY CONFLICT

For war in its Clausewitzian paradigm to function properly, two conditions are presupposed: polarity between sides (to define an enemy), and
the association of strategic audiences with either side (to define the war's
outcome against the enemy). In this traditional conception of war, the
use of force provides a military outcome which sets conditions for a
political solution. When these prerequisites are compromised, so too is
war's ability to provide an outcome: if both sides can go to war and
legitimately claim victory, war is largely redundant as a political instrument to achieve a decision.

Polarity, and the subsequent association of strategic audiences with
either side, encourages a stable interpretive environment, which allows
war's mechanism to function; when polarity gives way to politically
kaleidoscopic, fragmentary conflict dynamics, which create unstable
interpretive environments, war's functionality is compromised.

However, a clear distinction between polarised and non-polarised
conflicts is simplistic. Strategic audiences beyond the enemy have always
existed; concerns by a war's participants about the reactions of wider
international audiences, or audiences within a state who do not identify
with it, are not new. By 'beyond the enemy' I mean that there exist
audiences who are particularly relevant to the war's outcome (from a
given strategic perspective) who are not part of either side. Globalisa-

tion, which is strongly associated with such concerns, is not new either. Exclusively polarised, or non-polarised, conflicts are therefore abstract poles; they are rarely, if ever, attained in reality. All conflicts have some form of polarity, however weak; conversely, even the outcomes of the most polarised conflicts are rarely sealed off from the responses of audiences unaligned to either side.

However, the extent and speed of inter-connectivity associated with contemporary globalisation can unhinge classical strategy. Contemporary globalisation challenges the two prerequisites of war in the Clausewitzian paradigm: first, in the proliferation of strategic audiences beyond the enemy; second, in the tendency for conflicts in general to be drawn further away from the pole of 'pure polarity' as strategy tends increasingly to be sensitive to the opinions of global audiences. The consequence is the erosion of the distinction between military and political activity.

Military outcomes in politically fragmented conflicts

War is not a single, fixed, interpretive construct because audiences can understand war in their own way. If we return to the metaphor of war as a street fight without any set rules, 'victory' and 'defeat' are often perceived states which are subjective, and have to be imposed on an opponent. War does not provide an independent 'judge' to hand out a verdict mutually recognised by the fighters themselves and the crowd. Unlike in a boxing match, or a legal trial, each side is its own judge. War is a competition to violently force the opponent to agree with one's judgement. The street fight may have an audience. If one of the fighters wants to impose a verdict on them too, things become far more complex. First, the audience are not in the fight (even if they can accidentally be hurt), so one cannot literally force them to subscribe to one's verdict, which one can do with the enemy. Second, the members of the audience are judges in their own right.

Strategy has a problem when war is used by the strategist to influence a non-combatant audience who does not subscribe to the same conception of the conflict as war, and so do not interpret the use of force in the manner desired by the strategist. The first line of General Sir Rupert Smith's seminal book *The Utility of Force* (2005) is: 'War no longer exists'.[1] He goes on in the paragraph to qualify this: 'War as cognitively known to most non-combatants, as war in a field between men and machinery, war as a massive deciding event in a dispute in international affairs: such war no longer exists'. He suggests a paradigm of 'war among the people' to replace the 'paradigm of inter-state war' in terms of how the use of force should be understood to give it political utility. The main inference of the mode of thought posited by General Smith is that, if the audience does not understand an action in military terms, the action effectively has a direct, and possibly unintended, political effect. The argument that in war military force sets conditions for a political settlement which is exclusively reached on the basis of the war's military outcome is untenable in such circumstances.

Today even relatively conventional wars are not fought entirely within a sealed military domain. The means of war are not just combat. While this has always been the case to some extent, it is accentuated by contemporary globalisation. The Russian-Georgian War in 2009, for example, was fought in front of a global audience. Russia enjoyed overwhelming military superiority. The Russian offensive stopped for political reasons. Whether Russia achieved its aims is debatable. Russia may deliberately have stopped where it did, although it did not achieve its aim of forcing the anti-Russian Georgian President Saakashvili from power. Strategic audiences outside the Russian-Georgian states mattered to the war's outcome, and Russian strategy was influenced, to an extent, by audiences such as the North Atlantic Treaty Organization (NATO) and the European Union (EU).

While the concept of outside alliances influencing wars is not new, globalisation in its contemporary form catalyses the importance of strategic audiences who are external to one's state or the enemy's state (or 'side' if the term state is inappropriate) in the definition of success in any war. Indeed there is a credible argument that Russia's main purpose was in fact to assert its displeasure over two issues: the NATO campaign in Kosovo, which Russia claimed had violated Serbian sovereignty without UN backing, and the eastwards expansion of NATO. The degree to which Russia effectively made this point to NATO countries is up for debate, and not our current subject. However, the fact that the war was for Russia broader than merely strategic audiences within Georgia is clear.

The 2006 war in Lebanon between Israel and Hezbollah is an alternative case study of the critical relationship between polarity and war's ability to provide a decisive outcome. As Patrick Porter has argued in *Military Orientalism* (2009), Israel's war objectives, which were not defined consistently, ranged from the local to the regional.[2] Certain Israeli war aims were defined against a polarised opponent—the enemy—in Hezbollah itself: the return of two Israeli soldiers abducted by Hezbollah; halting the firing of rockets against Israel; destroying Hezbollah as a military organisation.

However, other war aims were defined against audiences who were not part of the enemy, namely the Lebanese people and government: to show them the costs of allowing Hezbollah to operate from their soil; to create a zone cleared of Hezbollah forces that Lebanese or international forces could then occupy; and to turn Lebanese mainstream opinion against militants. To an extent Israeli aims were defined beyond Hezbollah and Lebanese audiences. As Porter notes, an Israeli foreign ministry spokesman after the war defined it as a 'blow to all extremist jihadist forces in the region'.

Porter's account emphasises how Hezbollah, on the other hand, kept things simple. Hezbollah's Sheik Hassan Nasrallah claimed that survival would be victory: 'he set a realistic goal, to pose as the vanguard of a Lebanese national resistance, who withstood Israel's coercion'.[3] In the event, Israel successfully destroyed many of Hezbollah's long-range missiles. Israel claimed to have killed a quarter of Hezbollah's fighters, roughly 530. Israel also killed at least 1,000 Lebanese civilians and caused widespread wreckage in the suburbs of Beirut.[4] Hezbollah was reasonably able to claim to have succeeded in its aim not to be destroyed; its reputation was in many ways enhanced. Israel's aims that were defined against the enemy, Hezbollah, could also legitimately be said to have partly succeeded, given the amount of physical damage to the organisation.

Yet the 2006 war was generally seen as a failure for Israel at the time. Although Israel did succeed in some ways against the enemy, its aims that were defined against audiences other than the enemy were not achieved. Israel's objective had been to send the intended political message to these wider audiences through a military defeat of Hezbollah. Israel's critical assumption was, therefore, that its actions in war would be interpreted by these other audiences in military terms: these audiences would form a political opinion based on the relative military balance of Israel and Hezbollah. In reality these audiences did not interpret Israel's actions in war in military terms.

Israel's actions in war were not interpreted by the Lebanese people and government, a key strategic audience, in accordance with Israel's interpretive structure of war. Thus what for Israel was part of a battle in Beirut was for the Lebanese the death of family or friends. The capture of a military objective for Israel was seen by various constituencies, particularly in parts of the Muslim world, as a heroic fight by Hezbollah for Palestinians in Gaza and Islamic militants generally.

Nor did the Lebanese people and government reserve their political interpretation of events until the war had produced a military decision. The residents of Beirut would not have subscribed to Israel's argument that the destruction in the city was an unfortunate military necessity; the world witnessed anger and mass civilian protests in Lebanon during the war. The *direct* political effect of Israel's actions had far more significance in terms of Lebanese perception than the military outcome of the fight with Hezbollah.

The 2006 war suggests that the meaning of military action is not self-contained if the audience subscribes to an alternative, non-military, frame of reference. This issue is illustrated in microcosm in a 2001 article written by General Dan Halutz, the Israeli Defence Force Chief of Staff during the war (who subsequently stepped down), which argued in 2001 that 'victory is a matter of consciousness'.[5] He advocated the value of air power, because it could 'influence consciousness in a meaningful fashion', implicitly assuming that air power has a permanent cognitive quality.[6] In Afghanistan today, the British military make the same assumptions. For example a 'show of force' can be requested to deter any enemy actions; this involves a jet screaming overhead at very low altitude. This is normally effective in deterring any potential enemy, who will interpret that action in military terms. Yet the Afghan population, who are also a strategic audience, may not see it as a 'show of force' within a military context; in my experience, especially in the countryside, they are usually worried and frightened by this bizarre event.

The Iraq War in 2003 exposed the problems of an operational approach focused on military success on the battlefield over political consequences after the initial high-intensity combat. 'Shock and Awe' was meant to shock and awe the enemy: to shatter the will of Baathist Iraq. 'Shock and Awe' worked very well in the initial phase of war between the US and Iraqi armies. However, 'Shock and Awe' was not compartmentalised within the first phase of the war against Saddam

Hussein's regular forces. The Iraqi people were a critical strategic audience in a war fought for democracy, among other things.

'Shock and Awe' was now a problem, because it had indeed shocked and awed the Iraqi people, but presumably not always in the way intended. The Iraqi people interpreted it in their own terms: some supported coalition troops, others fought them. The phases of war by which the military plans and distinguishes between high intensity combat and less violent postures are an irrelevance for the civilian who lives through them and sees the whole as one experience. In Iraq, people mattered to the coalition's own definition of the war's success; democracy, for one, would have required popular consent. While there were entirely legitimate considerations that clearly were military, such as defeating the Iraqi army, the activity of coalition armed forces in terms of its reception by target audiences went beyond the traditional notion of a compartmentalised military cognitive sphere.

In terms of military jargon, one has to distinguish between 'means' and 'effects'. Any action, whether in war or not, has an 'effect'. The axiom that 'one cannot not communicate' posits that any behaviour is a form of communication, whether intended or not. The 'effect' of an action (from the highest to the lowest level of war, and indeed the war itself as an action) is thus its meaning as interpreted by an audience, whether that was the intended meaning of the actor or not.

The mistake is to assume that 'effects' are contained within the 'means', the action itself: assuming that an aerial 'show of force', for example, will always be understood to have been a 'show of force'—it is actually a low pass by a military jet—while the effect is how that is interpreted, which will vary. Israel assumed that its war in 2006 would 'send a message'; in the event it sent messages, only some of which were the ones intended.[7] The 2003 war in Iraq was intended, at least in part, to be seen as an intervention that would be understood by the Iraqi people as a signal to embrace freedom and democracy. The error of confusing means and effects can be witnessed in terms of the unintended consequences of an action: the angry Afghan villager after a show of force; the Israeli alienation of many Lebanese people after the 2006 war; and the actual Iraqi responses to the war in Iraq.

The confusion between means and effects relates directly to the interpretation of Clausewitz's dictum of war being an extension of policy by other means. The narrow interpretation of this dictum recognises only the actual use of force as the 'instrument' that war provides to policy. However, war itself as the interpretive structure which gives meaning to that force is equally an instrument. If the strategist fails to understand this, strategy will associate a 'message' with a given means; that confusion of means and effects is intrinsically associated with a conception of war as a fixed, single, interpretive structure, in which the actions of armed forces will be interpreted in terms of their military significance.

Strategy can get away with the confusion of means and effects if the parties to a conflict have an essentially symmetrical understanding of the conflict, as was discussed in Chapter 1. If the fighters and the audience of our street fight all interpret the fight according to the same rules, the idea that there is a mutually recognised military outcome is sustainable. In these circumstances war can act as a mechanism in which the armed forces provide a military outcome which sets conditions for a political solution.

However, we have seen that not only can the enemy use an alternative interpretive structure, as the North Vietnamese did in Vietnam; so too can audiences beyond the enemy see the war in their own terms. In this case, if one wants to persuade that audience in accordance with one's policy aims, one needs to think in terms of how they will interpret the action. This is compounded by the fact that in many contemporary conflicts insurgents are also part of the civilian population. This informs the paradox in counter-insurgency that the 'best weapons don't shoot'.[8] The death of an insurgent can create many more insurgents from his family and friends. Lieutenant General Sir Graeme Lamb states in his guidance for commanders engaged in counter-insurgency:

If you think you are doing well then think again: for it's not what you think, it's what they think that matters. If they think you are doing badly then you probably are. Review your progress from your own front line, from domestic and international perspectives, then reverse the telescope and look at it from the insurgent, the local, Arab [this quotation is related to the context of Iraq] and regional point of view. Always weigh in favour of the latter and not your own assessment of the success of the plan.[9]

General Lamb's succinct guidance perhaps seeks to militate against the fact that war as a cognitive unit as it is employed today often fails to achieve purchase on a strategic audience because it seeks to allocate military meaning to situations in which force actually has a direct political effect on that audience.

Armed force has frequently in the past been used outside war for direct political effect; but these cases are not understood in terms of war, or a military outcome. This has often been the case with what is publicly known of direct political action sponsored by intelligence agencies. Even if direct political action is used within war, it is usually kept secret precisely because it is different from normal military action. The key point is that this direct political use of armed force has not employed the cognitive construct of war.

Where force has direct political significance, but is used within an interpretive construct of war in the Clausewitzian, or inter-state paradigm, war's mechanism is compromised. Clausewitzian paradigms of war stop working when they cannot invest the use of armed force with military significance. To use an analogy, the market is an interpretive structure whose function is to impose a specific type of meaning, a price, on a product. When the market cannot allocate a price (which is one of its basic functions), its mechanism breaks down and it loses utility. This happened in the financial crisis of 2008, when many derivatives were so complex that the market could not price them. The market seized up as its basic mechanism stopped working. When an action in war can be interpreted in a multitude of different ways depending on the prejudice of the audience, it is very hard to make armed force have political utility in a Clausewitzian conception of war: for a military outcome to set conditions for a political solution it needs to be recognised as such.

In summary, the extent and speed of inter-connectivity associated with contemporary globalisation has great potential to unhinge classical strategy because of the proliferation of audiences beyond the enemy. Just as Clausewitz emphasised that social forces were primarily what transformed war after the French Revolution, so too does globalisation in its contemporary form, as a social force, change war again.

Contemporary globalisation undermines the two pillars of war in the Clausewitzian paradigm: first, the assumption that strategic audiences are contained within the state; second, the principle of polarity. In an inter-connected world there is a massive extension of the size of potential strategic audiences beyond one's side/state and the enemy's, which strategy will struggle not to recognise as relevant. The fact that they are all very unlikely to see the war in the same way means that a notion of definite 'victory' is significantly diluted; we speak instead more about 'success'.

While the term 'success' may indicate a middle ground between victory and defeat, the term is more revealing in the sense that it shares common ground with the language usually used to describe domestic politics. A party in office is not 'victorious' but 'successful' if it achieves its goals while balancing the interests of the government's various constituencies. This is not coincidental, but reflective of the politicisation of many contemporary conflicts down to the tactical level; indeed, more familiar political problems, such as the economy, are often continuously managed rather than having finite and definite solutions. If we now return to Afghanistan, it is clear that the dynamics that characterise contemporary conflict there, in which the 'war' is better understood as a direct extension of political activity—the attempt to convince a set of audiences of a given political 'narrative'—are not anomalous.

Afghanistan and the trajectory of contemporary conflict

The political fragmentation that characterises the Afghan conflict is likely to point to the future of contemporary conflict rather than prove to be an anomaly. In Afghanistan the coalition, in partnership with the Afghan government, has to convince a disparate group of people, including insurgents, to accept its strategic narrative. In one sense this strategic narrative is in competition with the strategic narrative of 'the enemy' in the insurgency. However, the conflict in Afghanistan cannot be described exclusively in terms of a polarised competition. A victory for one side is not necessarily a defeat for the other, particularly because there are not two clear sides. Rather than two polarised 'sides' there are endless 'actors' and 'audiences', which often overlap. These can be individuals or groups. The conflict in Afghanistan is far more of a game of political musical chairs than a two-way fight.

In terms of the 'enemy' there are broadly three groups against whom the coalition fights: the Taliban, associated more with southern Afghanistan and the city of Quetta; the Haqqani Network; and Hizb-i-Islami Gulbuddin (HiG), associated more with the east and the cities of Peshawar/Miram Shah. Beyond this are a number of syndicates who may operate in Afghanistan but whose focus is primarily in Pakistan or in central Asian states.[10] The al-Qaeda presence is very small.

However, the insurgency in Afghanistan, at the time of writing, can be broken down further into endless sub-groups who fight for different reasons. Many are insurgents with a legitimate grievance, many of whom see themselves as defending their land rather than fighting for any wider motive, as Kilcullen's concept of the 'accidental guerrilla' posits.[11] The official Afghan government language promoting the reintegration of insurgent fighters refers to them as 'lost brothers', or 'angry brothers' (in many cases legitimately) who need to be brought back on side. This confuses the idea of polarised sides. Other insurgent motivations vary widely: crime, drugs, money, a certain interpretation of Islam, revenge, excitement, war against the foreigner. The list goes on and motivations are usually found in combination. Having questioned captured insurgents myself, many are unclear in their own mind of their motivations; their self-identification as 'Mujahideen', which is one of the common features of most insurgents, belies a large range of possible meanings.

Self-interest, rather than commitment to a wider movement, is the predominant motivation of many of the Taliban's field commanders in southern Afghanistan. They obey Quetta's direction when it suits them. At the tactical level, Taliban fighting groups frequently fail to come to one another's support in battle; such selfishness is rational in the sense that they do not strongly identify with one another. To try to understand the tactical actions of the Taliban in terms of a wider 'operational intent' is thus usually wrong. Only rarely can the Taliban actually achieve this level of coordination when a particularly influential commander can temporarily unite different groups. When they do, it can be effective and catch coalition forces off guard; the fact that really serious insurgent ambushes or deliberate attacks are actually quite rare are the exceptions that prove the general rule.

For instance, in August 2010 a platoon-sized group of insurgents tried to overrun one of the checkpoints in our battle-group area in a coordinated operation which involved a preliminary diversionary attack and proper fire support; this led to an intense fight lasting well into the night. A handful of soldiers from the Mercian Regiment, attached to the Gurkha Battlegroup, successfully fought off insurgents on their perimeter, with the assistance of considerable fire support, after all the Afghan soldiers in their checkpoint had been wounded. Yet this was a highly anomalous event which had been coordinated by an unusually dynamic insurgent commander. Most Taliban 'operational' commanders actually struggle to coordinate the actions of 'their' fighting groups, who often only agree to a plan when it suits them.

The counter-argument would be that there does seem to be clear intent behind much of what 'the' insurgency does in terms of deliberate operations. The suicide bombings and assassinations, for example, are against carefully selected political targets. Many of the 'spectacular' attacks are designed to humiliate the Afghan government politically at particular points, such as during the visit of VIPs, or to coincide with international conferences. I would agree with such a line of argument. The Taliban senior leadership and the other groups associated with the insurgency do clearly have a capability to translate a political intent formulated by the senior leadership into actions on the ground. However, spectacular attacks do not require many people; they are much easier to coordinate than the day-to-day activity of all insurgent groups in a district, let alone across the country. In many ways the Taliban leadership's spectacular attacks are just as much about the encouragement of an idea that has themselves at the head of an organised movement, and thus legitimise their own position, as about the political impact against their enemies.

The Taliban fail to define themselves. In one study by Martine van Bijlert of Uruzgan Province (published in 2009) the term 'Taliban' had many different senses: *Taliban-e jangi* or *Taliban-e shuri* (fighting or insurgent Taliban) as opposed to *Taliban-e darsi* (madrassa students), some of whom may exclusively be students and not fight; *Taliban-e alsi* (the real Taliban) or *Taliban-e pak* (the clean Taliban) which referred to the honest Taliban committed to Islamic principles of justice as opposed to opportunistic Taliban, and sometimes opposed to *Taliban-e Pakistani*, who do Pakistan's bidding; *Taliban-e duzd* (the thief Taliban), who were local bandits; *Taliban-e mahali* (local Taliban), as opposed to outsiders (van Bijlert notes that the local Taliban were not always seen as less violent to the civilian population than outsiders); some were previously known as *zalem* (cruel) or *badmash* (no-good); *Taliban-e khana-neshin* (Taliban sitting at home) who are generally those associated with the 1990s Taliban, who are not currently active, but may have taken refuge in places such as Quetta, Helmand or Kandahar.

Van Bijlert also writes that such descriptions are often associated with concepts such as *majbur* (forced) and *naraz* (dissatisfied) to nuance the explanation of the behaviour of leaders associated with the Taliban. *Majbur* implies that the individual was persecuted by local authorities or international forces for associations with the original Taliban and now had no option but to fight for the new Taliban.[12] *Naraz* implies that the individual has been humiliated in some way, perhaps as a result of not having been offered any government role, or not being treated in accordance with his social standing. Van Bijlert argues that in both cases loss of face in front of their tribe or constituency has been the key driver of the rise of the Taliban in Uruzgan. Van Bijlert points out that a conceptual framework that recognises that the Taliban is not a unified organisation could legitimately be used to describe the original Taliban of the 1990s; she acknowledges the enduring validity of Bernt Glatzer's description of the original Taliban as 'a caravan to which different people attached themselves for various reasons'.[13]

The Taliban, when the term is used as a label to describe the whole insurgency rather than just its leadership, is better understood as a franchise than as a unified, centrally controlled movement. There are several audiences among the insurgency, whose political stances are frequently different from one another; what convinces one actor to stop fighting may not persuade another.

That the Taliban insurgency is a franchise movement is part of the problem with trying to negotiate a political solution with the Taliban leadership. When the Taliban leadership takes credit for the actions of those in the franchise, they may seem to exert real control over the movement, which in reality they do not. If the leadership were to negotiate a political solution only to have it ignored by the groups it claims to control, it would lose all credibility. The Taliban leadership possibly knows this, and understands that a deal might result in their political marginalisation. That does not mean it is not in their interests to negotiate, for while they do so, they increase the legitimacy of their claim to represent the movement and gain power. The coalition's application of a polarised model of war ironically gives the leadership of the insurgency more credibility than it really has. A distinct, but related, point is that the difficulties inherent in the coalition achieving decisive top-down solutions make the case for attempting bottom-up solutions; this in turn requires a close understanding of the conflict on its own terms at the local political level.

A further complication to a political settlement is the perception among some insurgents that reconciliation with the Afghan government essentially equates to honourable surrender. In Northern Ireland, the Good Friday Agreement was based on the existence of opposing parties who could provide a political channel for insurgent grievances. One of the key issues with Irish Republican Army (IRA) weapons decommissioning was the possibility that it would be perceived as the IRA apologising for having fought. The political approach to reconciliation in Afghanistan is different from a model in which the appeal to insurgents is to resolve their problems through non-violent political means. No party in the Afghan government represents the Taliban.

Adam Holloway MP sagely argued in 2009 that what he terms the 'patriotic' elements of the Taliban, who have legitimate political grievances, 'must be allowed to claim much of the success in local areas for reducing the presence of international forces and the establishment of order'.[14] As Daniel Marston writes in his chapter on Afghanistan in *Counterinsurgency in Modern Warfare* (2010): 'it is critical to remember that today's so-called enemy is likely to be part of tomorrow's solution. This has always been true, throughout the history of counterinsurgency'.[15]

The Afghan government is as much a franchise as the insurgency. The self-interest of the majority of the key players is more in evidence than a sense of ideological commitment to the government. Ahmed Wali Karzai, the President's half-brother, was the key government figure in Kandahar until his assassination in July 2011. The majority of coalition security contracts, a huge sum of money, went through his businesses, or those owned by his relatives. His allegedly close connections to powerful narcotics factions, inside and outside the government, were widely known. The government was very profitable for him. Ahmed Rashid, a leading authority on the insurgency in Afghanistan and Pakistan, writes that Tajik and Uzbek warlords in the north of the country are reported to have become so 'rich and powerful that they barely listen to [President] Karzai'. He adds that governors of northern provinces have created their own fiefdoms that are left alone by NATO forces based there because removing them would create further instability.[16]

The Afghan Army also exhibits characteristics of a franchise. In some areas they are very effective. The most obvious example of this is in close quarter combat, where their warriors (the Afghan National Army term for private soldier) have consistently shown themselves to be very brave. One domain where the franchise factor does come into play is in their logistics. The notion that army resources belong to the state, not to the individual officer, still finds significant resistance in many quarters. This may be an unfair criticism. To expect the Afghan National Army to model its logistic arrangements on a Western system is perhaps to go against the grain of how armed forces can operate reasonably effectively through a patronage-based system. Where a common conception of loyalty to the state cannot be assumed, other mechanisms of maintaining unity could perhaps be seen as the more pragmatic option.[17]

Nor are the government and insurgent franchises exclusive. Family, social, business and political connections cut across the government-insurgent divide. Many of the Taliban, particularly at the local level, are literally the relatives of those on the government side. For many Afghan district governors, or Afghans of the urban landowning class, to have friends in the Taliban is entirely common (and probably, in their own mind, sensible). Many are old Mujahideen fighting companions of the 1980s now on different sides of the fence, but still friends. For example, the Afghan government district governor of Musa Qala, Mullah Saalam, in 2007 said that a major Taliban commander called Abdul Bari 'is our friend'; to understand such comments as unusual would be to misunderstand the dynamics of the conflict.[18]

Other actors in the political kaleidoscope of the Afghan conflict have real power, but are not clearly identifiable with the government or the insurgency. Antonio Giustozzi, in the article, 'Armed Politics and Political Competition in Afghanistan' (2011), analyses in far more depth than is offered here the dynamics of armed political competition by non-state actors that have been extensive in post-2001 Afghanistan.[19] Several militia groups which were officially disbanded in 2005 continue to hold real power, often within the Afghan police. Moreover, the old Mujahideen parties endure as important political constituencies. Giustozzi makes particularly evocative use of political maps (see Figures 5 and 6) to show the extent of affiliation of various Afghan provincial governors and MPs to the two main branches of Afghanistan's Islamic movement: Jamiat-i Islami, formerly led by Ahmed Shah Masood, who were the core of the Northern Alliance of 2001; Hizb-i Islami, the movement whose part led by Gulbudin Hekmatyar now forms the core of the insurgency in eastern Afghanistan, but who have a legal identity as a legitimate political movement within Afghanistan, which disassociates itself from Hekmatyar.

We have to understand the conflict in Afghanistan on its own terms. In a personal example, diluted for security, an Afghan district governor I

Figure 5: Giustozzi's map of governorship positions in 2002, by affiliation.[20]

knew explained that certain elements of the insurgency in his district were not of great concern to him personally. He and his peer group were landlords, and these elements of the insurgency were mostly the sons of some of their tenants. These 'Taliban' represent only a limited threat to them, although the out of area insurgent fighters were a genuine concern. This governor was on a day-to-day basis more concerned about a large militia that was on the government side, but he did not see it as being on his side. The militia was tied into a faction based on the Barakzai tribe which competed for power in Gereshk; the governor was not from that faction. He could not have effectively exercised authority without ISAF being there as a counter-balance to the militia's authority. Therefore the governor and the militia were both on the ISAF side, but not on each

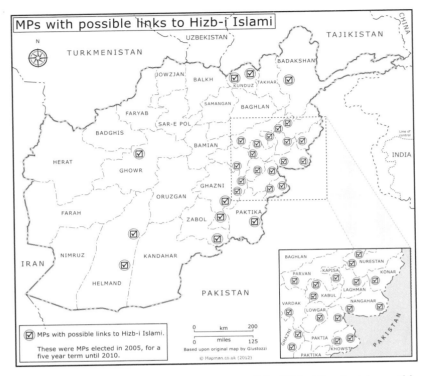

Figure 6: Giustozzi's map of MPs (members of the Wolesi Jirga) with possible links to Hizb-i Islami. These were MPs elected in 2005, for a five-year term until 2010.[21]

other's sides. The governor's main concern was to position himself politically for the future. He and the man commanding the militia were actors in their own right, affiliated more to themselves than to their side. These examples are not anomalies; they are the norm. There are endless examples of linkages between those on the 'Taliban' side and those on the 'government' side. This is illogical in a strictly polarised conception of conflict, but makes sense when understood in terms of a politically kaleidoscopic frame.

The 1980s Afghan conflict exhibited similar political dynamics. The two-way fight between the Mujahideen and the government was the most visible dynamic during the conflict. Yet the government side was continuously fractured between different interest groups, most obviously the two factions of the Communist People's Democratic Party of Afghanistan (Parcham and Khalq). Moreover, any assumption that there was an underlying two-way ideological polarity which defined friend and enemy would have to contend with what happened in the subsequent 'Mujahideen' period of the early 1990s. The Mujahideen fought one another. Many changed sides and backed what was left of the Afghan government side; the original Taliban then fought the Mujahideen, most of whom merged into the new Taliban. A polarised conception of war cannot comprehend situations in which force is used directly in the interplay of normal, untidy, political intercourse.

The political loyalties of the Afghan people are complicated. The majority of civilians in Afghanistan do not want to be ruled by the radical elements among the Taliban; that is consistently clear in private conversation, even if Afghans will rarely say so publicly. The north of Afghanistan in particular generally has strong antipathy towards the Taliban. That does not, however, necessarily translate into support for the government of Afghanistan, against which many civilians have legitimate grievances. Often the problem for coalition efforts is that locals often want ISAF, whom they essentially trust, and whose presence they want, but are more wary of parts of the Afghan security forces. Yet the same people that plead for coalition troops not to leave will enthusiastically rehearse the somewhat enervating rumours of secret foreign plots to occupy Afghanistan, which are ubiquitous. One of the most common rumours is that America and Britain are secretly backing the Taliban to facilitate a Pakistani takeover. The fact that such a ludicrous proposition is genuinely so widespread is an indication of how vulnerable people are to superstitious nonsense after thirty years of violence.

At the local level the most important motivation for the inhabitants is self-preservation. The people have been in war, more or less, since 1979; if they were not good at survival they would probably already be dead. In light of self-preservation, the relative benefits of life under either side proposed by the competing narratives are peripheral: people become actors in their own right. For locals to have family associations to both the Taliban and the Afghan government, sometimes with a son in both, is not uncommon, and is logical from their point of view. As one Afghan village elder once put it to Major Shaun Chandler, in a quintessentially memorable expression: 'everyone holds two watermelons in one hand'.

Finally, conflict evolves. The conflict in Afghanistan I have described here is only its present state. There are several variables which can significantly change the dynamics. If the Pakistani state, for example, should amplify its support for the insurgency after coalition forces have left, the conflict might move closer to being a more genuine war. Pakistani state support was a key factor in the original Taliban's success at taking power in 1994–6. Whether this scenario will be repeated is perhaps a 'known unknown'.

Strategic thought tends to reject the idea that 'gang warfare' is really war. Gangs and criminals use force for direct advantage rather than within a mechanism that provides a military decision on which a political outcome is based. This is political advantage in the broad sense of an adjustment of circumstances in one's favour, as opposed to just describing competition for state offices. Yet this is close to the way in which force is used by many actors in the war in Afghanistan, although it does not make the use of violence any less lethal.

In the Clausewitzian paradigm of war, the enemy is coerced into subscription to one's strategic narrative: he dies, or becomes no longer relevant. This makes the translation of force into political meaning relatively simple. Even if the enemy utilises a different interpretive structure, one can ultimately force an outcome upon him. While armed conflict continues to be at its core a clash of organised violence, the Clausewitzian notion that attack is the 'positive' and defence the 'negative' component of translating force into political meaning, a war's 'decision', is compromised in Afghanistan. Ultimately the more fragmented a political environment, the more actions are interpreted individually in directly political terms rather than as part of the military balance in the scale of a conflict's military outcome. The proliferation of strategic audiences beyond the enemy means that force no longer has a clear target: one cannot 'force' an outcome on a strategic audience that is not the enemy; they may well be free to ignore the war's military outcome.

The effect of violence in fragmented political environments

Clausewitz saw three elements at play in war: policy, passion and war's uncertain dynamics, 'the play of chance and probability'. He referred to this as the 'trinity' of war, in that these three elements formed the 'one', which was war. These three elements of war were for Clausewitz represented in his conception of the state at war. Reason (or policy) was represented by the government (bearing in mind that Clausewitz's Prussia was a monarchy) and passion by the people. The army did not strictly represent war's dynamics, but was the component of the state that had to confront the uncertainty inherent in combat.[22]

The nature of war was for Clausewitz constant, even though its character evolved. By situating war's nature in terms of the interaction of three variables, his definition remains flexible. While the Afghan conflict is not war in an inter-state sense, its basic nature can still be comprehended in terms of an interaction of these three elements. However, unlike in conventional inter-state war (in which policy tends to be the dominant characteristic), as there are a multitude of political actors, the role of human passion, and the unpredictable, potentially explosive, dynamics of violent clash, increasingly infrom the conflict's basic definition.

The consequence of the use of violence in war is often that fighting generates an antagonism of its own that distances people from their political common ground. Clausewitz acknowledged this: 'even where there is no national hatred and no animosity to start with, the fighting itself will stir up hostile feelings'.[23] Clausewitz understood violence to be an explosive, reciprocal force. The idea that 'violence begets violence' has always been part of human conflict; as Tacitus put it: 'once killing starts, it is difficult to draw the line'.[24] However, while the Clausewitzian paradigm recognises that violence may accentuate, or entirely generate, emotional antagonism, that antagonism is delimited by the strategic audiences' location within two polarised constituencies, typically the state parties to a conflict.

Where force is used within a fragmented political environment, it creates new enemies, who are not necessarily linked to any state. The essential feature of such an environment is that violence is not bound within the bilateral, polarised conception of two states at war; it has unpredictable, and often tragic, political outputs. The sectarian violence following the break-up of Yugoslavia, and in Iraq, occurred between communities who had previously co-existed, but were torn apart by the reciprocal hatred which violence causes.

This dynamic would appear to run in parallel with what Stathis N. Kalyvas has so persuasively argued in *The Logic of Violence in Civil War* (2006).[25] He posits that the mainstream narratives of most civil wars tend to locate violence in terms of macro-level emotions, ideologies or cultures. However, the empirical evidence points to a far more complex and fragmented analysis. What can be incorrectly labelled as 'madness' (i.e. complex, fragmented and irregular patterns of violence) actually has logic, but this is often to be found at the micro, not the macro level: 'because of the domination of national-level cleavages, grassroots dynamics are often perceived merely as their local manifestations. Likewise, local actors are only seen as local replicas of central actors'.[26] Violence at the local level is often produced by actors trying to avoid the worst and taking opportunities:

> For many people who are not naturally bloodthirsty and abhor direct involvement in violence, civil war offers irresistible opportunities to harm everyday enemies… Rather than just politicizing private life, civil war works the other way around as well: it privatises politics. Civil War often transforms local and personal grievances into lethal violence; once it occurs, this violence becomes endowed with a political meaning that may be quickly naturalised into new and enduring identities. Typically, the trivial origins of these new identities are lost in the fog of memory or reconstructed according to the new politics fostered by the war.[27]

Kalyvas argues that agency in the violence of civil wars is partly a function of 'alliance' between the centre and the periphery in that both use the other to their advantage. This allows for multiple, not unitary actors. He recognises that 'master-narratives' can legitimately identify the 'master-cleavage' in a civil war, but it is usually accorded too much significance post-conflict in the desire to 'simplify, streamline, and ultimately erase the war's complexities, contradiction and ambiguities'. Hence:

> Actions in civil war, including 'political violence', are not necessarily political, and do not always reflect deep ideological polarisation … an approach positing unitary actors, inferring the dynamics of identity and action exclusively from the master-cleavage, and framing civil wars in binary terms is misleading… Civil war fosters a process of interaction between actors with distinct identities and interests. It is the convergence between local motives and supralocal that endows civil war with its intimate character and leads to joint violence that straddles the divide between the political and the private, the collective and the individual.[28]

When the interpretive framework of Clausewitzian war is dragged into a situation which is closer to being a direct extension of policy through 'armed politics', be it in civil war as analysed by Kalyvas, or in the current politically kaleidoscopic Afghan conflict, serious strategic confusion can occur. The key difference being that the interpretive framework of war in the Clausewitzian tradition presupposes a bilateral polarity which channels violence and a stability of association between strategic audiences and their state. Thus violence may well escalate hostilities, but it exaggerates them rather than creating new ones.

The use of political violence for a prolonged period of time outside of the interpretive framework of 'war' is not a new phenomenon. The British attempt to keep in check the Pathan (now known as Pashtun) tribes on India's North-West Frontier with Afghanistan saw virtually not a single year pass between 1849 and 1947 without one or more military campaigns in the region (there were 60 campaigns pre-1900 alone). David Loyn in *Butcher and Bolt* (2008) has described this as 'an intensity of conflict unique in the world'.[29] The 1897 General Uprising against the British led to the deployment of an army 44,000 strong in the Tirah Campaign of 1897–98; this was the largest force ever deployed by the British in Asia to that point, and even then, it was outnumbered by the tribesmen.[30] Each campaign was intended to reach some kind of political settlement with the various tribes; force was used with an admixture of money and threats to maintain a delicate political balance for almost a century.

While this approach can legitimately be seen as successful from one perspective, the long-term fusion of military and political activity had destabilising consequences. British policy on the North-West Frontier provided an ideological counter-point for the radicalisation of people into Islamic extremists. David Loyn documents how the Wahabbi-inspired Deobandi strand of Islamic thought produced militants who sought to integrate themselves with the Pathan tribes. By 1849, for example, militants controlled the Swat Valley. The Ambeyla campaign in 1863 to eject them cost the British over 800 dead; prototype 'bomb factories' were found by the troops that cleared their base. Twelve-thousand-five-hundred men were needed five years later to dislodge militants who had made common cause with tribesmen in Sittana. Fanatical militants, called 'ghazis', used to fight alongside the Pathan tribes under the green banner of Islam as distinct units, travelling to conduct jihad.[31]

David Loyn states that the first recorded attempt at a suicide attack on British troops in Afghanistan was in Kandahar on 17 January 1880: a man calling himself a *Talib-ul-ulm* ran up to a British Engineer Sergeant and tried to kill him but was stopped.[32] In 1895 Mullah Powin-dah, a fundamentalist mystic, led his network of militants into the Swat Valley and joined forces with the Wahabists there under Mullah Sadhullah. Their call for jihad against the British was backed by the Afghan king, Abdur Rahman. Loyn notes how Abdur Rahman quoted the same passages from the Koran as Osama Bin Laden later used.[33] This Islamic narrative was inter-twined with the Pathan General Uprising of 1897. After their defeat in the Tirah campaign, the militants moved to an even more remote area and even started to publish a newspaper called *Mujaheed*.[34]

Loyn's remarkable account of this century of political violence, which can only be summarised in its most basic form here, illustrates the unstable and unpredictable consequences of the use of force outside the interpretive structure of war in the Clausewitzian sense. Loyn's argument is perhaps encapsulated by his assertion that the same villages in Waziristan that were the first to rise up against Great Britain and back the ghazis, later backed the Mujahideen, and now back Al Qaeda.

A counter-point to the rather austere radicalising trends at play during the century Loyn describes is provided by John Masters, a Gurkha officer who describes his experience living and fighting on the North-West Frontier, particularly from 1936–7, in the first of his autobiographical books, *Bugles and a Tiger* (1956). He recounts, for instance, that after each campaigning season 'scores of Pathans' who had been fighting against the British Indian army would earnestly apply to their British political agent for the Frontier Medal (the medal more typically awarded to soldiers of the British Indian army rather than to the 'enemy'!) with the appropriate clasp; after all, in their view they had valiantly fought in the same actions.[35] Masters' retrospective account of the texture of the British Empire's interaction with the peoples of the North-West Frontier at its twilight is a reminder that there were more subtle narratives at play in that period too: the notion of the politically kaleidoscopic battle-space is a long-standing feature of conflict that the contemporary context merely exaggerates.

To this point *War From the Ground Up* has sought to draw attention to what characterises the concept of war in contemporary conflict, in particular to identify the continuities, evolutions, or breaks with war as more traditionally defined in its inter-state paradigm; the concept as posited by Clausewitz being the primary point of comparison. Clausewitz wrote about war shortly after its transformation by Napoleon; war today is again being transformed by the information revolution, which forces liberal powers to reconsider strategic thought in relation to their use of armed force. The remainder of the book examines how the West can operate in the politically fragmented, and interpretively unstable, environments which tend to characterise contemporary conflicts.

4

STRATEGIC DIALOGUE AND POLITICAL CHOICE

When in contemporary conflict the application of force moves towards being a direct extension of policy, but is shoehorned into the interpretive structure of war in its more traditional, Clausewitzian sense, armed force frequently fails to connect to political utility. The following three pairs of chapters examine possible responses to this problem by liberal powers. Three themes are developed: the construction of the political context of conflict through strategic dialogue (Chapters 4 and 5); the construction of operational approaches (Chapters 6 and 7); and the construction of strategic narratives, which connect operational approaches to their political context (Chapters 8 and 9).

Strategic dialogue is the reciprocal interaction between policy, in the sense of the political decisions and intentions of the state, and how policy is articulated as actual operations: the interaction between what is desired and what is possible. I make a distinction between the organisation of strategic dialogue, in terms of the procedural configuration of how strategy is made within the state, and the substantive output that dialogue produces: the strategy itself. This chapter considers strategic dialogue in terms of what political choice means in contemporary conflict. The next chapter considers how well liberal powers, particularly in terms of their civil-military structures, are configured to conduct effective strategic dialogue.

When tactical actions are highly politicised, strategy needs to ensure that policy is politically coherent down to the tactical level; this is consistent with the role of strategy in armed conflict as a bridge between political and operational activity. Yet when liberal powers do not understand a problem on its own terms, applying instead a distorting paradigm of war, proper strategic dialogue is frustrated. This is primarily because conventional war is often understood as a decisive, finite, event; the flow of direction is one way, from policy through various levels to tactical execution; the military execute, but do not question policy. Moreover, strategic dialogue is blocked the other way too: when a default association is made between the action of armed forces taking place within the military domain of 'war', the traditional view is that civilian politicians, once their policy direction has been given, should 'stay out' of military activity. That view is misguided; policy makers should be as close as possible, realistically, in a vicarious sense, to the political pulse of the conflict on the ground.

The strategic 'level' in contemporary conflict

Strategy links deliberate action to political outcomes. In the Clausewitzian paradigm, while the lines of policy continue into war and drive military action, actions within war seek intermediate military, not directly political, objectives. In this context the strategic 'level' can legitimately be understood to be at the juncture of military and political activity, the boundary perhaps between war and international politics; this would normally be defined procedurally in terms of the interaction of politicians and generals. Below that level is the domain of operational military planning that ultimately serves a political end, but is itself military. In this context, for the policy-maker to consult 'ground truth' means to consult generals, not the soldiers below them, about the feasibility of achieving a given policy.

In the Second World War, for example, the experience of the common solider was clearly ground truth of a sort, but not the kind that mattered to policy. The interaction between military action and policy—strategic dialogue—occurred much higher in the chain of command. This made sense as the juncture of military and political actions was usually at the level of whole corps and army groups. For instance, General Patton's push into Czechoslovakia with his Third Army Group in the dying days of the war in 1945 was primarily driven by political factors in terms of the race against Soviet occupation rather than the German military threat.

There is an important distinction to be made between two possible significations of what the 'strategic level' means in the context of armed conflict. First, it means a location of strategic authority, in the sense that a person, usually of very senior military or diplomatic rank, makes decisions that formulate and adjust the strategic basis of operational plans in light of policy, and potentially makes recommendations to policy-makers to adjust policy in light of operational reality. Second, the strategic level can be understood as a domain in which an action has a political quality.

In traditionally defined conventional war there tends to be an overlap between the location of strategic authority and the location at which people make decisions that have a political quality, as in the example of General Patton above. In contemporary conflicts, however, the tendency is for there not to be a neat overlap, but an expansion of the strategic domain. This domain includes, but also goes far beyond, those who have strategic authority, like one circle expanding beyond another. Relatively junior commanders find themselves making decisions which although nowhere near as significant in scale as 'strategic' decisions made by those who have strategic authority, nonetheless have a directly political quality, however insignificant those actions in themselves may be, and so are also, in an alternative sense, 'strategic'.

This creates something of a mismatch, and can change the role of the commander with strategic authority, especially in emphasising his or her co-ordaining function across several tactical sub-units/agencies, military and civilian, relative to the function more traditionally associated with the strategic commander, of delivering decisive blows to the enemy.

In contemporary conflict, tactical action frequently does have directly political significance. This is not just when a tactical event is picked up by the global media, but also on a routine basis. The political outcome of a conflict is the accumulated outcome of innumerable individual actions as opposed to decisive blows against the enemy. This type of cumulative campaign has been described in the context of Iraq and Afghanistan by Dr Conrad Crane as a 'mosaic' conflict.[1] This term encapsulates the idea that the war is best represented by the accumulated effect of a multitude of sub-narratives, none of which is decisive in itself. In this context, strategy looks to brigades, battlegroups and companies, and their respective civilian equivalents and host nation partners, to deliver political results. Each may be pursuing very different activities, ranging from high-intensity combat to humanitarian work, even within a small physical space. Figures 7 and 8 exemplify mosaic conflict in the context of the coalition effort in Iraq in 2004.[2]

In such circumstances strategic considerations have to inform tactical action, in order to link tactical actions to political purpose. There may still be a 'strategic level' in the sense that it denotes a particular grade of civilian/military authority, but this should not be confused with the location of strategic effect, that is, the strategic domain. Strategic effect in many contemporary conflicts, including Afghanistan, is fragmentary: 'in counter-insurgency, the levels of war are all flattened'.[3]

The problem of how to have strategic effect in a fragmented conflict environment was considered in 1967 by Admiral J. C. Wylie, who distinguished between 'sequential' and 'cumulative' strategies.[4] Sequential strategies were linear. To achieve the goal of policy, step A led to B, led to C. He uses General MacArthur's island-hopping campaign in the Pacific during the Second World War as an example. Decisiveness, traditionally the feature by which an action has been defined as 'strategic' (rather than 'tactical'), is stamped on history with every step taken along a single path to the ultimate objective.

Cumulative strategies could be just as decisive, but far less perceptibly so. The US navy's wider contribution to the war in the Pacific is used as an example. The cumulative effect of each Japanese naval and merchant ship sunk, for instance, gradually choked the Japanese economy, a critical component of the US Pacific war effort. For Admiral Wylie these strategies were not mutually exclusive, as their unity in the overall Pacific campaign makes clear. In some ways Wylie's 'cumulative' strategy is about how to conceptualise an attritional strategy: the final result may be decisive, but the distance from the destination may not be signposted as clearly as an outcome arrived at through a series of decisive battles.

In Afghanistan, Wylie's argument is equally applicable. Decisive, sequential, strategic actions may legitimately be pursued, such as some form of negotiated settlement with the Taliban. Certain military actions may also have decisive strategic effect in themselves: the 2011 Osama Bin Laden raid being an example. However, in parallel with sequential approaches, the coalition is pursuing a cumulative campaign gradually to reconfigure the political landscape, namely by attempting to connect people to the Afghan government.

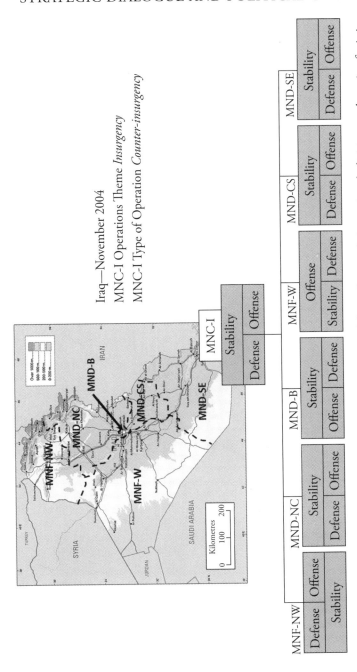

Figure 7: The 'mosaic' nature of US operations in Iraq in 2004. Each box refers in relation to its sub-divisions to the ratio of mission types that the formation was conducting. (MNC-I is Multi National Corps Iraq, MNF is Multi National Force, MND is Multi National Division, with a corresponding geographic orientation direction, or 'B' for Baghdad).

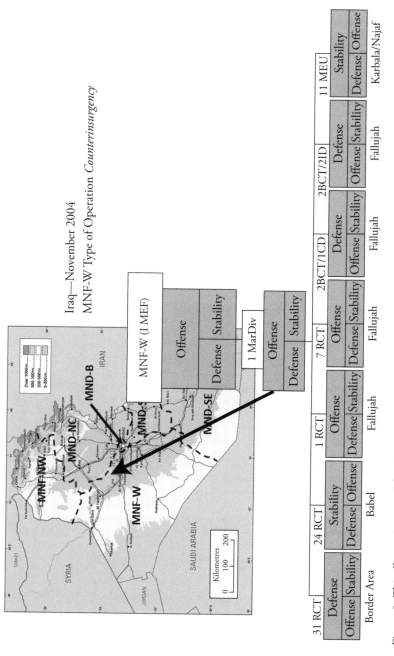

Iraq—November 2004
MNF-W Type of Operation *Counterinsurgency*

Figure 8: This illustration amplifies the situation in Multi National Force West, which was at the time held by 1 MEF (Marine Expeditionary Force). The mosaic nature of conflict is replicated within each of its RCTs and BCTs (Regimental/Brigade Combat Teams) and the MEU (Marine Expeditionary Unit).

To use a phrase from the world of political theory: 'all politics is local'. For armed force to be of political utility in mosaic conflicts, tactical actions often need to be considered primarily in terms of their local political effect, even if in their own right, such political effect is very small. This is different from situations in which armed forces only need to think about their actions in military terms. For instance, a decision to attack one group, or support another, whether desired or not (one may not know the affiliation of the insurgents one fights, or be able to avoid the fact that most projects empower some groups over others), will attract some realignment in the local political situation; that needs to fit in with one's broader strategy, or one's actions will politically be incoherent, like a politician who takes contradictory positions vis-à-vis the constituencies that he seeks to keep in balance. The critical implication is that political choices constantly need to be made at the tactical level.

As President Abraham Lincoln famously stated, 'you cannot please all the people all of the time'; this being the case, one cannot avoid making political choices. The key is how far they are planned and coherent, because one recognises the political quality of the action, or unplanned and incoherent, because one does not.

Contemporary conflict through the lens of domestic politics

The dynamics of the conflict in Afghanistan, like many other contemporary conflicts, are in many ways analogous to that of domestic politics in liberal democracies: strategy has to operate within a complex political environment that nobody can ever fully understand. Within this environment actors tend to act in a kaleidoscopic manner on the basis of self-interest.

The British army Jungle Warfare Advisor Course teaches that the 'jungle is neutral', after the famous book by F. Spencer Chapman.[5] This environment may be complex and intimidating, but has no favourites. To reject this complexity because one is unaccustomed to operating within it is a mistake. As in jungle warfare, one has an advantage once one accepts complexity and stops trying to fight against it by forcing it into the more straightforward polarised concept of war. The endless foliage of the jungle, like the infinite complexity of human societies, stops being an exhausting barrier to progress once one relaxes in that environment and comes to see its advantages, since its demanding texture is the same for everyone: most political environments are complex; that is normal.

The following vignette is from an exchange reported by Bob Woodward in his book *Obama's Wars* (2010) between General Stanley McChrystal and President Obama in 2009:

McChrystal presented a map of Kandahar and its suburbs that attempted to lay out the tribal dynamics. It was a crazy quilt of overlapping colors that resembled a piece of modern art... A spaghetti soup of dotted lines, dashed-dotted lines and double-dotted lines reflected what were believed to be the relationships and tribal loyalties. Some are Barakzais, others such as Karzai are Popalzais, and on and on. Some of the narcotics kingpins were listed...The President reflected on the Kandahar map and the power broker chart. 'This reminds me of Chicago politics', Obama said. 'You're asking me to understand the interrelationships and interconnections between ward bosses and district chiefs and the tribes of Chicago like the tribes of Kandahar. And I've got to tell you, I've lived in Chicago for a long time, and I don't understand that'.[6]

For Woodward, a highly experienced political journalist, to describe such complexity as 'crazy' in a military context is noteworthy. President Obama's reaction to this diagram reveals that he would be familiar with this way of conceptualising a problem in the context of domestic politics; and presumably, in a domestic political context, so would a political analyst of such skill as Woodward. A US political consultant, in the context of an election, would think about strategy precisely in terms of how to achieve political effect, in terms of overall public opinion, through the cumulative effects of fragmented local actions. The complexity of this diagram may appear unnerving as a military problem; yet the political environment it represents is very similar to the competition between a multitude of actors and interest groups in normal, messy, domestic politics.

General McChrystal's subsequent response to President Obama in Woodward's book is 'if it were Chicago we'd need far more troops!' While funny, there is some irony in the fact that the President has intuitively and immediately seen the problem in its own terms. That line of thought is, however, seen as a funny quirk, since this is not Chicago, it is 'war'. The President does not appear to see it as a legitimate line of thought with which to interrogate a policy problem.

Professional politicians have to be comfortable operating in uncertainty; nobody can ever fully understand any political environment, because human societies are so complex. Yet political theory exists that has successfully figured out how, broadly, to have effect in such an environment. US political marketing is perhaps the best example of this. Through detailed analysis of interest groups, one selects target audiences. Political messages, both in terms of actions and words, are carefully nuanced to achieve a change of perception among target audiences, and draw them towards one's narrative. While liberal democracies are entirely familiar with the application of such theory in the context of domestic politics, when it comes to war, or armed conflict, even when the dynamics are broadly analogous, to reject such complexity in favour of a simplified polarised narrative is the norm.

Admittedly, one will never have a complete political picture; that is impossible. One can always find out more about a society. In many ways the longer one spends in conflict environments such as Afghanistan, the more one realises how much one does not know. Yet to reduce what complexity one does acknowledge to a simple insurgent versus government model, just because one has an incomplete picture, is misguided. Reduction of complexity to black and white encourages the very type of anti-intellectualism that prevents strategy from understanding a problem on its own terms: we need to embrace complexity and deal with it, not reject it.

The conceptual crux of the problem is that Western liberal democracies often assume that military action consists of one concept when in fact it consists of two: military action means the use of armed force itself; it also refers to a military interpretive structure in which the application of armed force sets conditions for a political solution. In the Clausewitzian paradigm these concepts are symbiotic, as was set out in Chapter 1. When armed force is employed as a direct extension of policy in contemporary conflict, military action largely, and frequently unconsciously, leaves behind the accompanying interpretive structure of war as a military domain. Problems occur when the conceptualisation of the enemy in such circumstances has not evolved, and still presumes a military interpretive context that may not exist.

The relationship of a strategist to the 'enemy' in normal domestic political activity is significantly different from the enemy in the paradigm of inter-state war. For in the paradigm of inter-state war the enemy is also the strategic audience against whom one's actions seek to have an effect. In domestic politics an individual, or a target audience, may support the opposition, but that person or audience are not themselves the enemy. A politician in an election ideally would win over all of the electorate to his point of view. This may involve defeating the enemy, the opposition party, but one does not seek to defeat the electorate itself. In the same way a group of 'accidental guerrillas' may support the Taliban, but one should not be seeking their defeat; rather one should be seeking to pull them out from the sway of the Taliban.

There is a big difference between thinking about counter-insurgency in terms of the defeat of insurgents (i.e. actual people), and the defeat of an insurgency, which is ultimately an idea, or a group of ideas.

The International Security and Assistance Force (ISAF) campaign plan, redrawn in 2009, was based on the notion that the Afghan population was the 'strategic centre of gravity'; that is, their perceptions were judged to be the most important variable to campaign success, and the campaign was therefore planned with the primary objective of gaining their support for the Afghan government. In presentations that I have attended, this was usually the first step of the argument. The next step was usually that Kandahar city was the Taliban's centre of gravity. The third step was then that the control of the population in Kandahar city was therefore to be the ISAF campaign main effort. This was presented as a linear argument whose deductions lead into one another. While this may well have been the best course of action, to present it as a linear argument is problematic.

Focusing the campaign's main effort on the perceptions of the population in Kandahar city sought to achieve a decisive blow against the insurgency. Such a move indeed resembles the purpose of defining a centre of gravity in conventional warfare, to identify where to concentrate for the decisive blow to knock out the enemy. How does this concept translate in terms of Afghan counter-insurgency? In political terms, to have identified Kandahar city as the decisive point was a bold move; however, for a political consultant in a US Presidential election, it would be like the Democratic Party investing massive resources in trying to win Texas, or the Republicans California, seeking a knock-out of the other party rather than a victory on points. To continue such an analogy, massive investment of resources to take on the opponent's home base means taking risk on the support of one's own home base, and in more marginal areas. As this analogy suggests, if the defeat of the enemy is a means to an end (as in an election), rather than an end in itself, one does not necessarily need to capture the enemy's home base; that is only one course of action.

This is encapsulated by General Sir Graeme Lamb, who worked with General Stanley McChrystal in 2009 when the latter was commander of ISAF. In his evidence to the House of Commons Defence Select Committee, General Lamb states that he briefed General McChrystal in 2009: 'we [ISAF/the coalition] had, for seven or eight years, asked the question, "Where is the enemy?" The question we should have asked was, "Where should we be?"'[7]

Plans are not made in retrospect, and I emphatically do not seek to second-guess decisions made in 2009, which might well have been the best course of action. The point is, however, that if we take as a starting point the deduction that the population's political affiliations are the campaign centre of gravity, what we have is a problem with which a political consultant would be familiar in the context of an election. The defeat of the Taliban, like the defeat of one party by another in an election, is a means to an end if one has defined one's end as the will of the people. Thus while the decision to take on the Taliban in Kandahar as the centrepiece of the campaign may have been the best option, the linear three-step argument that is usually presented to justify it does seem to present a tension between the conception of a centre of gravity in conventional war and in Afghan counter-insurgency; the key variable being the difference of what the 'enemy' represents in either case.

This confusion of concepts gives rise to a paradox in the coalition approach to conflict in Afghanistan and the 'Long War' more generally. On the one hand, the liberal powers involved recognise that they are in a political war for perception and ideas on a global scale. However, when liberal powers are tempted to think about war in essentially inter-state terms, this assumption is insufficiently challenged: that military activity sets conditions for a political solution, but is itself apolitical. This can encourage liberal powers to think of military outcomes in absolute terms of 'winning' and 'losing', absolute standards of success or failure that are rarely evidenced in domestic politics. Every time the question 'are we winning in Afghanistan?' is asked, is the latent fixation with all armed conflict being understood implicitly in terms of inter-state war revealed.

*Armed politics: understanding and shaping the environment
in political terms*

David Kilcullen has characterised counter-insurgency as an 'armed variant of domestic politics'.[8] Antonio Giustozzi has used the term 'armed politics' to describe 'the distortion caused by the presence of non-state armed groups on the competitiveness of an otherwise open political system'.[9] Both of these definitions capture the essence of the problem: in such conflicts armed forces are required to have effect in an environment in which actors use an eclectic range of means, violent and non-violent, to compete vis-à-vis one another for political advantage (in the broad sense of power rather than just political advantage within state structures).

When one is fixated with the interpretation of any organised violence through the prism of inter-state war, whoever shoots at you becomes 'the enemy'. This encourages a mentality in which the enemy is treated as a unified political entity, and an assumption of a reasonable degree of coherence in their agenda, which confuses strategic planning. The last chapter argued this point in the context of Afghanistan. Yet neither does the 'terrorist' enemy of the Long War act with a single rationale. Application of a Clausewitzian paradigm distorts the situation. As Lieutenant General Sir Graeme Lamb, when the Commander of the Field Army, wrote on the front page of his *Counter-Insurgency Commander's Guidance* (2009): 'an insurgent fights for change, for the freedoms he believes in and a better life. You fight for change, for the freedoms you believe in and for a better life. What's the difference?'[10]

In the summer of 2010 the 1st Battalion Royal Gurkha Rifles (1 RGR) was based in central Helmand. While our purposes remained distinct, at one point the local insurgents started to build a road in imitation of a road we were building for the people. Conversely, the fact that the apparently efficient, if brutal, justice system offered by the Taliban is quite popular is a major incentive for the coalition to improve the Afghan justice system. These are but two of a number of examples of how, while we vilify one another, we can imitate one another in competition. This operates in the tactical domain too. While we seek to 'out-guerrilla the guerrilla', they copy some of our tactical methods. Patrick Porter, who looks at the theme of cultural mirror-imaging in *Military Orientalism*, cites a rather amusing quotation from the 2002 al-Qaeda 'newsletter': 'the time has come for the Islamic movements facing a general crusader offensive to internalise the rules of fourth-generation warfare'. Porter notes the irony of the fact that this concept was coined by Bill Lind, an American cultural conservative, in the US Marine Corps *Gazette* of 1989.[11]

The idea that many wars have resulted from political misunderstanding is well established. Neil Sheehan stresses this in *Bright Shining Lie* (1989), his account of the Vietnam War.[12] America saw Ho Chi Minh's forces as part of a wider communist threat rather than as a nationalist movement which used communism as a vehicle: 'anti-communism contributed to it [the Vietnam War] in the sense that because of their mindset, they [US leaders] wanted to see the world in black and white, they didn't want to see any shades of gray, and so you got a simple-minded anti-communism ... their instincts led them to look for simple-minded solutions and they then followed those simple-minded solutions to our grief'.[13]

The essential deduction is that, if force is to have political utility, one needs to understand the nature of the problem on its own terms, not through dogmatically applied ideological or doctrinal lenses. In contemporary conflict, if actions at the tactical level have direct political effect, they need to be planned with that in mind. Sheehan portrays Lieutenant Colonel John Paul Vann, the protagonist through which he often views the Vietnam War, stating: 'this is a political war, and it calls for discrimination in killing'.[14] The measures of such campaigns are the political opinions of target audiences. For Vann, the Hamlet Evaluation System, which graded each village in terms of its political sympathies, would become 'the body count of pacification'.[15]

If one fails to understand one's environment in its own political terms, one does not know what political effect one will have. Military action gains an element of lottery; one may arrest or kill insurgents because they are part of the 'enemy', but not know who they are in political terms. The political effect may be beneficial or hugely damaging: one simply does not know in advance. In wars of ideas, and battles for perception, merely to attack 'the enemy' in such a context is to push political buttons in the dark. As General Sir Frank Kitson wrote in *Low Intensity Operations* (1971), there is a need for both 'political intelligence' and 'operational intelligence' in these types of conflicts. This lesson, like many others in General Kitson's incisive book, has had to be relearned by the coalition forces in Iraq and Afghanistan.[16]

In response to this problem, one approach to counter-insurgency, used by 1 RGR in Afghanistan, sought to understand and shape the operating environment to have political effect, and to prosecute what

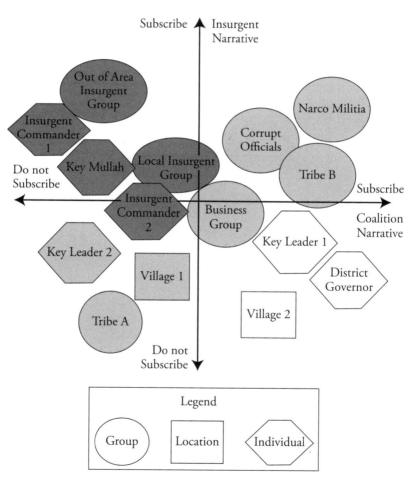

Figure 9: Basic target audience analysis chart (fictional).

might be termed 'legitimacy-centric counter-insurgency', in line with General McChrystal's direction at the time: to define how actors within the political environment subscribed to the narrative of the government of Afghanistan, and attempt to draw them towards it. Once one has some form of political understanding, one can tailor the strategic narrative to each audience. The chart at Figure 9 shows the different political affiliations of a fictional society based on an Afghan district. This particular model is not complicated, and one can clearly come up with more sophisticated political models. Simplicity, however, has a utility of its own so long as it distils rather than distorts a political environment. The real utility is the creation of a common political operating picture that can be mutually understood by coalition soldiers, civilian counterparts and Afghan partners.

The model breaks down a society into target audiences in much the same way as a politician in a domestic political environment would do. The colouring of these audiences is in relation to their proximity to the Afghan government narrative, ranging from white, meaning they generally subscribe, to grey denoting ambivalence, to black, for those who reject it. In the bottom right-hand corner are those who support the Afghan government narrative but not the insurgent narrative. In the top left-hand corner are those who support the insurgent narrative but not the Afghan government's. In the bottom left we have those who are alienated from both sides; the majority of people in the Afghan conflict will be found here, be they 'accidental guerrillas' or disenfranchised farmers. In the top right we have those who back both narratives to gain personal advantage, such as big narco-militias and warlords. These people usually have connections to the insurgency and the government.

The essential deduction this model presents is that to have political effect, one needs to make political choices at the tactical level to tailor the overall narrative to have purchase in one's operating environment; or potentially, to show that the overall narrative really does not work in one's own area and requires adjustment higher up.

Can the moderate insurgents be broken off from the hardcore? If so, how do we configure our operations to make sure we are putting pressure on the hardcore without alienating the moderates? How does one deal with the audiences in the top right? An overly aggressive posture risks inflating the size of the insurgency; not dealing with them risks losing credibility among the bottom left groups. Does one use resources to bolster the position of those in the bottom right, who already support the narrative, or reach out to less committed constituencies, potentially alienating one's home base? These are examples of any number of questions one could ask. They have to be asked when one decides how to attack an insurgent base area, where to build a road, where the local police force should recruit, and to whom one should award contracts. Without such information, or where there is not a common political picture across time and space, a circumstance all too common, actions will be politically incoherent.

The approach also dispenses with the notion of an isolated enemy picture; that is, a picture which only presents the insurgency, often in the form of tree diagrams, in terms of its operational set-up. While such charts are obviously vital, political context is essential: who are these insurgents in social and political terms? Without that information, one can attack a network, and even destroy it, but the political effects of doing so, both in terms of positive and negative outcomes, will be uncertain.

One needs to locate the insurgency in its political context before one can even start to think about how to deal with it. Are they fighting because of genuine ideological attachment to the Taliban? Perhaps they are fighting because they are marginalised in local politics, and want greater power locally; perhaps they are criminals, perhaps they are 'accidental guerrillas' who see themselves as defending their land against foreign forces, but do not have a problem with Afghan government forces.

An insurgent commander in Afghanistan may also be the relative of a prominent local political figure. His death or arrest may alienate that political figure from the Afghan government. The military benefits of attacking the insurgent network may well be outweighed by the political consequences of the action. Alternatively, if that political figure is corrupt, one may use the threat of arrest against his insurgent relative as leverage to stop his corrupt practices. Yet if one does not configure one's information so as to situate insurgents within their 'civilian' environment, these links will not be visible, precluding the possibility of anticipating risks and opportunities in the first place.

The identification of political leaders who are marginalised, be they insurgents or not, is also vital. This is an important counter-balance to the preoccupation with 'key leaders' that tends to dominate ISAF political engagement at all levels. If ISAF is only seen to engage with leaders who are already in power, the appeal to a narrow political base is exaggerated, and may well alienate marginalised communities.

In summary, as counter-insurgency involves armed politics, it requires making real political choices, even at the tactical level. If one company secures an area by empowering one tribe, and the adjacent company empowers another in their area, an illusion of stability may be created that falls apart as soon as the coalition have left should it turn out that the two groups are hostile to one another. One cannot refuse to engage in political activity: the empowerment or marginalising of individuals and groups will occur through coalition actions, whether deliberate or not.

The difficulty that having to make real political choices on the ground presents can be illustrated with reference to the British experience in Afghanistan. On the one hand, the British military and its civilian counterparts are fighting for 'a better life for the Afghan people'. However, the British effort is also premised on a narrative that emphasises British national security. This depends on the denial of the Afghan state for terrorist use. The desire for a stable Afghanistan to safeguard regional security, especially given the insurgency in Pakistan, is also perhaps considered in rational terms to be more important than a just and democratic Afghanistan. The problem with this is as follows: if the tactical actions that strategy orchestrates cannot satisfy all of it political aims, a political choice must be made between courses of action; if that choice is not made, tactical actions are pulled in different directions and will not be coherent.

The anti-narcotics policy goal in Helmand, for example, might be said to frustrate other policy goals, and pulls the effort there in different directions. The idea that destroying poppy removes the insurgency's main income may be true; yet it also removes the income of the rest of the population, as it is the basis of the economy. In this respect a blanket ban on poppy may appeal to domestic political sensitivities, but it does not help to win anyone's support in Helmand. If poppy were destroyed selectively as a form of political pressure (a means rather than an end) it would be a very effective tool. Yet that is not possible if one subscribes to a blanket ban. On the other side of the argument is the belief that drugs fuel corruption, and the West should not tolerate drug dealers given its own domestic stance on the issue.

While there are legitimate arguments on both sides, the approach is currently in limbo as the need to avoid pushing peasants towards the insurgency by burning their crops is usually the more pragmatic choice. The question here is not the policy itself, but how the absence of proper strategic dialogue has led to stagnation.

On 1 December 2007 C Company 1 RGR, in which I served, fought its most successful battle of the tour in the village of Siah Choy, in a combined operation with Canadian infantry and armour on the banks of the Arghandab River, west of Kandahar city. We caught the insurgents by surprise and routed them. One memorable feature of the battle was the fact that one of the contacts found my platoon running around village streets that were full of drying marijuana, which was both surreal and an indication of the huge scale necessary for any undertaking to eradicate the crop. Properly resourced and prosecuted, it is possible (poppy was successfully eradicated from some districts of Helmand, such as Nawa). However, there is no comparable crop with which to replace people's livelihoods. This remains the case today. For anyone on the ground, the need to establish some coherence in the approach, while recognising that there are legitimate views on either side of the argument, is plain to see.

This is not a point about narcotics; that is just one example of a much wider problem that realistic policy cannot be made unless there is frank official debate and willingness to actually confront very hard policy choices and ultimately make those choices. This is further complicated by the nature of coalition operations, and the difficulty of establishing coherent strategic dialogue with so many actors on the Afghan government-ISAF side alone. The anti-narcotics policy is just one example of the difficulties of wanting to eat one's own cake. The coalition wants to satisfy several audiences, which include both the domestic public and the Helmandi public, among others. This is the equivalent of a politician in domestic politics trying to win an election by refusing to commit decisively to an issue and thus have broad appeal. This approach may gain support for a while, but will come to grief when actual choices need to be made, especially since most of the real power in Helmand is held not by the Taliban but by tribal factions dependent on narcotics, who will simply not back anyone whose official policy is anti-poppy.

As transition takes place to full Afghan government control there, the coalition will need to make hard choices between different agendas; yet the likelihood of those hard choices actually being made is very low. Failure to make real policy choices will simply result in the coalition being overtaken by reality on the ground.

The next chapter considers how well liberal powers are configured to conduct strategic dialogue in order to make such political choices, to tailor what is desired in the light of what is possible.

5

LIBERAL POWERS AND STRATEGIC DIALOGUE

Because liberal powers tend to organise strategic dialogue through procedures in which the military executes, but does not adjust policy, adequate substantive output from strategic dialogue—sound strategy—is often frustrated in contemporary conflict. To use armed force to have political effect as a direct extension of policy, those on one's side whose actions involve making political choices, which typically will extend down to the tactical level, need to contribute to policy to keep the gap between desire and possibility as small as possible. The neat policy-operational distinction, an idea firmly entrenched in both constitutional and strategic thought, is untenable in many contemporary conflicts, not least in Afghanistan.

Civil-military relations and strategic dialogue

Strategic dialogue is essential for the desire of policy and the possibility of its implementation reciprocally to inform one another, in order to craft coherent actions that serve the end of policy. In *On War* Carl von Clausewitz deals with the interaction of policy and war during conflict. He advocates that the head of the Army should have a place in the Cabinet so that the reciprocal interaction between military possibility and political intention can take place.[1] The importance Clausewitz attached to the understanding of the position of the commander-in-chief is revealed by his promise to the reader in book 8 to write a 'special chapter' on 'the structure of supreme command' to conclude *On War*.[2] However, he died before it was written.

In reality the relationships between senior military commanders, senior civil servants and politicians (if indeed there has been a distinction) in any conflict have produced a strategic dialogue particular to that circumstance. While there are many possible variations in the processes by which strategy has been formulated, what consistently comes to the surface is that personality seems to be a more powerful variable than the official state system.

Samuel Huntington's *The Soldier and the State* (1957) was one of the most influential post-1945 texts on the subject of civil-military relations.[3] While Clausewitz does not figure prominently in this text, Huntington draws on Clausewitz to emphasise the concept of war as an instrument of policy. However, Huntington's interpretation of Clausewitz is particularly partial, as he makes a connection between war's instrumentality and robotic military obedience that Clausewitz's own argument does not sustain.[4] Clausewitz's own view was that: 'when people talk, as they often do, about harmful political influence on the management of war, they are not saying what they really mean. If the policy is right—that is, successful—any intentional effect it has on the conduct of war can only be to the good. If it has the opposite effect the policy itself is wrong'.[5] Clausewitz's work engages with how policy and war interact during conflict. To see the military as a politically inert executor of policy in a one-way system is to misread Clausewitz.

Huntington locates his propositions in an inaccurate interpretation of Clausewitz's historical reception. Thus he posits that as 'disciples of Clausewitz' von Moltke and von Schlieffen, both chiefs of the Prussian/German General Staff, were strict adherents to this interpretation of the instrumental view, in which war and politics were clearly separated. However, one of Huntington's problems in terms of argumentative clarity is that he rarely distinguishes, including in this instance, between party politics and government policy.[6] This is not only a partial interpretation of Clausewitz but of historical fact. Moltke's arguments with Bismarck, his civilian master, during the siege of Paris in 1870–71, for example, went against this idea in practice. Huntington asserts that 'since political direction only comes from the top, the means of the profession [the officer corps] has to be organised into a hierarchy of obedience…

His goal [the 'military man'] is to perfect an instrument of obedience; the use to which that instrument is put is beyond his responsibility'.[7]

Huntington associates military professionalism, which he sees at the core of this instrumental, robotic, military ethic, as the ideal to which officers should aspire. This military ethic (for Huntington based on a philosophy of 'conservative realism') apparently informs the 'military mind', which 'emphasises the permanence, irrationality, weakness, and evil in human nature'. The supposed qualities that make up Huntington's military ethic elevate it to a cult to which all military officers subscribe. Huntington makes a fetish of the officer corps, and even makes an absurd claim that enlisted personnel 'can never develop professional motivation and the sense of professional responsibility characteristic of the West Point or St Cyr [US and French Officer Academies] graduate'.[8] Did Huntington ever meet a sergeant major during his brief time in the US army?

Huntington's arguments about the military are seriously out of date, if they ever were in date. Officers think for themselves; they are not robotically programmed by a conservative realist ethic; to argue that enlisted men cannot have the same level of professional commitment is utter nonsense. There is some irony in the fact that a text which jars with the reality of military experience is today still a reference point in the widely held military view that the military should only execute, and not contribute to, policy.

The Soldier and the State makes more sense when read in its historical context. The arguments advancing a clear distinction between policy and the execution of war were already established in US military thought prior to the Second World War. Huntington cites a US Command and General Staff School publication of 1936: 'Politics and strategy are radically and fundamentally things apart. Strategy begins where politics ends. All that soldiers ask is that once policy is settled, strategy and command shall be regarded as being in a sphere apart from politics… The line of demarcation must be drawn between politics and strategy, supply, and operations. Having found this line, all sides must abstain from trespassing'.[9]

Huntington saw the Second World War as an unwelcome departure from this principle, as he argued that military chiefs held too much power, which expanded beyond the military domain into diplomacy, politics and economics. He argued that the fixation with victory in war, which obscured the importance of thinking about political consequences subsequent to that victory, was driven by a military domination of policy over civilian authority. He took issue with the fact that by 1945 the War Department was enmeshed in US foreign policy. By the end of the war more than half of the papers of the Operations Division of the General Staff were devoted to matters that went beyond the US army's traditional military domain.[10] Huntington made an astute point that the absence of real opposition to the military's views on war policy was not necessarily a sign of a well-functioning process: 'too much harmony is just as much a symptom of bad organisation as too much conflict'.[11]

Huntington's key reference point, writing in 1957, was of course the showdown between General MacArthur and President Truman over policy in the Korean War, which led to the former's dismissal from command. Huntington analysed MacArthur's desire to expand the war to win in absolute terms as a continuation of the military domination of policy during the Second World War. That MacArthur should challenge the President's authority was for Huntington an attitude not present before the Second World War, but it had become so overly inflated by 1945 that Admiral Leahy, the Chief of Staff to the Commander-in-Chief (President Roosevelt), and effectively (though not in title) the first Chairman of the Joint Chiefs of Staff, could 'quite frankly and truthfully say' that 'The Joint Chiefs of Staff at the present time are under no civilian control whatsoever'.[12]

Huntington argues that in the Second World War the American people traded 'military victory for military security', as the military domination of policy led to an end state based on total victory that did not necessarily leave the United States in a more secure position.[13] He makes the connection with MacArthur's position in Korea, in which his obsession with total victory, which might have involved the deployment of atomic weapons against China, was not in the US security interest, at least in the President's view. Hence Huntington's thesis is not just about constitutional stability, although he is concerned about the 'weakening of liberalism' in the Cold War environment.[14] His main argument concerns the effectiveness of the US strategy-making process.

Huntington's advocacy of the military ethic and of an apolitical military officer corps, which should 'serve with silence' and in so doing 'remain true to themselves', made more sense in the years following the Korean War.[15] Given the possibility of escalation to nuclear war, to limit war, rather than to think of war in terms of total victory, was eminently sensible. This required a challenge to what Huntington saw as military domination of policy and a rehabilitation of the tradition of civilian control. This may explain why Huntington does not distinguish between policy and politics: it made strategic (policy) and constitutional (politics) sense for the military to stay away from both. To back up this argument he elevated military professionalism, the inward-looking cult of the 'military man' and the officer corps, its guardians, to a state that did not correspond to historical or contemporary reality.

The problem with his thesis is that he requires an ideal to serve his broader argument; in trying to present this ideal as reality he loses purchase on the actual historical record and does not relate to the modern military. In today's context Huntington's argument would have the military in contemporary conflict pursue exclusively military goals in the name of professionalism—this would not work in mosaic conflicts, in which tactical actions have a political quality: to refuse to engage in politics would just mean not knowing what political effect one is having, or refusing to discriminate between military courses of actions on a political basis, leading to chaotic outcomes. Huntington's ideas taken literally today, outside their legitimating Cold War context, isolate the military from wider society. This frustrates, rather than balances, strategic dialogue.

The Soldier and the State is a seminal reference point for the theory of civil-military relations. While its constitutional arguments still make sense, its strategic arguments only made sense in their Cold War context. In contemporary conflict, the effectiveness of strategy must be predicated on an inclusion, not a total separation, of the military in policy. To reject this possibility is either to deny the reality that activity, civilian and military, at the tactical level tends to be highly politicised in contemporary conflict, or to accept this, but to maintain that, even this being so, the military should not have a viewpoint on policy.

While the political nature of war is clearly not a new idea, the extent of the penetration of the military domain by political factors even at the lowest level is a key evolution. Thus when Clausewitz envisions an interaction between political and military officers, he is concerned that generals commanding whole armies, not majors commanding companies, have their opinions on policy heard. While strategic dialogue between statesmen and generals may well be established in Clausewitz, in contemporary conflict, where tactical actions have policy implications in a small but cumulative manner, strategic dialogue needs to be extended much lower down the chain of command.

In short, the necessity of linking political choices at the tactical level with policy outcomes is a strategic necessity in today's mosaic conflicts. Only in this way can strategy and its expression as strategic narrative be adjusted to local circumstances and actually work coherently. The way in which the West tends to think about strategy frustrates this because it is frequently not understood that strategy is a relationship between policy and tactical action in which both should be adjusted in the light of the other; it is not a one-way road from policy to tactical action.

Strategy has been defined succinctly as a convergence of ends (objectives), ways (actions) and means (resources).[16] Colonel (retired) Harry Yarger's pithy definition of strategy is equally convincing: 'the calculation of objectives, concepts, and resources within acceptable bands of risk to create more favourable outcomes than might otherwise exist by chance or at the hands of others'.[17]

Essentially strategy is the dialectical relationship, or the dialogue, between desire and possibility. At the core of strategy is inevitably the problem of whether desire or possibility comes first. Does one start with the abstract idea of what is desired, or should one commence by consideration of what is realistically possible? This is a chicken and egg situation.

The two should ideally be in perpetual dialogue, not just before but also during a conflict. Desire must be grounded in possibility; possibility clearly requires an idea in the first place which informs any analysis of possibility. In the colloquial language often used to describe actual strategic process, this could be described as the continuous tension between 'top-down' and 'bottom-up' approaches to a problem set. Ideas coming from the top need to be rooted in ground truth; yet an un-coordinated bottom-up approach based only on what works locally lacks a unifying purpose and will be incoherent. This is comprehended in Admiral J. C. Wylie's argument that the plan produced by strategy 'is a vehicle for conversion of an idea to a deed', but as a dynamic process: 'the link between a thought pattern and reality'.[18]

Understood as dialogue between desire and possibility, strategy is as much the process that handles this dialogue as the output of the dialogue itself. The former can be seen as the procedural element of strategy (how an actor, typically a state, organises its processes to set up dialogue between policy intention and ground truth); the latter can be seen as the substantive element of strategy (the actual strategy that is produced). This dialogue is very hard to get right in practice. Historical examples in which there has been satisfactory equilibrium are far more seldom found than instances in which desire has not been rooted in reality, or when actions have not had any unifying purpose. Often these last two scenarios are two sides of the same coin.

Taken as concepts, policy, strategy and tactics are representative of distinct types of thought that are universal in all situations. In the abstract, all human action can be understood in terms of the physical expression of intention, or desire. Strategy requires an abstract starting point, an idea, which is typically understood as policy. Clausewitz stated that 'policy is nothing in itself ... we can only treat policy as representative of all the interests of the community'.[19] In reality, to reconcile all the interests of the community in relation to a given conflict is often impossible. Even those constituencies who support a military action may well do so for different, and potentially contradictory, motives. The further one moves away from wars fought for national survival, the more likely is one to detect such inconsistencies.

The requirement for strategic narrative to bind its audiences is crucial; that is hard to do when different parts of the audience expect substantially different outcomes, and strategic choices arise that make it impossible to keep juggling alternative versions. To take policy as representative of all the interests of the community, as Clausewitz does, is not a situation one would often expect to find in reality. Yet any analysis of a circular system, in this case strategic dialogue, requires a starting point, and this abstract, simplified notion of representation provides this. The point is stressed in this chapter to make the distinction between abstract analysis and practical reality. While an abstract understanding of strategic dialogue is important, in reality the policy starting point will be far more complicated. Policy aims in reality tend to be woven together and expressed as a strategic narrative; the construction and coherence of strategic narrative is the subject of Chapters 8 and 9. This chapter, however, continues to examine the abstract position.

The actual expression of that abstract desire, in the context of strategic theory, has been described variously as an outcome, an objective, an end, a result, a goal. This expressed idea is also comprehended by policy. The distinction between an end (policy in the abstract) and an end-state (policy achieved) might be illustrated as a line which shows the expression of the idea: it starts with the abstract desire and finishes with the actual accomplishment of that desire. In this sense policy represents not just the starting point, but also the end point: strategic dialogue is a circular system.

The accomplishment of policy is achieved through deliberate action. In war this has traditionally been understood to come about through the use of military force. How one configures and orchestrates that force is an area of technical expertise, and requires specific knowledge. This had traditionally been understood as tactics. Clausewitz defined tactics as the coordination of actions within battle, which he termed the engagement. Tactical thought was distinct and lent itself more to scientific analysis: principles of battle, technical knowledge of military equipment and geometry, for example, were for Clausewitz associated with tactical thought.[20]

Clausewitz defined strategy as the use of the engagement (battle) for the purposes of war.[21] This was more of an art. Hew Strachan has argued that strategic thought in this sense had originated from the growth of standing, professional armies in the eighteenth century as the type of theory which dealt with the general's plans and manoeuvres in the lead-up to battle.[22] As war expanded in scale, predominantly due to technological advances in communication and transportation, what Clausewitz understood as strategy was significantly stretched.

Julian Corbett, the British strategist of the early twentieth century, distinguished between 'major strategy' and 'minor strategy'. 'Minor strategy' is what would now be termed 'operational' thought, which related to action within war, but outside combat. 'Major strategy' was for Corbett the coordination of all military tools of the state to achieve the ends of policy. As Strachan argues, this prefigured conceptions of 'grand strategy', or 'national strategy' as it is usually termed today.[23] Thus, while for Corbett major strategy principally meant coordinating the actions of the army and the navy, this mode of thought has expanded to include within the military, air forces, space and cyber. Beyond the military, national strategy also coordinates diplomacy, economic options and the role of international aid. In this 'major' sense, strategy is very close to state policy, and national strategy is indeed decided in most countries at the political level.

The stretching of the distance between policy and tactics can distort the fact that strategy is fundamentally the relationship between the two rather than just a 'level' between them. Nonetheless, linear models which see strategy as a 'level' of war are more typically encountered than a conception which understands strategy as a relationship. A common formulation is the policy-national strategy-military strategy-operational-tactical 'levels of war' model (see Figure 10).

This can be a legitimate model if one recognises that policy is the origin and the destination of strategy: the idea and its expressed form. In this sense strategy not only adjusts actions in light of what is desired, but desire is also adjusted in light of practical possibility. Strategy seeks to reach a destination, and must adjust policy if that destination is not

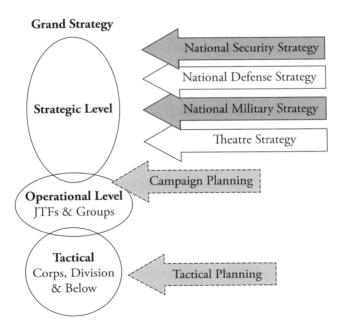

Figure 10: Levels of war and hierarchy of strategy (in a US context). (A 'JTF' is a Joint Task Force.)[24]

attainable. Strategy is therefore not a one-way road from policy to tactical action (which is the way such a model is often, mistakenly, interpreted); strategy should be a dialogue between the two.

Strategic dialogue ideally produces strategy that situates the desire of policy in the possibility of its execution. This juncture between desire and possibility, the strategic domain, is located at the point where actions have a political quality: the course of action potentially impacts on both the policy aims themselves, and the audiences against whom they are defined. In conventional war that juncture would be very high up the military chain of command, usually at army group or corps level. Thus there is an overlap between the commander of an army group, a very senior military officer that one would expect to have strategic authority, and the location of the strategic domain: while the action of the whole army group may have a political quality, actions of smaller formations and units within it seek a preliminary military outcome which only connect to the policy aim indirectly in their contribution to the actions of the whole army group; the key point is that commanders within the army group lower in the chain of command, the vast majority, do not need to make political choices when discriminating between courses of action. How strategic dialogue is configured in conventional war is therefore relatively straightforward, since it is essentially limited to how politicians and generals interact with one another to adjust policy and actions in light of one another.

The issue is then how effective such interaction is in producing balanced strategy. This depends on constitutional civil-military configuration, and the force of individual personalities. In the case of a military force micro-managed by a military dictator, for example, strategy would probably adjust policy seamlessly. In most liberal powers, strategists tend not to be the primary policy-makers, so this involves the strategists informing the policy-maker that a policy aim is unattainable, or requires adjustment in terms of its content and/or the audiences against whom it is defined.

In conventional war the overlap between strategic authority and the strategic domain means that politicians, if they do listen to their generals, have to consult a relatively small number of people. The problem in contemporary conflict is that the strategic domain often expands far beyond strategic authority, as discussed in the previous chapter: junior commanders routinely make political choices, either consciously or by implication through a course of action; their actions may be of less significance in a mosaic, cumulative sense. The problem is that effective strategic dialogue in this circumstance requires the integration into that dialogue of all those who operate within their strategic domain, which typically includes junior commanders at the tactical level.

Liberal democracies are not constitutionally configured to do that: the notion that the strategic domain and the tactical level can overlap is a reality of contemporary conflict that is deeply uncomfortable because it pits constitutional and strategic arguments against one another.

Constitutional and strategic arguments are only aligned when liberal democracies (mis) understand strategy as a one-way process, in which strategy is an expression of policy, but does not adjust policy; where soldiers do not question the objectives of policy, as posited by Huntington in *The Soldier and the State*. The endurance of this one-way interpretation of the 'levels of war' model is evidenced in the perception of the armed forces in liberal democracies as theoretically apolitical organisations. In a debate at Oxford University in 2010 on how far the military should contribute to policy-making, Professor Vernon Bogdanor, an expert in British constitutional law, argued that:

The distinction between policy questions and operational questions is not an easy one to observe, and perhaps especially difficult in military matters. Nevertheless, the chiefs of staff ought to do all they can to maintain it. It is important for the processes of democratic accountability that the dividing line is not blurred.[25]

The crux of Professor Bogdanor's argument is constitutional stability. The idea that the military are controlled by civilians and democratically accountable to them is standard in liberal democracies. This argument is entirely legitimate, and makes sense in a constitutional context. However, it does not make sense in the strategic context of contemporary conflict. This is a major paradox for liberal democracies. The military is often in the best place to assess whether policy is realistic. If the soldier on the ground can see that policy is unrealistic, but is unable to challenge it because he is at the end of a one-way flow of policy direction, policy cannot be adjusted in light of practical possibility. To my mind, while the military, and their civilian counter-parts who act in conflict environments (such as diplomats and development experts), should be involved in policy, they should stay out of politics (which is admittedly difficult to do in practice); this is a fine line, but seems the only way to balance constitutional and strategic arguments.

The enduring prevalence of a Huntingtonian conception of civil-military relations is exemplified by the ineffectiveness of the strategic dialogue that liberal powers have conducted during the coalition campaign in Afghanistan. The coalition narrative has, at the time of writing, shifted essentially to the avoidance of state failure. As of January 2012 the International Security and Assistance Force (ISAF) mission was stated as follows:

In support of the Government of the Islamic Republic of Afghanistan, ISAF conducts operations in Afghanistan to reduce the capability and will of the insurgency, support the growth in capacity and capability of the Afghan National Security Forces (ANSF), and facilitate improvements in governance and socio-economic development in order to provide a secure environment for sustainable stability that is observable to the population.[26]

General Stanley McChrystal's re-assessment of the situation on his assumption of the ISAF command, which encouraged an alignment of desire in the light of practical possibility, took place in 2009, although the process had been started by General David McKiernan before him.[27] However, it was evident earlier than 2009 that wide policy goals were unrealistic. The assumption that the coalition's actions earlier in the campaign were always leading to the same end point is an understandable teleological perspective, encouraged by a retrospective viewpoint from the more coherent strategic context that emerged after 2009; but it distorts the historical reality. Many of the coalition's actions were going a different way before 2009, to satisfy different policy objectives that were at best confused.

The British Secretary of Defence at the time thought of the deployment of British troops into Helmand in 2006 primarily as a reconstruction mission. This was not an illegitimate viewpoint given the absence of a serious pre-existing insurgency. However, that narrative was not agile enough to maintain coherence once real fighting started, and yet it did not evolve, causing a gap to open. As an infantry platoon commander, I met no soldiers or junior officers in my 2007–8 tour in Afghanistan who actually thought that our more idealistic aims were really achievable, at least without a long and well-resourced commitment in most rural parts of southern Afghanistan. At this time Prime Minister Brown would describe in Parliament what British forces were doing in terms which emphasised schools, governance and drug eradication. This may well have been his view, but had little to do with the army's operations at the time, which were focused on clearing out the Taliban from populated areas through aggressive combat operations.

The Prime Minister by late 2008 came to stop mentioning his previous view of the more idealistic interpretation of the army's actions, and focused instead on securing Afghanistan from terrorism in terms of UK national security.[28] From then on the 'chain of terror from Afghanistan to the UK' argument has dominated, although this is increasingly failing to convince people.[29] Justification tends now to focus on the mission's other, to my mind legitimate, goals: state and regional stability, the credibility of NATO and the moral commitment to the Afghan people.

Having moved away from more ambitious policy goals, Western politicians now tend to define the narrative in the negative: 'we are not building Hampshire in Helmand' or 'Switzerland in Afghanistan' are both expressions that have been used by British politicians. In his speech of 27 March 2009, President Obama declared the objective to be to 'Disrupt, Dismantle and Defeat al-Qaeda in Afghanistan and Pakistan', primarily in the context of Western security and regional stability, a significantly clearer and more narrowly focused mission. Afghanistan would need to be secure to achieve this. In terms of the Afghan state, President Obama has been reported to have spoken (confidentially at the time) in the US National Security Council about not having the resources to 'build a perfect Afghan state', and possibly achieving 'Bangladesh levels of corruption'; this is fairly depressing, especially since it is an aspiration.[30]

However, President Obama's more pragmatic approach is entirely sensible and more realistic, given what is within the realm of the possible on the ground. Ultimately, to have significantly reduced the policy aims of the war is common sense on the basis that one needs to align what is desired with what is possible.

Discrepancies between aims and their achievability became apparent as both the NATO footprint and the insurgency expanded from 2005–9. The December 2005 revision to the plan (NATO OPLAN 10302, Revise 1) which set out the extension of the NATO footprint into southern and eastern Afghanistan (following the earlier expansion into the North and West) set out a narrow 'Alliance Political End State': 'a self-sustaining, moderate, and democratic Afghan government able to exercise its sovereign authority, independently, throughout Afghanistan' (note that anti-terrorist operations were still to be conducted under separate authority, such as Operation Enduring Freedom, distinct from the NATO plan).[31]

To achieve the end state, the plan set out NATO's mission in Afghanistan: essentially, that in coordination with Afghan security forces, the NATO force would assist with security, the development of Afghan governance structures, and assist reconstruction/humanitarian efforts.[32] As far as expansion into southern Afghanistan was concerned: 'the strategic intent of the southern expansion is twofold. First, to expand the beneficial ISAF effect in Afghanistan by deploying NATO-led PRTs [Provincial Reconstruction Teams] into the Southern Provinces. Secondly, expansion to the south will establish conditions for the assimilation of the remaining provinces into the NATO-led mission...'[33]

The three levels used here as examples (political end-state, strategic mission, regional application of strategic intent) at which the NATO plan engages can in one interpretation be seen as fairly narrow in their objectives. If the lower level regional direction is read in the light of the political end-state, their ambition is limited to a fairly stable Afghan state, which is not far from the present aim. However, these examples also show that if read individually, and more broadly than was probably intended by the plan's drafters, there is the potential here to understand the mission more in terms of nation building. Moreover, there was not a large-scale insurgency to frustrate the plan at the time it was published in December 2005. By the time it was being implemented, and partly given the expansion of the insurgency in response to its implementation, the beneficial effects of NATO's expansion into the south were far less detectable than the vicious fighting that was taking place. Even if the destruction that such fighting brought with it was actually localised, wider audiences were at the time more disposed to have understood the conflict through the lens of aggressive combat operations than reconstruction.

The NATO 2005 plan read how, I think, its drafters would have intended it to have been read makes sense and was not overly ambitious. However, the scope for interpreting it in a broader, more ambitious sense was made apparent by the potentially confusing narratives advertised by Westerners, from political leaders speaking to their electorates to soldiers explaining to Afghans why they were there, sometimes during combat patrols on their land. In the background of the picture was the idea of reconstruction; in the foreground was intense violence, at least in the southern and eastern peripheral areas of Afghanistan. The strategic narrative did not paint a coherent tableau; its conflicting themes were only re-harmonised in 2009 in terms of aims, the resourcing of those aims and their operational execution. The speed at which strategic dialogue was able to harmonise desire and possibility was too slow, and was outpaced by events on the ground.

Afghanistan illustrates how, in any circumstance, possibility will ultimately catch up with desire. If one cannot change the facts on the ground with the means allocated to do so, the facts will catch up with one's policy and force it to change, or make it fail. If policy is unrealistic, there will come a point when that becomes clear. The key question in a liberal democratic context is to whom it is clear, and the time it takes between being clear to those on the ground, to the policy-makers, and ultimately to the public, their auditors. The lag between perception and reality can be identified when the strategic narrative does not correspond to the reality on the ground. If ground truth and the perception of ground truth by those who make policy are different, the closing of the lag between the two can be politically embarrassing, and worse, lethal.

The alternative to changing policy ungracefully because it is publicly obvious that it is unrealistic is regularly to adjust aims in light of what is possible; thus intention and possibility are not allowed to move too far apart. That implies early recognition of the point at which aims are not being realised on the ground. As this is typically most obvious to those on the ground, it means incorporating them into strategic dialogue.

This may seem to be common sense, but it is by no means common practice. In a Westminster Hall debate on Helmand in 2009, Adam Holloway MP, an ex-army officer, stated:

I wonder what on earth the Government have been doing. The Defence and International Development Committees go out there regularly. Every time we are given the same good news story, but it is not reflected on the ground. It is like smoke and mirrors, with everyone lying and deluding themselves. That is certainly how it feels from my perspective. As one Government employee put it to me yesterday: 'We realise it is now time to start taking it seriously'.[34]

There is an argument that the UK government cannot make strategic decisions as a junior partner in an American-led coalition. The need to maintain the credibility of NATO and keep the UK under the US security umbrella are legitimate objectives. However, the lack of clarity over the political command and control of the mission from a junior partner's point of view in a coalition can lead to correspondingly confused political engagement with the campaign, especially in terms of the expectations of the domestic population. The handover of Sangin (a town in Helmand) to the US Marine Corps in 2010 made complete sense in operational terms, as it allowed UK forces to concentrate their efforts in central Helmand. This set conditions for the relative success which the British army, with adequate force ratios, has had in securing its three districts of central Helmand since then.

However, the fact that so many British lives had been lost in Sangin consumed most of the media attention of the handover; the media coverage also highlighted the corresponding military concern that it would be seen as a British defeat or forced withdrawal. In one sense, to remember British casualties is entirely understandable and correct. In another sense, however, the concern that such a move would be seen as a British defeat (which it was not) exemplifies how the temptation remains for the domestic populations of junior coalition partners to see the conflict too rigidly through the experience of their own troops.

The British public tend to identify Afghanistan with Helmand, for example. A coalition campaign will only work if the coalition maintains political coherence, which often means junior partners acknowledging that policy is made higher up, even if they have some input. To talk about 'British policy aims' in Afghanistan only makes sense when understood that this is in a coalition context, unless one is specifically alluding to reasons for British participation in the conflict that are ulterior to what the coalition is seeking to achieve in Afghanistan.

Proper strategic dialogue involves the adjustment of policy in the light of practical reality in relation to various audiences. Such dialogue should be continuous, as it is in domestic politics; politicians are wary of overly idealistic policy, precisely because they understand that it can cause political embarrassment when it fails.

The grammar of war

One of war's defining features is its strong tendency to evolve in unexpected directions. Clausewitz identified how policy cannot entirely regulate war. In war the particular logic that is brought into being when there is a clash of organised violence had a subordinate, but independent role. Clausewitz described the 'explosive' quality of war's logic, namely its capacity to escalate into something beyond the desire of the policy-maker, and beyond even the desire of both sides: 'war is an act of force and there is no logical limit to the application of that force. Each side, therefore, compels his opponent to follow suit; a reciprocal action is started which must lead, in theory, to extremes'.[35]

While war itself was for Clausewitz subordinate to policy, the relationship was certainly not one way. War itself, its internal logic brought about by the clash of violence, either actual or anticipated, had an active role which could push back on policy and change it. Thus policy would 'permeate all military operations, and so far as their violent nature will admit, it will have continuous influence upon them'. For Clausewitz 'the political aim is not a tyrant. It must adapt itself to its chosen means, a process which can radically change it; yet the political aim remains the first consideration'.[36] Clausewitz summarised the relationship between the uncertainties of violent clashes that war brought into play, which he termed war's 'grammar', and policy, in the argument that war's 'grammar, indeed, may be its own, but not its logic'.[37] The point is that policy does ultimately regulate war by providing its 'logic'; yet violence in war produces dynamics which policy cannot fully control.

The capacity of war's 'grammar', even as the subordinate agent, to unhinge policy has revealed itself to some degree in every war. Admiral J. C. Wylie argued that, rather than being a continuation of policy, 'war for a non-aggressor nation is actually a near collapse of policy'.[38] The defeat of one side is the obvious example of this throughout history: the final collapse of policy in war. In this case war is still animated by policy, but the enemy's rather than one's own. War can unhinge the policy of the victors too. France and Britain were among the victors of the First World War. Yet the Great War for them was not the war it was supposed to be. It was not over by Christmas 1914; their empires were mortgaged to pay for the conflict; in the long-term it marked the start of the end of a period of European world domination.

War can also unhinge the policy of the victor in other ways than the 'Pyrrhic Victory'. A victor can find himself so powerful that the outcome of the war forces new pressures on policy which can take it in new directions. The US emerged from the Second World War the pre-eminent Western superpower. The war's outcome did not unhinge policy in the sense of US failure—quite the opposite; but it did unhinge US policy in the broader sense of the marginalisation of the isolationist position which had acted as a balance in pre-war policy debates.

Clausewitz's argument about the need for policy to adapt to war's evolution is problematic for liberal powers today, given their configuration of civil-military relations.[39] The political debate concerning whether to go to war in liberal democracies takes place (in theory) before the war has started. Logically, the 'war' formally debated in public is war in the abstract because it has not yet started. If politicians adjust war aims during the actual rather than the abstract war they tend to lose credibility, and are considered flip-floppers. Yet the charge of flip-flopping is dangerous because it inhibits the need to tailor policy in light of the reality that war is inherently unstable and will evolve. For liberal powers to insist on political accountability for a war's original intention is often illogical.

The frequent result, to use a metaphor, can be likened to driving a car through the rear-view mirror rather than looking at the road ahead: it swerves all over the place and may crash. War in reality has so many variables that for policy to insist on the maintenance of aims that were established in the abstract before the main fighting started is to deny the possibility that the original aims are not in fact attainable in reality and should be adjusted. This gives politicians little room for manoeuvre, which does not encourage an agile strategic dialogue. What we are often left with is a public increasingly confused by war aims which correspond to a version of the war which is not the war actually being fought. Moreover the war actually being fought may not correspond to the war policy claims it is conducting. This frustrates the adjustment of policy in the light of how a war evolves. The consequence is that policy usually waits until it is being overtaken by events on the ground before adjusting: only when it is abundantly obvious that current policy is heading for failure is it changed.

The counter-argument would be that states invest huge credibility in conflict, and thus perceive that decisively to adjust their aim is to compromise that credibility. In some circumstances that may be right, although to pursue an unachievable aim is by logic just delaying rather than solving the eventual loss of credibility; and during that delay, soldiers die. The key point here is that big alterations in policy aims are indeed to be avoided if possible on grounds of credibility, but that it is precisely by retaining flexibility, and constantly making small adjustments (which cumulatively, and imperceptibly over time, may add up to a big adjustment), that desire and possibility are kept close. Dogmatically to retain a political aim in conflicts which are of lower stakes than national survival is potentially to push military activity further than its political utility.

For liberal powers continually to adjust policy so that the gap between desire and possibility is as small as possible would be more sensible. This in turn means recognising that the convergence of policy and action in contemporary conflict goes down to the tactical level. Thus political (not just military) analysis at the tactical level must feed into strategic dialogue. Chapter 4 and this chapter have examined the interaction of strategy with its political context in contemporary conflict; the next chapter looks at the interaction of strategy and the operational actions which it orchestrates.

6

PRAGMATISM AND OPERATIONAL THOUGHT

Counter-insurgency in Afghanistan is frequently described as a strategy. It isn't. Counter-insurgency is an operational approach: a method which organises actions in service of a strategy, but not a strategy in itself. The countering of an insurgency is a means to an end. A strategy connects an operational approach to its ends, the objectives of policy, and adjusts both in so doing. While counter-insurgency is a legitimate and necessary operational approach in the context of Afghanistan, to talk about a 'counter-insurgency strategy' is potentially confusing shorthand: it can erroneously suggest that counter-insurgency doctrine can be applied regardless of political context as a strategy in itself, as opposed to being the operational component of a strategy.

This chapter argues that although contemporary conflict tends to be different from war in its Clausewitzian paradigm, the basic conception of strategy that one finds in Clausewitz's writings still makes sense: the military domain is an extension of policy, not a conceptually sealed-off environment. Strategy's role is to situate an operational approach within a particular political problem, which requires pragmatic interpretation of military doctrine. If an operational approach is cut off from its political context, it may well become self-referencing, looking inwardly to satisfy abstract military principles rather than connecting outwardly towards its political goals. When an operational approach is thought of as a strategy, or even a policy, what can result are campaigns primarily driven by internal military logic, rather than political objectives.

Clausewitz's centre of gravity: the association of military action with political effect

Clausewitz's strategic theory was premised on his conception of war as a political instrument. The strategist in war was required to orchestrate military actions so that they translated into a political meaning, and therefore had to look outwards to policy, not just inwards to battle; hence Clausewitz's defined strategy as 'the use of the engagement for the purposes of war'.[1] This was to be achieved by the identification of, and decisive strike at, the enemy's *schwerpunkt*, which can be translated as 'centre of gravity' (or 'focal/decisive point').[2] The centre of gravity was a physical representation of the centre of the enemy's 'will': 'by constantly seeking out the centre of power … one will really defeat an enemy'. This is a far more sophisticated idea than defeat corresponding to an arbitrary level of destruction. The centre of gravity would usually be the enemy army, but only in so far as it represented the core of the enemy's will. In certain circumstances, the destruction of his army would not stop an enemy from fighting on. The centre of gravity could therefore be different. It could be the enemy capital, especially in 'countries subject to domestic strife'; it could lie in communal 'interests' in the case of an alliance; and it could lie in public opinion, especially in cases of uprisings.[3]

The centre of gravity was simply what mattered to an opponent, or more specifically what could be made to matter. Admiral J. C. Wylie in *Military Strategy: A General Theory of Power Control* (1967) explains this through the example of Scipio the Elder and Hannibal in the Second Punic War: Scipio ignored the fact that Hannibal's army was in Italy threatening Rome and deployed his Roman army to Africa, threatening Carthage. Hannibal chased him, and was drawn away from Rome. Scipio was then able to defeat Hannibal on ground of his own choosing at the Battle of Zama in 202 BCE. However, Hannibal did not have to chase Scipio any more than Hannibal's threat to Rome had to keep Scipio in Italy; Scipio effectively imposed his will over Hannibal. The point Wylie makes is that the strategist needs to use physical force, or its threat, to manipulate the will of his opponent, not just focus on destruction as an end in itself.

The originality of Clausewitz's centre of gravity lay in its association of military action with a particular psychological, essentially political, result in the minds of an audience. Although Clausewitz did not use the term audience, the key audience was implicitly the enemy in the context of *On War*. That the centre of gravity connected operational action to a political outcome underscores how Clausewitz did not advocate strategic theory which exclusively looked inwards to a sealed-off military domain.

However, general military principles could be developed once they were situated within a generic scenario, which assumed as a starting point, for example, that the enemy army was the centre of gravity. To avoid confusion, what Clausewitz described as 'strategy' and its associated strategic theory is today generally equated with the 'operational' level of war: a domain which lies within war, but outside battle. The strategic theory ('operational principles' in today's parlance) that Clausewitz advocates in *On War* is primarily concerned with how to deal with war in its near absolute state.[4]

Thus having situated the centre of gravity within this generic context, he defines general principles that would serve to defeat an enemy: to seek out the enemy main force, converge on it with all available force, and destroy it in a major, decisive battle, the *hauptschlacht*.[5] In the context of near-absolute war, which Clausewitz strongly associated with Napoleonic warfare, a major battle 'provided a provisional centre of gravity for the entire campaign'.[6] Andreas Herberg-Rothe has argued that this deduction was particularly associated with Clausewitz's analysis of the Battle of Waterloo in his study of the 1815 campaign: 'Clausewitz stresses that no victory has ever had greater moral force than that of Waterloo, which led directly to Napoleon's abdication'.[7] The *hauptschlacht* was not an inwardly looking military concept, but a means to strike decisively at a political target.

Clausewitz's operational principles, as they would be described today, were designed to function in a particular context, not in the abstract in any military situation. When the political context changed, these operational principles would have to be adapted. Clausewitz recognised that there were two forms of war: absolute and limited. They were not neatly categorisable, and were defined by degree by distance from the pole of absolute war. Absolute war aimed at the total overthrow of the enemy. Yet the majority of wars, he acknowledged, aimed at more limited political outcomes. Military principles thus had to be attuned to any 'modification … in the absolute form of war'.[8]

The central difference is that in absolute war, war only provides a single decision (a single outcome); a more limited political outcome is by logic excluded: 'within the concept of absolute war, war is indivisible, and its component parts (the individual victories) are of value only in their relation to the whole'.[9] In wars which are moderations of the absolute form, individual components can be objectives in their own right, because armed force can be used for direct political advantage. The capture of a fortress, for example, may be of no military significance in absolute war, but may be significant as a prize in wars fought for more limited political advantage. Clausewitz makes clear that the operational approach he advocates applies to wars which approach an absolute state; the more war is 'tame and half hearted, the less solid are the bases available to theory [theory which deals with war in its 'ideal' or 'absolute' state]'.[10] The more war is a moderation of its absolute form, the less stable a body of operational principles becomes, as progressively greater intrusion of political considerations within the military domain takes place.[11]

The distinction between absolute war and limited war is necessary to understand Clausewitz's strategic ideas. When Clausewitz is prescriptive about focusing on the destruction of the enemy army in a decisive battle, he writes about absolute war. However, the centre of gravity concept works just as well in any conflict environment, although it must be differentiated from the operational principles that typically accompany the concept in absolute war. Contemporary conflict is characterised by the fragmentation of strategic audiences beyond the enemy, and thus a corresponding fragmentation of centres of gravity develops. This scenario was not the norm in Clausewitz's time, but neither was it inconceivable (in coalition warfare, for example) or inconsistent with Clausewitz's ideas: 'where it would not be realistic to reduce several centres of gravity to one ... There is realistically no alternative but to act as if there were two wars or even more, each with its own object'.[12]

Military principles and operational approaches

The identification of a centre of gravity is essentially a political appreciation of a conflict situation. It situates the subsequent application of armed force against that centre of gravity within a political intent. To converge on all axes to strike at the enemy main force in a decisive battle makes sense if the enemy has a main force which has been identified as the centre of gravity. Problems occur when 'principles of war' are applied without a prior political appreciation having taken place. In many cases, especially in contemporary conflict, a focus on the destruction of the enemy is encouraged by such an application of military principles in the abstract. Principles are not wrong in themselves; they are a vital handrail for planners. However, military principles need to be applied pragmatically to suit specific political conditions, not generically in any circumstance of armed conflict.

In 1827 Clausewitz was asked by Major von Roeder of the Prussian staff to solve a military problem in the abstract. The problem was described in exclusively military terms: if Austria attacked in such a way with so many men, how should Prussia respond given its military dispositions. In his reply Clausewitz argued that one could not draw up a strategic answer without knowing the political context.[13] For the mature Clausewitz, policy came first; principles should be adapted to form an operational plan tailored to a particular problem, understood on its own terms.[14] This informed Clausewitz's view that it was not possible to formulate 'a set of all-encompassing principles, rules, and methods':

History has certainly not guided us to any recurrent forms … it is plain that circumstances exert an influence that cuts across all general principles… A critic has no right to rank the various styles and methods that emerge as if they were stages of excellence, subordinating one to the other. They exist side by side, and their use must be judged on its merits in each individual case.[15]

While Clausewitz's emphasis on pragmatism in the application of military principles makes sense, such an approach is at odds with the endurance, and prevalence, of a tradition of military theory which argues that universal military principles do exist. The most influential military theorist of the nineteenth century was not Clausewitz but Antoine-Henri Jomini (1779–1869), a French officer from Switzerland who served under Napoleon.[16] Jomini's work, which also took Napoleonic warfare as a model, presented an approach based on universal scientific and geometric principles.[17] Peter Paret, the American military historian, cites the opening of Jomini's *Résumé des principes généraux de l'art de la guerre* (1806): 'at all times there have been fundamental principles on which good results in warfare depend … these principles are immutable, independent of types of weapon, time, and country'.[18]

Jomini's essential conception of strategy involved the application of these principles, namely to operate on 'interior lines' to the enemy, and to strike the enemy through concentration at a decisive point.[19]

The actual principles that Jomini advanced were in many respects very similar to Clausewitz's, particularly the idea of concentration on the decisive point. The principles themselves made sense in a post-Napoleonic context. The conceptual difference with Clausewitz is therefore not so much the actual principles as the idea that they can be applied indiscriminately and without reference to a political context.[20] However, Paret emphasises that the difference in authorial intentions between Jomini and Clausewitz is important to any comparison: 'Jomini, we might say, writes about warfare rather than war. Clausewitz, on the other contrary, writes to explain war, shaped by society and politics, as it functions according to means and ends'.[21] Hence while Jomini's work takes the general's perspective and looks down onto the battlefield, Clausewitz examines war as a whole and its interaction with its political context. Moreover, as John Shy has argued, Jomini writes about 'conventional' war; his principles may be universal, but within a particular context. He was clearly aware that war among the people was a different phenomenon.[22]

While an objective comparison of Jomini and Clausewitz indicates how many of their ideas were similar, there is nonetheless a tradition of strategic thought premised on the validity of universal military principles which has taken Jomini as its origin.[23] As Daniel Moran has argued, Jomini has only been the most prominent representative of a tradition of military thought that conceptualises the use of force outside a political context:

Jomini detached Napoleon's achievements from their Revolutionary roots and infused military theory with a political and social naivety from which it still struggles to free itself. Jomini's work purported to show that the essence of military success lay in rational decision-making, designed to bring opposing armies together in a sequence of violent clashes whose political implications would be readily apparent.[24]

This tradition of military thought endures. The British Army teaches the '10 principles of war' in the first week at Sandhurst. While these make sense in conventional, high-intensity warfare at the operational level, they are not universal military principles to apply in all circumstances of armed conflict, although this is sometimes how they are interpreted. 'Concentration of force', for example, is often cited as an enduring military principle at the operational level. This analysis is inaccurate outside its legitimising context, which could be seen as the experience of Western conventional armies. Most successful insurgencies have succeeded because they have avoided concentration. 'Selection and maintenance of the aim' is the holy grail of military principles. Bold strokes and tenacious pursuit of an objective have been the hallmark of several successful campaigns in conventional war. Yet in conflicts which are highly politicised at the tactical level, to have an aim which cannot be adjusted in light of practical reality because it is an immutable principle not to do so can become problematic.

An operational approach must connect back to its political purpose, or risk that self-referencing military logic drive a war much further than its political utility. Karl-Heinz Frieser argues in *The Blitzkrieg Legend: The 1940 Campaign in the West* (2005) that the German army's invasion of France was not based on any preconceived notion of *Blitzkrieg*, but was a series of actions developed by pragmatic responses to the situation on the ground.[25] The German army had itself expected the invasion of France to take longer. The formalisation of *Blitzkrieg* as doctrine came later in the invasion of the Soviet Union in 1941. It did not link back at this later stage to a political goal, because operational thought had been elevated to the level of policy and become an end in itself. The politically indiscriminate application of *Blitzkrieg* left the German army massively over-extended on the Eastern Front.[26]

Germany's response to its experience in the First World War provides clues to its strategic experience in the Second World War, and emphasises the importance of distinguishing operational principles from policy. Hew Strachan argues that 'the German army entered the First World War convinced that there was only one way to fight a war, and that was a strategy of annihilation resulting in complete German victory: its operational thought was scaled up to the level of policy'.[27] Yet the physical destruction of the First World War was not taken into the heart of German territory because the war was (ultimately) regulated by policy. The outcome for Germany in 1945 was far more destructive. Germany's experience in the Second World War can be linked, Strachan argues, to the fusion of war and policy, with the *Führer* as the head of state and the military. It was General Ludendorff, among others, who suggested in

1922 that a *Führer* should unite policy and *Kriegführung*.[28] This idea contributed not only to the confusion of operational thought and policy but to the exaggeration of the war's consequences.

The necessity to distinguish between operational principles according to political context is a theme which can be detected more widely than the two World Wars. The Vietnam War provides a case study of how the failure to understand a conflict on its own terms encouraged military objectives to become disconnected from political purpose. General Victor Krulak of the US Marine Corps understood that military action had to link into a political outcome. He endorsed the pacification approach that was adopted by the US Marines in I Corps, the northern part of South Vietnam, in 1966. This was an approach which recognised the local political dimension of the conflict, and sought to link villagers to the authority of the South Vietnamese government.

General Krulak was dismayed, however, at the military metrics that General Westmoreland and Secretary of Defense Robert McNamara were using to evaluate campaign progress. These metrics were most obviously symbolised by the body-count, but also emphasised geographical control relative to the enemy as opposed to political measures. Hence for Krulak the question of 'who held what in the mountains was meaningless because there was nothing of value there'; this was in the context of much military effort being expended in contesting remote areas.

In 1966 General Krulak wrote a private letter to another US marine general in response to a remark by a US army general that the US was 'winning militarily' in Vietnam, stating that this was 'meaningless': 'you have to win totally, or you are not winning at all'.[29] The possibility that one can 'win militarily' but lose a war is indeed perverse logic; it totally unhinges strategic theory, as it disconnects the use of force from political purpose.

Part of the problem seems to have been an institutional culture which saw the army primarily as a tool of conventional war. A RAND Corporation study of 1970 cited a senior US officer in Saigon so as to illustrate the problem of an organisation characterised by inward-looking, self-justifying principles: 'I'll be damned if I permit the United States army, its institutions, its doctrine and its traditions, to be destroyed just to win this lousy war'.[30] This view encapsulates the problem of military thought which is focused inwards on itself, privileging the satisfaction of military principles—principles that may not be wrong in themselves but that have been inappropriately configured in relation to the nature of the conflict—above the need to adapt and win a conflict.

There is an argument that the US had achieved its aims by 1972: the defeat of the North Vietnamese Easter offensive in that year would support this view. The application of mass US air power prevented a rout of the South Vietnamese armed forces (although this equally suggests a South Vietnamese dependence on extensive US military support, which would indicate that the conflict was not over, especially in terms of the resources and political will required to sustain it). There is a counterfactual argument that if the US had provided the same support in 1975, South Vietnam could have survived. The outcome of the surge in Iraq in 2007 may plausibly lend more credence to such a revision of the historiography of the Vietnam War. This would depend on the evolution of the situation in Iraq, which is unclear at the time of writing.

However, the cost of war to both the Vietnamese and Iraqi peoples, and the costs to the US, must be considered in order to ground such revisionist arguments in the actual political, human and financial realities of what such strategy involves: was it worth it? That question is not the subject of this book; however, it is critical for our actual subject; strategy. Strategy must be clear that it serves policy (even if strategy can adjust policy if necessary, strategy should never be self-serving), and must consider the application of force in relation to the policy objective. Strategy must not allow military 'metrics' to become inward-looking and self-referencing.

Military thought today sometimes makes a helpful distinction between 'measures of performance' (measurements of actions being taken) and 'measures of effect' (measurements of the outcome of those actions). By linking measures of performance to measures of effect the former is not allowed to become self-referencing. Night raids, for example, can be very effective at making the insurgent feel insecure, but may make other people feel anxious. The number of night raids would be a measure of performance, but the number of people coming to the market, responding to improved security, could be a measure of effect. The point is that the purpose is to make the community feel more secure, which depends on how they react to attempts to secure them. If they respond positively, do more of the same; if not, actions need to be adjusted. This is more sophisticated than just measuring performance, such as the 'body-count' in Vietnam, which locates a measure against an arbitrary and generic standard that may well not relate to the actual nature of the conflict. The dual measure system is better because it links internal military actions into their broader purpose as defined in real life.

The proposition that the military realm is autonomous from its political context has been encouraged historically by the cultural associations of the verdict of battle with honour. Because the idea of the 'fair fight' is culturally conditioned, the degree to which one can gain the moral victory in military terms despite losing the war in general terms depends on the audience. In Afghanistan the coalition characterises the Taliban as dishonourable in their use of roadside bombs and guerrilla tactics. The default Taliban response, which is frequently encountered in banter between the Taliban and the Afghan police on unsecure radio traffic (along with the trading of colourful and amusing insults), is that they would prefer gun-fights but are denied the opportunity for a 'manly' fight by the coalition's unfair use of air power. This would seem fairly sensible from their point of view. (At one point in 2010 an insurgent in our area, who may well have been smoking something, was known to claim that 'the ISAF have captured a giant milk-fish', which was in fact a reference to our use of a white Zeppelin-like surveillance balloon that floated above the base tied down by a rope: whether the reader accepts the insurgent's opinion or mine, this asset was clearly unfair!)

The argument against the 'fair fight' idea in relation to tactical methods can be summarised in a saying coined by Conrad Crane of the US Army War College: 'there are two types of warfare: asymmetric and stupid'. Abstract cultural conditions which allocate military victory or defeat are subjective criteria and are as powerful, or irrelevant, as the audience's prejudices. That is not to say that there are no boundaries. Certain practices are deemed to be so universally distasteful, such as the use of poisoned gas, or torture, as to have been banned by international law.

War, and armed conflict more broadly, is subject not just to its political context, but also to its cultural context. For an operational approach to locate itself within a military realm separated from its political and cultural context is misguided. The extent to which an operational approach is governed by abstract military principles is a tension that lies at the heart of strategic thought today.

As Hew Strachan has argued, during the Cold War strategic theory became increasingly focused on the use of force short of war, such as nuclear deterrence, which made it more abstract as it drew on theoretical scenarios in the future, rather than actual historical experiences. It also moved strategic theory from the domain of the professional soldier to a domain dominated by civilians. This left a void in terms of the theory of actual war-fighting and the contribution to theory of military practitioners.[31] The conceptualisation of the operational level of war in terms of 'operational art' filled this void in the 1980s. This was especially in response to a renewed US focus on conventional warfare post-Vietnam, and a NATO re-assessment of its conventional response to the Soviet threat. Strachan posits that such a conception of operational art could take its geo-political and strategic context for granted, and so focus on battle: 'although presented as a bridge between strategy and tactics, the orientation of the operational level in the late 1980s was towards tactics, not strategy'.[32]

While successful on the battlefield in the First Gulf War in 1990–91, the geo-political and strategic context of contemporary conflict is significantly different. Yet the divide between strategy-policy and the operational level survives, and has been applied to non-conventional conflicts. This is most clearly articulated in the endurance of the idea that while political direction comes from politicians alone, the military should be left alone to execute that policy. Strachan cites General Tommy Franks' comment to Paul Wolfowitz, Under Secretary of Defence at the Pentagon during planning for the 2003 Iraq War: 'keep Washington focused on policy and strategy. *Leave me the hell alone to run the war* [emphasis original]'.[33] The result was that 'there was no strategy that united the military and the civilian, the operational to the political, with the result that the operational level of war also became the de facto strategy, and its focus meant that a wider awareness of where the war was going was excluded'.[34]

When military thought is devised outside of a political context, real or generic, it rapidly loses meaning. Edward Luttwak, for example, has pointed out how the distinction between strategic and tactical air power lost meaning because it confused means with ends. Since the Second World War the adjective 'strategic' has been used to describe long-range aircraft as opposed to 'tactical' short-range aircraft. Luttwak locates the origin of the distinction in the Second World War: long-range bombers were called 'strategic' because their effects in terms of bombing cities were strategic; short-range planes provided 'tactical' support to ground forces.

Luttwak traces how the adjective evolved from describing an end, to become the means by which that end had been achieved; thus 'strategic' became associated with long range and 'tactical' with short range. However, in the 1991 Gulf War 'tactical' F-117 aircraft were used to attack headquarters in Baghdad, while 'strategic' B-52 bombers were employed to attack troop concentrations in Kuwait and other tactical targets. Luttwak also cites examples from the Kosovo War, in which 'strategic' B-52, B-1A and B-2 bombers attacked Serbian ground forces, while all the strategic targets in Serbia were attacked by 'tactical' F-15Es, F-117s and other such aircraft. Luttwak's brief history of this distinction exemplifies neatly how no means possesses intrinsic strategic or tactical value, as that can only describe an end, which depends on the particular context in which that means is employed.[35]

In the same spirit as Luttwak's analysis, wars and armed conflicts in general are typically classified in terms of their means, not their ends. Thus conventional warfare usually describes the phenomenon of two armies clashing in battle rather than a fight over absolute political objectives. The First Gulf War, for example, was a conventional war because of the clash of regular armed forces. Yet it was fought for limited political objectives. Several non-conventional wars have been fought for far higher stakes. Counter-insurgency is part of a tradition of conflict identified in terms of methods rather than of political objectives: small war, imperial policing, low-intensity conflict and counter-revolutionary warfare, among others. Those who advocate that 'hybrid war' is the next paradigm also emphasise method over objective. To classify conflict in this manner is not incorrect, as there are evidently methods which are transferrable. What this type of classification excludes, however, is a particular political context.

General military principles clearly retain value in constructing operational approaches to contemporary conflicts. John Shy makes a compelling case when he argues that such abstract principles, which are frequently dismissed as too rigid and unrealistic, have, for the sensible reason of giving planners a handrail, remained popular in strategic thought since Jomini. He argues that Jomini's identification of strategic decision-making as a specific area of knowledge remains important; certain principles can help in strategic decisions (as opposed to overly prescriptive theories).[36] Indeed the term 'lines of operations', which is current in operational thought today, was popularised by Jomini's advocacy of thinking in terms of *lignes d'opérations*.[37] Shy's point indicates that following principles in itself can be a useful planning method; the real issue is whether the appropriate principles have been relied upon in the first place, which is a question resolved by the strategic context in which they are applied.

Counter-insurgency operational doctrine usually comprises three generic lines of operation: security, governance and development. In Afghanistan the government of Afghanistan-ISAF has expanded upon this template to create six theatre-specific lines of operation (as of 2011): protect the population, neutralise insurgent networks, develop Afghan security forces, neutralise corruption and organised crime that threatens the campaign (effectively all part of the security line of operation in generic counter-insurgency doctrine), support governance and support socio-economic development. These provide a very useful method of organising effort across an international civilian-military coalition, and with Afghan partners. The point here is that the abstract doctrine has been applied to reality within the specific political context of the Afghan conflict, and thus has more purchase on the reality of the situation.

In summary, properly to situate 'Jominian' thought in terms of strategic theory, Peter Paret's distinction between warfare and war remains crucial. That professional military officers should seek to formulate general principles for generic problems is common sense. However, when that doctrine does not link into its political context, or is used as a substitute for that context, it oversteps its limits.

Pragmatism and counter-insurgency

Counter-insurgency is often understood as a subset of state stabilisation. Stabilisation doctrine, the generic guidance for UK forces involved in this activity, is necessary in order to draw up contingency plans, to train, and to configure state resources appropriately in the anticipation of involvement in future stabilisation missions. The UK military's operational stabilisation doctrine sets out primacy of political purpose as its foremost principle: 'The purpose of UK military participation in security and stabilisation is the achievement of the desired UK political aim. This should be at the forefront of the commander's campaign planning, implementation, and assessment efforts, noting that this may require adaption where political aims change in light of the conduct of the campaign'.[38]

However, as in conventional war, were operational doctrine to be up-scaled to the level of policy, there would be a risk that it would crowd out real strategic debate: hard political choices about what political end-state is to be sought may well be neglected, as the generic policy aims of doctrine, such as 'avoiding state failure', become the actual policy aims. A policy aiming to avoid state failure is a definition in the negative. The definition of a state as having been 'stabilised', or as not having failed, is exceptionally broad. Such an end state could range from supporting a repressive tyrannical regime to achieving a stable democracy. Because stabilisation does not provide an end state defined in the positive, it means little in itself.

The result may be a campaign that lacks direction. Susan Woodward, who had extensive experience of stabilisation in the Balkans during the 1990s, has argued that the real issue of state failure today is to do with its consequences, not state failure itself, which is actually very hard to define in practice.[39] She argues that genuine strategic dialogue has to be defined against the outcomes of state failure, not the failing of the state itself. Hence the policy component of a strategy is of far more utility if it states what it wants rather than, or in conjunction with, what it does not want.

Like its parent, stabilisation doctrine, counter-insurgency doctrine demands a political context, as it concerns the conduct of armed politics. In the absence of positively defined policy objectives, which should properly be based on an understanding of the conflict on its own terms, an operational approach might well generate an artificial political context: the hypothetical political scenarios upon which the operational doctrine is based, such as generic support for a government versus an insurgency, may be imposed as a template over the actual facts on the ground; the doctrine now fills the policy vacuum and becomes a policy in itself.

When counter-insurgency is (mis)applied in this manner, its critics have a point. Colonel Gian P. Gentile of the US army, for instance, has described counter-insurgency (as articulated in the *US Army and Marine Corps Counter-Insurgency Field Manual*) as a 'strategy of tactics', disconnected from wider political objectives.[40] His preference for conventional war is tied to the argument that the US should only engage in wars which it can win decisively, rather than have a conflict's outcome be heavily influenced by factors largely beyond an operational commander's control, such as corrupt and incompetent local partners.

PRAGMATISM AND OPERATIONAL THOUGHT

Colonel Gentile's argument presents an important policy choice between two legitimate positions, but does not present an operational choice in the context of the policy objectives of the Afghanistan campaign today. To satisfy the policy goals which the US-led coalition has sought in Afghanistan, an operational approach that excludes counter-insurgency doctrine would be problematic. To conduct exclusively what has been characterised as counter-terrorism would only satisfy significantly distilled policy objectives; conversely, to beat the insurgency through conventional battle would require indiscriminate killing, which would be a massive change of policy which liberal powers would not tolerate.

To distinguish between policy and operational choices is helpful in answering some of the questions that have arisen in the debate about whether counter-insurgency is the right option in Afghanistan, and in future conflict. Edward Luttwak, for example, characterised US counter-insurgency in an article of 2007 as 'military malpractice'.[41] He pointed out that the most successful counter-insurgents, such as the German Army in the Second World War, were successful because they out-terrorised the local population through reprisals. He states, of course, that the United States cannot engage in such activity.

That seems to me to be the point: liberal powers would not want to engage in terrorising populations. Luttwak legitimately points out the limitations of counter-insurgency as applied by the coalition in Afghanistan; but the limitations are there for good reason, and counter-insurgency remains the best operational choice given current policy demands in Afghanistan. Any jettisoning of counter-insurgency, and replacement with a more, or less, intense operational approach, would entail major policy changes; hence the concerns that Luttwak raises, as with Gentile, are to my mind primarily policy problems.

The public debate over counter-insurgency's utility in contemporary conflict suffers from confusion as to whether counter-insurgency is an operational approach, a strategy or a policy. An article in the *Financial Times* in March 2011 used all three terms to discuss a change in US approach to the conflict in Afghanistan.[42] The title of the article was 'US shifts Afghan tactics to target Taliban'; the first paragraph stated: 'the US is escalating its attacks on the Taliban and its supply lines in a shift in strategy in Afghanistan'; the next paragraph asserted: 'the move, which comes as the Obama administration debates the future of its military presence in Afghanistan after a troop drawdown begins in July, is a sign of the difficulties of the counter-insurgency policy'.

There is legitimate scope for confusion in journalism, not just because it would be unfair to expect journalists to use military lexicon with consistent precision, but also given the US government's lack of clarity as to whether it understands counter-insurgency in Afghanistan as a policy, strategy or operational approach. The critical policy-level debates relating to the Afghan conflict by the Obama administration in 2009 appeared to be more concerned with operational approaches—whether to prosecute a counter-insurgency or a counter-terrorism campaign— than with policy objectives.

Counter-insurgency is a useful, and necessary, approach to contemporary conflict within a context that recognises two criteria for its use: first, that it is an operational approach; second, that like all operational approaches it must be applied pragmatically. Let us deal with each of these in turn.

The utility of counter-insurgency in contemporary conflict has been most prominently argued in debate between Colonel Gentile and Lieutenant Colonel (retired) John Nagl, both of the US army.[43] Nagl argues that counter-insurgency is the most effective approach to many contemporary conflicts. He argues that it has been an effective operational approach in Iraq and Afghanistan, and that coalition forces should adapt to become as effective as possible in this approach to win the wars that they are in.[44]

In Nagl's earlier book, *Learning to Eat Soup with a Knife* (2005), he argues convincingly, by way of comparing the British experience in Malaya with the US experience in Vietnam, that the ability to learn and adapt is the vital variable in armed conflict, more so perhaps than being well prepared at the outset, as reality often unhinges the best laid plans.[45] The campaigns of both the British in Malaya, and the United States in Vietnam, experienced low points early on, but differed in their ability to adapt and evolve, as a result of difference in institutional culture. The dramatic changes that General David Petraeus brought about in Iraq in 2007–8 would support Nagl's thesis. Nagl cites Brigadier General H. R. McMaster to make the point that the conflict we now see in Afghanistan will probably not be anomalous in the future:

Correcting the persistent flawed thinking about future conflict requires overcoming significant obstacles and acknowledging that adversaries will force real

146

rather than imaginary wars upon military forces until those forces demonstrate the ability to defeat them.[46]

This makes sense. Until there exists a more effective operational approach that can gain purchase in the fragmented political environment of Afghanistan (and its regional context) to achieve current policy goals, counter-insurgency remains the best operational approach. A more conventional approach would require, for a start, a clear enemy, which there is not in Afghanistan. When the coalition tries to force insurgents to fight conventional battles, they generally refuse, leaving a small group to fight a delaying battle while the rest are temporarily evacuated. This was the standard reaction that the Gurkha battlegroup I was part of experienced in 2007–8 across southern Afghanistan; and it was precisely our role to act as the Regional Command South Manoeuvre Battlegroup to strike insurgent base areas.

That the coalition in Afghanistan conducted counter-insurgency adequately across the civilian-military effort before General McChrystal's 2009 reforms seems untenable, because even if commanders were thinking in terms of 'armed politics' (and many, military and civilian, were), resources and structures did not sustain such an approach. Counter-insurgency requires civilian-military cooperation (which is traditionally understood as a policy-level issue) at the tactical level; until the 'civilian surge' post-2009 there were very few civilians operating at the tactical level in contested areas, so even if military commanders wanted to apply counter-insurgency pre-2009, there was a basic resourcing issue in terms of the relevant civilian expertise. As Figure 11 illustrates, the configuration of intelligence resources illustrates the same point: in counter-insurgency, most intelligence comes from the ground up, not from the top down, yet the pyramid was until recently still resourced for conventional war.

The second criterion proposed here for counter-insurgency to be used as an effective operational approach is that its doctrine must be interpreted pragmatically. Bob Woodward in *Obama's Wars* describes one side of the US Afghan policy debate in 2009 in terms of how 'failure to perform a textbook counter-insurgency would doom the US mission'.[47] He describes counter-insurgency in the Glossary as 'the doctrine for using military force to protect a local population'.[48] While criticism of Woodward is unfair, since he is not a counter-insurgency specialist, his definition is noteworthy because it captures how tranches of the public

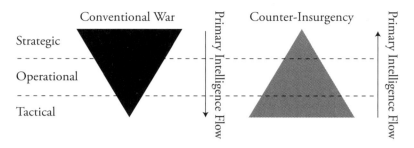

Figure 11: The infill of these pyramids is intelligence resources, human and technological, that are required in conventional war and counter-insurgency. There is a direct correlation between readjustment of resources and operational effectiveness. Counter-insurgency is not just a mindset of 'armed politics'; it is just as much about the configuration of resources and processes to enable such a mindset to translate into operational effectiveness. This model is idealised to make a point about being top-heavy. In reality resources need to be configured in relation to the particular conflict and may resemble more of a column than a triangle, given the circumstances.

might well understand counter-insurgency as this narrow, fixed practice of protecting the people to gain their support.

Colonel Gentile is right to challenge dogmatism in application of counter-insurgency doctrine. He takes issue with the maxim that 'the people are the prize' in all counter-insurgency operations. The 'prize' in any armed conflict is defined according to the goal of policy, which may, or may not, have to do with the political affiliations of the population.[49] In my view, in Helmand, for British brigade commanders to have defined the people as the prize (which I think British soldiers started saying colloquially around 2007) was actually a legitimate slogan in that context; it was a useful way at the time of modifying an overly enemy-centric mentality. But Gentile is right that the slogan is not necessarily transferable. Gentile also acknowledges that counter-insurgency as a military method, rather than a strategy, can have utility in certain circumstances, although he specifically defines counter-insurgency in terms of its 'population-centric' version, which is a narrower method and a less flexible conception than what is actually available within counter-insurgency as a whole.[50]

Counter-insurgency theory is the distilled experience of how insurgencies have successfully been countered in the past. In practice, counter-insurgency is simply the countering of insurgency, an end-state which is meaningless outside of a specific political context. Insurgencies have been countered successfully by a diverse range of methods suited to a particular political context. In some cases this has involved large troop numbers, in other cases very few troops have been successful. The appropriate level of force used is subjective and variable. Field Marshal Sir Gerald Templer stated that counter-insurgency was '20 percent military and 80 percent political', but that was said in reference to the specific political context of the Malayan Emergency. This ratio is all too often dogmatically restated in significantly different contexts.

A distortion to the current debate has been caused by those who see 'population-centric' and 'enemy-centric' forms of counter-insurgency as mutually exclusive. This is incorrect: each situation is distinct, and will require a particular application of means; to emphasise one approach over the other in the abstract rejects the notion that in many circumstances they can be combined, and that their relative configuration will be situationally dependent. To argue in the abstract about the value of any operational approach can be to get into debates with dead-ends. The Roman General Pompey, for example, 'on hearing that his soldiers were disorderly in their journeys' ordered his soldiers to put a wax seal on their scabbards during an operation in Sicily in 82 BC, and demanded an explanation for any broken seals.[51] His emphasis on restraint to maintain the consent of the local population was common sense. Neither was Pompey averse to highly aggressive combat operations; he was, after all, known as the 'teenage butcher' as a young general. He could be said to have blended population-centric and enemy-centric methods!

The need to deal with the enemy threat is common sense in any population-focused approach. One can build medical clinics and schools, and conduct other developmental activity, but if the population cannot use them for fear of insurgent intimidation, they achieve little. Lieutenant Colonel John Paul Vann, in the context of Vietnam, expressed this pithily: 'security may be 10 percent of the problem, or it may be 90 percent, but whichever it is, it's the first 10 percent or the first 90 percent. Without security nothing else will last'.[52] General Sir Frank Kitson anticipated the need to combine both in his conclusion to *Low Intensity Operations* (1971). Kitson stated that the operational emphasis of counter-insurgency operations:

will swing away from the process of destroying relatively large groups of armed insurgents towards the business of divorcing extremist elements from the population which they are trying to subvert. This means that persuasion will become more important in comparison with armed offensive action, although both will continue to be required, and both will equally depend on good information.[53]

Yet the killing or arrest of insurgents in combat, or aggressive targeting of insurgent commanders by special forces, is often reported as not being 'hearts and minds' nor 'not counter-insurgency'.[54] Such statements cannot be made in the abstract. The killing or arrest of insurgents who make a peasant's life a misery may be very well received; conversely, they may be his children: one can only make such judgements in context with reference to one's actual audiences. The post-1945 history of countering insurgency shows that the pragmatic selection and application of doctrine in relation to a specific, not an abstract, political context is what has distinguished successful campaigns. There is not space here for a full survey, but a few vignettes exemplify the utility of pragmatism in the construction of an operational approach to deal with an insurgency by tailoring it to the particular political problem, and thus dealing with it on its own terms.

'Classical' counter-insurgency, which is often associated with the British experience in Malaya 1948–60, was far more about population control than about popular support. 'Hearts and minds' in Malaya involved forcing 400,000 ethnic Chinese peasants into 'strategic hamlets' which were guarded with barbed wire and searchlights.[55] Hearts and minds were meant to attack the insurgency as an idea through a combination of practices, which comprised both carrots and sticks. Basic rights were removed from whole communities unless they stopped supporting the insurgency. Many of these methods would be illegal today. Although Malaya is sometimes taken as an example which underscores the principles of being seen to act within the law, this was clearly a subjective concept. Alex Marshall has argued that the emphasis on action within the rule of law loses meaning when the counter-insurgent is also the colonial sovereign power which has legislative authority.[56]

The operational approach that worked in Malaya succeeded in a very specific political context. The British had over a century to build up a colonial state, even though interrupted by Japanese occupation during the Second World War. This was essential to the concept of having the military act with legitimacy in support of the civil power. Moreover, the

British were aiming to leave. The entire premise of the campaign was the handover of authority to a Malay-dominated government, and not being seen as an occupying power. The communist insurgency in Malaya was strongly associated with the ethnic Chinese community. Hence separation of the insurgent from the population was in many cases the forced internment of the Chinese population which played on existing divisions within Malay society and essentially backed the majority group as the basis of a stable government.

In the early 1960s Sir Robert Thompson, one of the key counter-insurgency theorists in Malaya, was invited to aid the American effort in Vietnam. He lifted the idea of the strategic hamlets programme, which had worked in Malaya, and encouraged its use in Vietnam by President Diem's regime. In the latter context, the relocation of thousands of peasants was a disaster. It infuriated the peasantry and further encouraged support for the Viet Cong. The programme was abandoned by 1964. The physical articulation of the disjuncture between operational idea and political context was what Neil Sheehan reported as 'the ghosts of strategic hamlets' that were visible on the roads in the provinces around Saigon; most of these hamlets remained only as statistics on charts.[57] Moreover, given the fine line between government village militias and the insurgents in many areas, several thousand US weapons went to the Viet Cong; one estimate puts the number at about 200,000.[58] Sheehan's narrative suggests that an abstract template, which saw war as polarised between two sides, failed to comprehend the complex political dynamics of the conflict on its own terms.

The Dhofar campaign of the 1960s and 1970s in southern Oman illustrates how a style of counter-insurgency different from that developed in Malaya worked equally well because it was suited to a particular context. While Malaya emphasised the need to have large troop numbers to secure populated areas, the campaign in Dhofar deliberately kept a very low profile. Mass deployment of British troops was not used, as it would have caused more political problems than it solved.

The most effective methods, used by the Special Air Service (SAS), involved the development of local forces, called *firqa*, who were mentored and could operate in that political and cultural environment far more successfully than foreigners. A report by a British adviser following a year of service with the *firqa* states that: 'the main reasons for joining and fighting for a *firqat* [sic] are financial and political in nature; political control of the individual's tribal area, and gains in cash, food, land or livestock... The aim must be to select a force of men who have their own motivation for fighting—not necessarily in tune with the aims and motivations of the advisers'.[59] This comment identifies how the political dynamics were understood on their own terms, and plans based on this; facts were not straitjacketed by idealised doctrinal models. Indeed the first *firqa* to be raised failed because it was recruited on a mixed tribal basis. The subsequent recruitment of *firqa* units on a single tribal basis encouraged the alignment of the tribesmen's own interests with that of the wider campaign.

The Dhofar conflict exemplifies the importance of the strategic relationship between tactical activity and its political context. The campaign was not going particularly well before 1970: the communist forces based in Yemen were swelling, and the province of Dhofar remained politically very unstable. The main reason for support for the communist cause was that the government did nothing for its people. Elderly Sultan Said Bin Taimur was not liked by many of the tribes, whom he treated badly. When he was deposed in a coup in 1970 and replaced by his son Sultan Quaboos, many of the tribesmen who had fought against the government joined the new Sultan's cause against what they saw as the godless communists. With very few exceptions, most of the *firqa* were ex-insurgents themselves, a key indicator of the importance of the change in political context.

This change of political context was a strategic opportunity, exploited by successful operational changes in the campaign after 1970: first, the introduction of the SAS to train indigenous forces; second, the abandoning of the practice of bombing all insurgents, and burning their homes and villages, with complete prohibition by 1972. Third, most crucially perhaps, there was no coherent doctrine of civil development pre-1970 (indeed Said bin Taimur routinely rejected the suggestions of his advisers to invest in civil development), whereas it was Sultan Qaboos's main promise to all his people after 1970 and perhaps the strongest leverage to get people to reject the insurgents, who offered nothing so tangible[60] (which by counterpoint exemplifies why official corruption is such a problem in Afghanistan, and to my mind is a significantly more relevant issue than the insurgency in terms of future state stability).

Another key lesson from Dhofar is that counter-insurgency does not require a large-scale overt presence of foreign troops. A small contingent of British troops, who fought as officers integrated into the Omani forces, as opposed to in discreet units, proved successful, while not 'taking ownership of the problem', the key concern with large-scale interventions.

Counter-insurgency post-1945 has also been practised by powers that are not liberal democracies; to ignore that experience is to be partial. Sometimes the methods used, even in recent conflict, have gone beyond what liberal powers would deem acceptable; but those powers, using a form of counter-insurgency, have achieved their aims nonetheless. Some insurgencies have simply been destroyed. For example, in terms of contemporary counter-insurgency, the Sri Lankan government and Russia both subdued two long-running insurgencies against the Tamil Tigers and Chechen separatists using methods which resemble conventional warfare in terms of means used. There are obvious criticisms that can be levelled against these approaches on moral grounds, namely the gross human rights violations involved in both cases. However, the idea that counter-insurgency is the application of fixed principles to any problem involving an insurgency without adaption to that specific political context is incorrect.

In summary, counter-insurgency doctrine allows the strategist to access a wide range of tools that have been successfully used in various historical circumstances. Those tools do not, however, have any intrinsic meaning outside a political context, past or present. Disregard of this caveat is at the core of the confusion about how to deal with contemporary conflicts on the ground. Confusion stems from the belief that operational approaches, and in particular counter-insurgency, are comprehensive solutions rather than tools.

Without wanting to get overly drawn here into technical doctrinal debate, Major Shaun Chandler and I have argued in the *British Army Review* that kinetic (violent) effects and non-kinetic (non-violent) effects, the current official terms of British military doctrine, do not exist as such.[61] They are not categories of effects, but categories of means, which are inert tools; it is how they are used and interpreted that has an effect. No tool inherently possesses the ability to deliver an effect. Thus effects are simply that—effects, usually on people—they are neither 'kinetic' nor 'non-kinetic'. However, the default idea that one should 'balance' violent and non-violent means in counter-insurgency is commonplace. Why, in the abstract, should one arbitrarily want to balance the use of two tools? The requirement to balance, if any, depends on the problem.

Kinetic means can be a powerful way positively to influence people (i.e. not by terrorising them, but the opposite, by attacking that which terrorises them). If a village is broadly supportive of the Afghan government, but is being intimidated by a particular group of alien insurgents, it matters not how many leaflets one gives them, or schools one builds; they will still be intimidated and will not subscribe to the Afghan government narrative. If the insurgents who intimidate them are killed or captured, change can come about. When Major Shaun Chandler was commanding a company of Gurkhas in 2010, in a remarkable episode, a group of locals actually came to one of his checkpoints to applaud after a contact in which an insurgent had been killed. This insurgent was part of a group that had been making the villagers' lives a misery, not least by indiscriminately planting bombs in the village which had killed children (and badly wounded some of our soldiers too). Conversely, in many other circumstances, the use of violent force, even if proportionate and targeted, may be a bad option. To seek the intervention of a local powerbroker may be the best solution.

The deduction is that means, violent and non-violent, do not have an intrinsic ability to influence people in a given way. A mistaken belief that they do can lead to artificial compartmentalisation which frustrates their more imaginative use in any number of combinations in time and space. Moreover, to compartmentalise operations as either 'kinetic' or 'non-kinetic' is simply an inefficient use of resources (i.e. as soon as one decides to have a 'kinetic effect' on a target audience, non-kinetic tools are excluded, and vice versa).[62]

The effect is the essence; all activity should point to it. This might be summarised in a particularly pithy piece of tactical direction I came across in 2010: 'Can I, should I, must I?'[63] 'Can I' is a legal question about rules of engagement; 'should I' is about the effect—does the potential action support the purpose of the wider operation; 'must I' is a practical moral question which seeks especially to keep potential civilian casualties to a minimum. This last question may seem obvious, but in reality can be the most demanding, and most ambiguous, in that the people who typically are required to answer it are junior commanders in vicious contacts, who have to balance the need for 'courageous restraint' with responsibility for their own men.

The key in counter-insurgency is to match actions and words so as to influence target audiences to subscribe to a given narrative. The tension

154

between 'enemy-centric' and 'population-centric' counter-insurgency introduces an artificial and unnecessary distinction. They are both categories of means, and should rather be used, potentially in combination, in a way that corresponds with the political context. In a fragmented political environment that requires flexibility, to mix and match means to suit particular localities. To insist that one method is, in the abstract, superior to the other would be to frustrate such pragmatic flexibility.

Pragmatism in the application of any operational approach helps to distinguish means from ends: while doctrinal principles are important to construct any operational approach, their attainment should not be goals in themselves. Strategy must not start by forcing the actual political problem presented by the conflict into preconceived categories, such as conventional war or counter-insurgency, and then apply in a literal manner the corresponding doctrine to the problem. The reverse sequence should be applied. Strategy should start by considering the political problem on its own terms and then pragmatically draw upon doctrine to create a tailored operational approach to that particular problem.

The application of counter-insurgency doctrine can be compared to that of a sales technique. One may be the best salesman, and apply the technique, but if the product is poor, one will still struggle to make the technique work. Strategy is about dialogue between the product and the relevant technique which adjusts both (or at least makes recommendations to adjust the product). A technique itself is an inanimate tool. To limit strategic discussion to criticism of operational methods can be like a bad workman blaming his tools, or even a good workman blaming his tools rather than considering whether his task is appropriate for the tools he has.

Clausewitz's theme of pragmatism in operational thought, which associates method with political intention through the centre of gravity, draws together what makes sense in both Nagl's and Gentile's arguments. An operational approach must work on the ground and the army must win the wars it fights; but for that to happen, it needs to operate within a properly forged political context, and that is the role of strategy. The next chapter takes the Borneo Confrontation of 1962–6 as an extended case study of this theme.

7

BRITISH STRATEGY IN THE BORNEO CONFRONTATION 1962–6

This chapter presents an extended case study to illustrate the theme of pragmatism in the construction of operational approaches discussed in Chapter 6. From the British perspective, the Borneo campaign is usually regarded (incorrectly) as an appendix of the Malayan Emergency 1948–60. The conflict, termed from the British perspective either the 'Borneo Confrontation' or the 'Indonesian Confrontation', provides an independent and valuable example of the utility of a pragmatic mentality in the construction and application of strategy. British strategy understood the problem on its own terms: both policy and operational approaches were adjusted relative to one another to formulate, and continuously review, a coherent campaign plan.

Throughout this case study the term British, for simplicity, is used to refer generally to all of the Commonwealth troops who fought in the campaign. Australian, New Zealand and Malaysian troops played an important role. Their respective governments were also actors in their own right. There is not space here for a full narrative, and the emphasis of this case study is on the quality of pragmatism in British strategic thinking. To that end the Commonwealth dimension of the conflict is significantly simplified.[1] I have also used evidence to support my account of combat on the ground largely from the history of my own regiment. This is simply because I have had better access to ex-Gurkhas who served in Borneo and the relevant records from the Gurkha Museum. I do not mean in any way to sideline the role played by other units, British and Commonwealth, and indeed Indonesian, in the campaign.

British Secretary of Defence Denis Healey's verdict to the House of Commons upon the successful conclusion of the Indonesian Confrontation was that 'in the history books it will be recorded as one of the most efficient uses of military force in the history of the world'.[2] Between 1962 and 1966 British and Commonwealth forces had been engaged in an armed confrontation against Indonesia, fought for the most part deep inside the jungles of Borneo. By 1964, 30,000 troops were committed in what was a major British combat operation. Yet contrary to Lord Healey's prediction, and despite some excellent specialist works, their exploits have been largely forgotten, failing to emerge from below the jungle canopy into the light of general knowledge. A short narrative is necessary.

For the British government, the Confrontation had its origins in the context of decolonisation and Cold War. Malaya had been granted independence in 1957 and Singapore in 1959. In colonial terms, Britain still retained interests on the island of Borneo in Sarawak, North Borneo (Sabah) and Brunei. The British plan was to federate these entities with Malaya and Singapore as 'Malaysia'. In the event Brunei did not join. Malaysia was born in September 1963, but Singapore left in 1965. In Cold War terms, Britain wanted to retain basing rights in Malaysia, particularly in Singapore. Britain had commitments to the region as a member of the anti-communist South East Asia Treaty Organisation (SEATO), which had been set up in 1955 following the Geneva Conference and Manila Pact in 1954.

The Indonesian President Ahmed Sukarno was hostile to both the 'imperialist' British presence in South East Asia and the concept of Malaysia. He hoped to assimilate the whole of Borneo into Indonesia (the other, much larger, territory of the Island of Borneo, Kalimantan, was already part of Indonesia). This was to be achieved by a policy of *Konfrontasi*. J. A. C. Mackie in *Konfrontasi: The Indonesia-Malaysia Dispute 1963–1966* (1974) states that at this stage the meaning of the policy was uncertain. The term had been coined at a press conference on 20 January 1963 by the Indonesian Foreign Minister Dr Subandrio who, when asked what it meant, stated: 'Confrontation does not include war, because it can be carried on without war'.[3]

Michael Leifer in *Indonesia's Foreign Policy* (1982) describes *Konfrontasi* in terms of 'coercive diplomacy', which had worked in the earlier Indonesian assimilation of West Irian (also known as West New Guinea, West Papua, or Irian Jaya), a remnant of the Dutch East Indies, in 1961–2. Sukarno played on US fears of alienating Indonesia and losing it to communism. The result was a UN settlement that demanded Dutch withdrawal. Leifer also stresses the other, equally important, purpose of *Konfrontasi*: it was a means for President Sukarno to stabilise his political position by binding together 'in adverse partnership' the two potentially antagonistic elements of his power base: the army and the Indonesian Communist Party (the PKI).[4]

The pattern of the Confrontation falls into four phases. In the first phase, Indonesia provided aid to the rebels who led the Brunei revolt of December 1962, although this was soon suppressed by British troops flown in from Singapore. In the second phase, from April 1963, Indonesian regular army officers led guerrilla 'volunteers' from Kalimantan on raids across the border, mainly into Sarawak. While lethal, these raids remained few and generally involved small numbers of less than platoon size. Their purpose was to back up Indonesia's negotiating position in the spring and summer of 1963, which opposed the formation of Malaysia. This period involved a rather complex series of events which will not be discussed here, but which involved the UK trying to establish Malaysia against Indonesian pressure, with other key actors involved, including the US and the UN.[5]

The conflict proper began in the following third phase, when the formation of Malaysia on 16 September 1963 triggered a violent Indonesian response. Symbolically, a mob smashed the British Embassy in Jakarta on that day.[6] More seriously, from late September, much bigger and more aggressive raids were conducted by Indonesian regular forces into Sarawak and Sabah. Indonesia began limited (and unsuccessful) sea and airborne raids on peninsular Malaysia in August 1964 that were conducted intermittently until March 1965. The fourth and final phase opened in October 1965. A successful Indonesian army counter-coup against an attempted PKI coup brought General Suharto to power. This resulted in the Confrontation winding down to the old pattern of guerrilla raids. Secret peace feelers were sent to Kuala Lumpur in March 1966, which resulted in the Confrontation formally ending on 11 August 1966.

In diplomatic terms, the central problem the British faced from the outset of the Confrontation was to convince the United States that British policy was not a self-serving colonial construct, but supported the fight against communism in Southeast Asia. The US was worried that Indonesia, with a population of 100 million, and with the PKI as the third largest communist party in the world, would become communist.

Matthew Jones in *Conflict and Confrontation in South East Asia, 1961–65* (2002) notes the powerful effect on President Kennedy of First Secretary Khrushchev's famous January 1961 speech encouraging anti-colonial revolutions in Africa and Asia. The effect in relation to the Indonesian situation was underscored by the fact that the Indonesian Army Chief of Staff, General Nasution, and the Foreign Minister, Dr Subandrio, were at that very time in Moscow to sign a $400 million contract for military hardware.[7] Jones also notes how by 1963 Indonesia's relationship with China, advertised by the visit of the People's Republic of China (PRC) Chairman, Liu Shaoqi, to Jakarta in April of that year, also became a pressing US concern, especially in the Southeast Asian regional context, in which several countries (not least Vietnam, Laos and Cambodia) appeared under threat.[8]

Britain's international position at the outset of the Confrontation was difficult, caught between Commonwealth and Cold War interests. Britain simply could not ignore Kennedy's position which was that, in defeating Indonesia militarily, Sukarno would lose face and the Indonesian Army might lose its political power, leaving the PKI dominant.

British policy-makers approached the problem with a pragmatic mindset. This was not pragmatism as a formal strategic approach; there is no evidence of that. Nor was it pragmatism in terms of trying to find the answer through a conscious notion of 'common sense', which is often associated with being pragmatic, because contradictory views on policy could legitimately claim to be based on common sense. Thus there were significant private disagreements on policy in 1963 between senior British officials. The key seam was formed between those who advocated negotiating a settlement with Indonesia (such as Peter Thorneycroft, the Minister of Defence) and those who wanted to hold the line militarily (such as Rab Butler, the Foreign Secretary). Both points of view were not particularly ideological; they were both anchored in practical 'common sense' considerations. The credibility of these views is reflected in the nature of Cabinet discussions, which entertained both seriously. Nor were more genuinely ideological ideas seen as suspect. The Cold War 'domino theory' played a significant role in shaping British policy. So what then was pragmatic?

Pragmatism can be identified as the mentality by which the coterie of senior British policy-makers, civil servants and soldiers involved in the Borneo Confrontation dealt with the problem on its own terms. They recognised ideological and doctrinal lenses through which to understand the issue, but were not slaves to them; they modified or discarded ideological positions when they did not suit the government's perception of its national interests. In this way the issue was dealt with not generically, but in terms particular to itself.

In January 1964 Butler presented the Cabinet with a major policy paper on Indonesia that reviewed possible options.[9] As this was the British government's key policy document in the conflict, it merits particular attention. The paper was acutely sensitive to how the conflict should be conceptually configured in relation to various target audiences. This had two benefits. First, the strategic narrative was formally considered at the highest level of government, which set definite and clear parameters within which the armed forces, the diplomatic service and other agencies could develop operational plans. Second, the government was clear in its own mind about which audiences were priorities, and evaluated various courses of action against the degree of purchase they would have in relation to those strategic audiences (the term 'strategic audience' was not actually used, but the sense was the same, of an audience against whom a policy aim was defined).

The first option was offensive military action. Butler recalled the Dutch failure to check Indonesian guerrillas during the war of Indonesian independence (1945–9); this was despite the fact that they were technologically superior and had twice inflicted major defeats on the Indonesians (even capturing Sukarno himself at one point): 'The importance of this is that no military action we contemplate could make it militarily impossible for the Indonesians to continue and even intensify guerrilla activity'. A military offensive could only succeed by breaking the will of the Indonesian government or their authority over their people. Yet, 'in the light of past experience it seems unlikely that military action on our part could achieve this, unless such action were of so drastic a character (i.e. nuclear bombing) that it would invite retaliation from, for instance, the Soviet Union'. Moreover, overt military action would probably hinder Britain's international position 'because international opinion generally does not regard fomenting a rebellion in someone else's country (which is all the Indonesians admit to doing) as justifying the victim in openly carrying the war into his tormentor's country'.

The second option was an appeal to the UN, which would bring the currently 'undeclared' conflict into the open and put pressure on Indonesia. While Malaysia had more support there than Indonesia, there was little support in the wider international community for the United Kingdom's military presence in Southeast Asia: Approaching the UN, argued Butler, would probably lead to either a vote of sympathy for Malaysia without sanctions against Indonesia, or a demand that Malaysia and Indonesia resume negotiations, but almost certainly not under the conditions demanded by Malaysia.

Even if the UN could be persuaded to send peace-keepers or observers, they would hamper the operations of British regular forces more than Indonesian infiltration and subversion. Essentially, the more the UN intervened, the more Malaysia would be subjected to international pressure to find a negotiated settlement: 'and once negotiations are internationalised, Malaysia will be subjected to pressure, as the price of peace with Indonesia, to abandon her defence agreement with us [the Anglo-Malaysian Defence Agreement of 1957] and to deprive us of the Singapore base'.[10] On balance, recourse to the UN would 'not significantly assist to end the Indonesian Confrontation on acceptable terms'.

All of these options would bring the conflict into the open. However, the benefits of this would be limited to Commonwealth and US public opinion. Elsewhere it would probably encourage a resumption of negotiations rather than support for Malaysia and Britain:

Its greatest disadvantage [bringing the conflict into the open] would be to diminish the range of options available to us. As long as our conflict with Indonesia remains unofficial and bilateral, we retain the initiative. We can choose either to intensify it or to seek a settlement. Once we either internationalise it or turn it into a war (declared or undeclared) against a wicked aggressor, Her Majesty's Government will be restricted in their freedom of action by both public opinion at home and by international pressure.[11]

Hence the policy paper advanced that bringing the conflict into the open would cause other problems, as the ambiguous conflict would evolve into a situation where neither side could withdraw without admitting defeat: 'the Indonesian Government, whose pretence that they are only giving limited help to an indigenous resistance movement, however irritating in its mendacity, does at least leave the possibility (which we should be careful not to destroy) of withdrawing from the Confrontation without intolerable loss of prestige'. The paper also stressed the limitation of information to avoid the British public perceiving that the military had been committed to an interminable conflict.

The course of action recommended by Butler was accepted, acted upon, and remained the basis of British policy during the Confrontation. This entailed: 'a prolonged but restricted struggle to protect Malaysia against Indonesia'.[12] This was not an ideal policy, namely because it sought to manage and contain the issue, rather than to offer a more definite solution. The plan was essentially to make Indonesia weary of the struggle, especially under the pressure of internal, especially economic, stresses. Indonesian weariness was to be expedited by soliciting international diplomatic and economic pressure.

Butler's policy paper steered a course between a set of bad options. It dealt with the problem in its particular terms, in the sense that each policy option was evaluated in terms of how given strategic audiences would react, namely: the UN, the US, the Indonesian army, the Indonesian communist party, President Sukarno, the new Malaysian state, Commonwealth allies and the British public. The utility of a pragmatic mentality realised itself when, by deliberately having retained flexibility in the presentation of the conflict, which in this particular context made sense, Britain was able to remain agile in terms of its strategic narrative.

With regard to the Indonesian Confrontation, the British government advantageously adapted its strategic narrative to what it perceived to be the British national interest as the international situation evolved. Two key moments of evolution can be identified.

The first, which Matthew Jones emphasises in his diplomatic account, followed Lyndon Johnson's assumption of the presidency after President Kennedy's death. In parallel, and in the forefront of US foreign policy, was the significant escalation in the US commitment to Vietnam. The British government deliberately altered its strategic narrative in late 1963/early 1964 by equating the US engagement in Vietnam with the British fighting in Borneo. This required a narrative that presented both conflicts as part of a larger fight over 'Western interests' in Southeast Asia. One of the key British arguments was that retention of British military bases in Malaysia, particularly in Singapore, would support this. John Subritzky in *Confronting Sukarno* (2000) stresses the significance of the Australian and New Zealand influence in the repackaging of the Commonwealth position.[13]

The new narrative was put forward at quadripartite talks in February 1964 between the US, Britain, Australia and New Zealand, which were followed by a separate meeting between Prime Minister Sir Alec Douglas-Home and President Johnson. The result of this last meeting was that, despite the endurance of US concerns as to Indonesia's internal political stability, the US gave its tacit political support to Britain in Borneo. In return, the US received British political support for its commitment to Vietnam.[14] This turned out to be a significant diplomatic achievement for the British government. Yet, as Subritzky argues, the actual linkage between the conflicts was 'not substantial'.[15]

The second key evolution in the British strategic narrative occurred shortly after fighting in the Borneo Confrontation had ended. While the Vietnam War was reaching its climax, the British government in 1967 announced that it would withdraw all forces from Malaysia and Singapore by the mid 1970s, and in January 1968 accelerated this to 1971. The British government's rapid jettisoning of the concept of 'Western interests' in Southeast Asia illustrates the pragmatic quality of British strategic thought: financial imperatives were prioritised in the face of the huge expense of maintaining forces east of Suez, and British troops were kept out of Vietnam. However, it also shows the limits of pragmatism. Britain did not follow through on the commitments to its US, Australian and New Zealand allies (who were all militarily involved in Vietnam) that stemmed from a strategic concept of a unified Western position in Southeast Asia which Britain had itself previously pushed for. Pragmatism may be the most effective way to associate strategic actions with the national interest, but its value in more general philosophical terms evidently depends on how the national interest is defined in a given case.

This is exemplified in a powerful vignette that Matthew Jones presents to illustrate the official US reaction to Britain's announcement of withdrawal east of Suez. In January 1968 Dean Rusk, the US Secretary of State (1961–9), said to an American colleague how he could not believe that the British viewed that 'free aspirin and false teeth were more important than Britain's role in the world'.[16] Rusk's argument would be divisive in Britain today, and illustrates that the utility of pragmatism in the case of British strategy in the Borneo Confrontation was as a mentality used to formulate strategy, which is to be distinguished from the ideological values that inform a given policy position.

To this point the case study has examined the theme of pragmatism above the jungle canopy, in the diplomatic arena. But a pragmatic mindset was also a feature below the canopy where the fighting actually took place, to which we shall now turn.

In line with Cabinet policy set out above, the armed forces were to contain the Indonesian threat until Sukarno desisted: the Commander of British Forces in Borneo, Major General Walter Walker, was ordered to 'contain Indonesian aggression without escalation to open war'.[17] The Cabinet policy of restricted conflict was based on the assessment of the British Chiefs of Staff that without heightened military action 'short of full-scale war', Confrontation could not be won by military means alone.[18]

To understand how government policy was translated into an operational approach, we have to examine the situation below the jungle canopy which faced the British military. The first Indonesian raid came on 12 April 1963, against a police station at Tebedu in Sarawak. It was conducted by Indonesian-trained guerrillas led by Indonesian army officers. The Indonesian raids became far more serious from 28 September 1963, when a force of 200 well-trained regular Indonesian soldiers attacked a remote British army outpost at Long Jawai. Throughout the Confrontation, Indonesia also supported the Chinese Communist Organisation (CCO), who conducted sabotage in Sarawak and Sabah.

The Indonesian threat was not small: at the start of the Confrontation, British Intelligence estimated that there might be some 24,000 Chinese sympathisers in Sarawak, while along the border were 10,000 Indonesian troops, supported by an unknown number of volunteer guerrillas.[19] Throughout Confrontation, Indonesian forces employed the tactics of guerrilla warfare: they would attempt raids against military, police or government targets inside Malaysian Borneo, which were frequently remote outposts.

The thick jungle terrain appeared to favour the Indonesians, as they could approach unseen, attack, and then melt back into the rainforest. The border itself was 970 miles long, and the sea coast considerably longer. The aboriginal inland populations (mainly Ibans) lived in kampongs (longhouse villages), many of which were inaccessible except by air, or river followed by a long trek. These kampongs were scattered all over the jungle, making it impossible to supervise each one. The terrain thus made the civilian population vulnerable to the Indonesians. To cover this huge area General Walker's forces stood at only 13 battalions (10,000 men) and 15 helicopters; this was increased by January 1965 to 16 battalions and 80 helicopters. Nonetheless, his four brigade front-ages remained seriously overextended, standing at 181, 442, 267 and 81 miles.

The Indonesian Confrontation was for the British armed forces a peculiar conflict. It had elements of a counter-insurgency campaign: the Indonesians used guerrilla methods and sponsored the CCO. Yet by late 1963 the Confrontation could also be seen as a small conventional war, as British troops were directly fighting the regular Indonesian army.

Rather than trying to shoehorn the problem into a pre-existing doc-trinal template of counter-insurgency or conventional war (the two types of conflict that British forces of the 1960s were oriented towards), the operational approach drew on both concepts to create a unique concept tailored to that particular situation. Two men were chiefly responsible for its development. The Commander-in-Chief Far East, Admiral Sir Varyl Begg, was responsible for all army, air and naval forces in the area. He delegated to the Commander of British Forces in Bor-neo, Major General Walker, who ran ground operations on a daily basis.

A light infantry man commissioned into the Indian Army in 1933, Walker had served on the North-West Frontier, Burma in 1942–5, and as a brigade commander in the Malayan Emergency. As the Director of the Malaya Jungle Warfare School, he had himself written the army manual for counter-insurgency operations in the jungle, stressing the need for platoon and company patrols and ambushes as being superior to big brigade clearance operations.[20] Walker's experience reinforces the fact that he had been sent to Borneo on account of his extensive opera-tional experience in the jungle.[21] In this sense the conflict was from the start recognised as one which required specialists in this type of terrain, rather than being a conventional small war which happened to be in the jungle.

Walker used many concepts from the Malayan Emergency. He was by his own account 'tremendously influenced' by Field Marshal Sir Gerald Templer.[22] The imperative of getting the civilian population on side was directly transplanted from Malaya to Borneo. Army-civilian-police committees were established at each level of command, as well as a campaign to win over people in the remote villages. Yet the Confrontation was not a re-run of Malaya, and Walker recognised this. Walker's task was not to put down an indigenous guerrilla movement, but to defend the local population from the Indonesian incursions while avoiding pushing Sukarno into open war. Neither was Walker's thinking limited to counter-insurgency; in Burma he had led a Gurkha battalion in some of the most savage conventional battles the British army experienced in the Second World War.

When Duncan Sandys, the Secretary of State for Commonwealth Relations, visited Malaysia in September 1963, he told Walker that: 'it is not the policy of Her Majesty's Government to become caught up in a war ... try to stop it from escalating. Do everything you can to stop it'. Walker thought this attitude smacked of defensive thinking.[23] He believed that the war having already started, the emphasis should be on ending it by winning: 'offensive action is the very essence of successful military operations when faced with guerrilla or terrorist forces'.[24] Indeed, while Sandys was thinking about Confrontation from above the jungle canopy (note how at this time British policy-makers were still very sensitive to the Kennedy White House's scepticism towards British military action in Borneo), Walker was thinking about the conflict from the ground upwards.

Walker saw that a defensive strategy would not work on the ground: the terrain made it impossible for the British to guard against Indonesian infiltration in such a large area: 'the Indonesians held the initiative because they could operate from safe bases in Kalimantan ... they knew the bases were safe from attack because there had been no official declaration of war'.[25] As policy-makers can sometimes forget, an armed conflict has to succeed on the ground as well as in terms of international politics. Let us examine Walker's plan in that context.

Walker's approach was based on an understanding of the terrain on its own terms. Bear in mind that the average contact distance with the enemy in the Confrontation was only 5–10 metres, which is the normal limit of visibility for infantry moving in that type of jungle.[26] Guerrillas could appear unseen and unheard, attack, and then vanish into the rainforest. Walker believed that unless commanders took a firm stand, they could very soon have all their forces tied down defending their bases. The only way to beat them was to make them feel insecure in the jungle by taking control of it. Walker notes that, as in counter-insurgency operations, there was no 'rear' area; every man in uniform had to be a potential front-line infantry soldier.

Patrol bases were designed to be defended by a third of their occupants, be it a section in a platoon base, or a platoon in a company base. The other two-thirds of the unit were out on patrol, dominating the jungle in an offensive role. Walker stressed that 'results could not be achieved by attacking and shooting the enemy then returning to base. He had to be played at his own game by living out in the jungle for weeks on end... The jungle has got to belong to you; you must own it; you must control and dominate it'.[27] Troops spent a very high proportion of time out on patrol. One Gurkha ambush stood for 40 days before the enemy arrived.[28] The domination of the jungle, in conjunction with hearts and minds, was intended to take advantage of the vast and intimidating jungle by taking control of the physical and political terrain.

Through colonial experience, a principle of 'minimum force' had developed to deal with civil disturbances and colonial insurrections. The principle was to apply the least force necessary to maintain order. Yet it would have made no sense to apply minimum force, a defining principle of the Malayan campaign, at the tactical level. Practically, commanders clearly could not order troops to spare enemy lives as far as possible if a contact occurred, especially since the enemy was the aggressive and professional Indonesian infantry, not the communist guerrillas of the Malayan Emergency who usually fled when attacked; it would just have seemed like incompetence.[29]

Walker pragmatically raised the level at which minimum force was applied from the tactical to the operational level. He intended to use minimum force within an offensive approach to dominate the jungle. In practice, this led to the development of operations codenamed 'Claret', which started in April 1964. These were top secret clandestine raids across the border into Indonesia, which regained the initiative from the Indonesians by making the Indonesians feel insecure everywhere. Claret operations, although used against regular troops, were an extension of the approach of psychological domination of the opponent by appearing to be everywhere at once. This is very close to the way insurgents normally operate. Improvised explosive devices (IEDs), for example, try to make soldiers feel nervous everywhere, even though there may only be a few devices in a big area. Walker had coined the phrase 'to out guerrilla the guerrillas' as a brigade commander in Malaya; he now used this pragmatically in a different context.[30]

Walker kept a tight control over the direction of Claret raids so as to limit Indonesian casualties in the theatre as a whole and thus avoid escalation of the conflict by not provoking Sukarno. He devised a set of seven "Golden Rules" to that end: he, as Director of Operations, would personally authorise every operation; only trained and tested troops were to be used; the penetration depth was to be limited, attacks being only to thwart enemy offensive action, never in retribution of one's casualties, and civilian casualties were never to be risked; there was to be no air support, except in extreme emergency; operations were to be planned and rehearsed for at least two weeks; every operation was to be planned and executed with maximum security, cover plans made, code names for each operation used, and soldiers sworn to secrecy, with no details to be discussed over radio or telephone, no ID disks worn and no identifiable material to be left in Kalimantan; and no soldiers were to be captured alive or dead.[31]

Hence Walker was using the jungle terrain to his advantage: instead of trying to fight a conventional war against the Indonesian guerrilla tactics, he fought them in the jungle using light infantry who beat them at their own game. The terrain was central to this approach: by keeping the conflict below the jungle canopy, Walker was able to raise the application of minimum force to the operational level, as the world could not see anything of what happened on the ground.

Claret operations connected to political objectives primarily by undermining the Indonesian army's morale for Sukarno's enterprise. A succession of extensions of the distance across the border for Claret operations were authorised in 1964 and 1965 in line with political conditions. For example, Secretary of Defence Denis Healey in November 1964 authorised an extension in response to Indonesian parachute landings in peninsular Malaysia.[32]

Soon after Major General George Lea took over from Walker as Director of Operations in March 1965, the Indonesian Army became more aggressive. On 27 April 1965 the Indonesians launched a full battalion-sized attack on a company base manned by British Paratroopers at Plaman Mapu in Sarawak, which was only just beaten off. In response Lea attempted to establish a no-man's-land 10,000 yards inside

Kalimantan by an intensive series of Claret operations 'to make absolutely clear to the Indonesians that their proper place was behind their own frontier'.[33] While a battalion in 1964 conducted an average of two Claret operations per month to ambush Indonesians, by mid-1965 eight per month was normal.[34]

2/10th Gurkha Rifles, for example, arrived in Sarawak in March 1965 and launched operation 'Super Shell' in August and 'High Hurdle' in September.[35] These were multi-company operations which involved simultaneous attacks on an Indonesian camp and the River Koemba that supplied it. This approach achieved its aim, as most of the fighting was confined to the Indonesian side of the border. In one instance, an Indonesian commander even sent a note to his British opposite number from 2/2nd Gurkha Rifles saying that he was retreating and wanted to be left alone.[36] These more daring operations did not provoke an Indonesian public response, even though it was evident that Commonwealth troops had violated the border. This was probably because the Indonesians did not want to lose face by admitting to military defeats.

One of the most gripping first-person narratives of Claret operations is Brigadier (then Captain) Christopher Bullock's *Journeys Hazardous: Gurkha Clandestine Operations in Borneo 1965* (1994). He emphasises the relentless tempo of cross-border operations that his company carried out. What is remarkable in his account is how particularly arduous these operations were, and the level of jungle experience required to beat the Indonesian regular forces, who were themselves a skilled enemy. This experience had been built up over years of regimental experience in the jungles of Malaya during the Emergency. Just as Walter Walker was a jungle specialist, so were many of his troops.[37]

Cross-border operations were regulated to suit the political dialogue at the international level. The authorisation for 'hot pursuit' across the border requested in 1964 was suspended until after the meetings of foreign ministers of Afro-Asian countries, the South East Asia Treaty Organisation (SEATO) ministerial meetings, and the Malaysian elections, in order to minimise the likely political fallout resulting from such operations. Lea started what was known as a 'be nice to Indonesians' period in October and December 1965 in response to events (the PKI coup and Indonesian Army counter-coup), which meant that all Claret operations were suspended. As the Indonesian Army started to fight the communists in late 1965, it was assured that the British would not exploit the situation. Hence the tempo and nature of cross-border operations were regulated at the operational level to ensure that the principle of minimum force was being applied.

British strategy also drew on ideas associated with Cold War doctrine, and intertwined them pragmatically with the counter-insurgency theory and jungle warfare that Walker was fusing on the ground. The British Ministry of Defence was created in 1964 from an amalgamation of the Admiralty, the War Office, the Air Ministry, the Ministry of Aviation and the old Ministry of Defence itself. The concept of joint command sought to fight a more effective Cold War battle by using each service to its greatest advantages, working in conjunction with the other services rather than encouraging doctrines that favoured only one service. Cold War doctrine was employed more obviously with regard to the role of air and naval power. Bombers and warships were based in Singapore under the command of Admiral Begg to remind Sukarno not to escalate

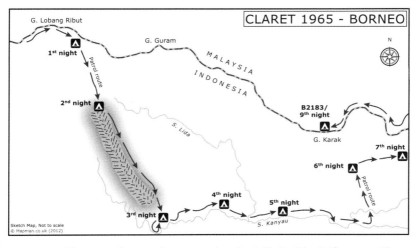

Figure 12: This map depicts the route taken by 2/2 Gurkha Rifles on a Claret operation in 1965. The ambush took place on the river at the loop depicted at the 3rd night location. The map indicates the level of risk that these operations involved, given the time spent in Indonesia and the difficulty of extraction in the jungle (which places in relief the significantly different and typically more nervous attitude towards taking risk today).[38]

the Confrontation himself, as Indonesia would suffer massive retaliation if it came to open war.

When Confrontation escalated in 1964 after Indonesian parachute landings on mainland Malaysia, the British Chiefs of Staff Committee agreed upon the requirement 'to convince Sukarno that should he turn aggressor we have the determination and capability to retaliate immediately and effectively'.[39] Britain sent a squadron of Vulcan jet bombers and Javelin jet fighters to Singapore, and more warships were sent to Malaysian waters. These were assets which could project a huge amount of firepower and were normally associated with Cold War deterrence. They were effectively used in that role: as a deterrent to remind Sukarno that escalation on his part would be lethal.

The language used in discussions concerning the deployment of bombers to Singapore is indicative of the facility with which the concepts of Cold War deterrence were interwoven into the operation: 'The best deterrent to the possibility of Indonesian air attack on Malaysia is the maintenance of a clear ability to destroy their air force by counter-air operations. Should the Indonesian air force nonetheless attack, our strike forces must be capable of immediate retaliation… Such a force might also deter Sukarno from resorting to other forms of overt aggression'.[40] In terms of what this book has described as the language of war, British strategy was successful in the sense that President Sukarno understood the threat in the terms desired by that strategy; nor was this a coincidence: the whole plan was carefully orchestrated around the theme of audiences and persuasion, as Butler's policy paper illustrates.

By the end of 1964, the British Far East Fleet comprised more than eighty warships, the largest naval presence in East Asia since the Korean War. The combined air and naval forces conducted numerous well-publicised exercises around Singapore as a demonstration of strength. For instance, a note from the Secretary of State for Defence to the Foreign Office of October 1964 affirmed that a squadron of 8 Canberra bombers would be sent over from Germany to Singapore for two weeks; a naval exercise in the South China Sea involving eight warships, including one Australian and one New Zealand vessel, would take place; and information was to be planted in Indonesian intelligence of a commando landing exercise on the north Malaysian coast. These measures were deemed to be 'adequate for the political purpose desired'.[41] This desired show of force reached its height when the British carrier HMS

Victorious sailed through the international waters of the Lombok Straits east of Bali, which was to be taken as a strong signal of Commonwealth self-confidence.

Although Commonwealth air and naval power were never used in retaliation, the contingency plans illustrate how the operational approach was intimately associated with the political context in which it was to be applied. In 1963 plan 'Addington' was developed to be implemented as an immediate response to an overt Indonesian assault. It envisaged large-scale air attacks on Indonesian military targets. In 1964 plan 'Mason' was devised as a possible measured response to continued Indonesian attacks on the Malaysian peninsula.[42] Although similar to Addington, Mason was never carried out: it would have involved raids on Indonesian bases in the Rhio Archipelago (south of Singapore) and Sumatra from where the Indonesians launched their attacks on west Malaysia.

Addington and Mason were contingency plans geared primarily to deliver a political effect, since militarily they would not in themselves stop the Indonesians. For both plans procedures were worked out for the Malaysian government to get to the UN Security Council before the Indonesians did, in order to complain under Article 51 of the UN Charter that they were victims of aggression and were acting with the support of allies in self-defence.[43] By framing the deterrence within a framework which only authorised action in response to Indonesian aggression, the British hoped to make best use of their advantage in firepower without compromising in the wider international community the image that Indonesia was at fault. Commenting upon this procedure, a Foreign Office document outlining plan Mason notes that 'we have been much influenced by the importance of avoiding anything which would damage the international image of Malaysia as the injured party'.[44] While the actual plans were highly classified, Sukarno clearly knew about such a possibility. In November 1964, Tunku Abdul Rahman advertised the threat of the Royal Air Force (RAF) 'hitting back' in a direct threat to Sukarno at a widely reported press conference.[45]

British strategy, as noted in the discussion of Rab Butler's January 1964 policy paper above, played on the fact that it suited both sides to keep the conflict unofficial and bilateral as far as possible (although Matthew Jones indicates accurately how it was never literally bilateral, since even actors on the same side acted independently of each other, not least the sovereign Malaysian government).[46] The presentation of the conflict to the outside world was therefore crucial. The terrain was the single most important factor in determining how Confrontation could be presented. British strategy had to be attuned mainly to four target audiences: the Indonesian government; the Malaysian civilian population (especially the indigenous tribes in Borneo); domestic opinion; and international opinion. The hearts and minds campaign was effectively how the Confrontation was presented to the indigenous tribes deep in the jungle. The tribes did not have much contact with the outside world, so the British forces could retain a monopoly on flows of information from inside the jungle to the outside world. As most of the fighting occurred in remote jungle, its only witnesses were usually soldiers themselves.

While Sukarno made speeches about the national quest to crush Malaysia, the Indonesians never admitted sending regular troops across the border. They claimed that the incursions were conducted by guerrillas, whose cause they nonetheless supported. Nor did the Indonesians make propaganda out of British cross-border incursions. The Indonesians were unlikely to publicise incursions for prestige reasons, as they had consistently shown themselves unwilling to admit the extent of casualties they suffered in the jungle. The British could not risk locking Sukarno into a situation from which he could not withdraw without loss of face, and so did not themselves publicise the conflict.

The role of the press was limited because reporters could only go to military bases to which the army took them. The official secrecy surrounding military operations prevented information coming out of unofficial channels, especially since troops were not allowed to go to towns and bars while on operational tour. The importance of managing the press can be brought into relief by comparison with the situation of the British counter-insurgency operation in Aden and South Arabia, which was going on concurrently. Here, journalists were far more exposed to the front-line troops. Mismanagement of this aspect of the campaign contributed to the British government announcing its intention to withdraw from the region while troops were still engaged in operations. Intelligence from local sources dried up immediately once locals realised that it was not worth endangering themselves for the British, who would shortly leave them to fend for themselves.

To summarise, a pragmatic mentality in the construction of British strategy in the Indonesian Confrontation was a key factor in its success: the conflict was understood on its own terms; there was proper dialogue between desire and possibility; the operational approach drew on existing concepts and tailored them to a particular situation, rather than applying them as an abstract template; the outcome of the campaign was understood in political terms, specifically in terms of responses from various strategic audiences. It was implicitly understood that strategy had two interrelated functions: to shape the political context in order to give meaning to actions (effectively the construction of an interpretive structure through the strategic narrative); and the selection of an operational approach. Strategy was not thought of as the application of actions based on inflexible ideological agendas. The decisive moment in the construction of strategic narrative occurred when the United States administration (albeit reluctantly) was persuaded to see the conflict in terms of an overall Western interest in Southeast Asia, where Britain's commitment to Malaysia equated to the US commitment to South Vietnam.

The British operational approach worked because, instead of trying to work round the terrain (both the physical and cultural terrain), it worked with it, in both political and military terms. The political and military elements of the campaign were not artificially separated. The texture of the Confrontation on the ground was understood in political terms. This encouraged a strategy that recognised the need to work both at the international level and in terms of combat below the jungle canopy.

Hence, political constraints having been satisfied, British strategy was largely able to contain the Confrontation to a pattern of conflict which took place on the jungle floor, and then decisively beat the Indonesians militarily in this arena by applying light infantry concepts that suited the British army's superior experience in jungle warfare at the time (following Burma and Malaya). 'Claret' operations succeeded in extending the principle of domination of the jungle from a defensive concept inside Malaysian Borneo to an offensive concept by delimiting a no-man's-land just inside the Indonesian border where most of the fighting took place. When the Indonesians tried to break out of this pattern, such as landing in west Malaysia, Cold War-type escalatory threats were brought to bear to bring them back into line. British forces did not attempt to fight a Cold War battle or a counter-insurgency campaign, but understood the conflict for what it was on the ground, and formulated a novel strategy that had elements of both doctrines which suited the particular nature of the conflict.

In 1969 General Walker, by then Commander of NATO's northern flank in Denmark, wrote an article at Denis Healey's request on 'How Borneo Was Won'.[47] It described the Indonesian Confrontation as a 'Limited War'. In one sense, this was merely a descriptive term which referred to conflicts which were not total war. In another sense, in 1969 'Limited War' was a conceptual term, which was at the time more obviously associated with the Vietnam War and the Cold War. The most influential Cold War political scientist to deal with this concept was Robert Osgood, who published the book *Limited War* in 1957.[48] Osgood's argument was that conventional 'proxy' wars between the superpowers, in which political aims and military means were deliberately limited, was the way to confront the spread of communism without escalation to a nuclear exchange. This was the type of war that America was attempting to wage in Vietnam.

In his article, Walker uses Vietnam as a counterpoint to Borneo. Although 'Limited War' as defined in the Indonesian Confrontation had developed organically in response to the Indonesian threat, Walker was now setting up Borneo as a paradigm of Limited War. This, however, was misguided. Britain succeeded in Borneo because an abstract template had not been imposed on the conflict.

Walker was really getting above himself in retrospectively describing the conceptual approach to the conflict in a way that had not actually been used at the time. He was trying to present his plan as the true articulation of Limited War, which the Americans were getting wrong in Vietnam. In reality, Vietnam was a far more complex conflict than Borneo, and of a completely different scale; the comparison was illegitimate. Later on Walker was effectively sacked from his NATO command. He had made a fetish of aggressive defence, a concept that had worked in Borneo but would have been catastrophic in a nuclear war context. The irony is that Walker the pragmatist had perhaps been intoxicated by his success and had become the ideologue.

Luck also played a major role. Lord Healey's account implies a linear narrative from military action to political outcome: 'a textbook demonstration of how to apply economy of force, under political guidance, for political ends'. As Christopher Tuck has argued, in his work on conflict termination in the context of the Borneo conflict, the 'end' that resulted was not as deliberate a goal as Lord Healey's retrospective view might imply.[49] Indeed, the Indonesian Army counter-coup in October-

BRITISH STRATEGY IN THE BORNEO CONFRONTATION

November 1965 was preceded by the PKI's coup, which might well have been successful.

Strategy, even when properly conducted, involves an element of luck, as conflict is unpredictable. After all, the same British government failed in the other major action which involved British troops at the time in South Arabia and Aden. The understandable hubris associated with entirely rational and linear retrospective narratives of why particular approaches succeed, often proposed by the victors, tend in many cases, as here in the case of Borneo, to overplay the role of any operational approach and to underplay the role of luck. This can encourage the mistaken notion that there genuinely exist certain approaches that work in any context.

Finally, although not actually part of the Confrontation, it must be mentioned that the Indonesian military counter-coup, which secured General Suharto's position, triggered the killing of around 500,000 Indonesian 'communists' in 1965–6. This is a separate story for which there is not space here to do justice, but it must be taken into consideration in any evaluation of the aftermath of the conflict.

The Indonesian Confrontation is an example of successful strategy that was able to control the narrative by understanding the language of force. The case study is an example primarily of the utility of a pragmatic mindset. The actual British operational approach that was developed to deal with Borneo was a product of its time, and cannot be transplanted to the present day. Moreover, the Borneo case study is an example of a strategy that was intimately attuned to the importance of information and audiences; operational thought needs to be constructed within a conception of strategy that recognises that strategy is not just the orchestration of tactical actions themselves (the use of force), but also the construction of an interpretive structure, the strategic narrative, which gives meaning to those actions.

One could well argue that a campaign such as the Indonesian Confrontation would be impossible for Britain today, in a far more open and complex information environment. That would probably be correct. (Of course there is an argument that if a conflict, or more typically, a behaviour within a conflict, is successfully kept secret it is not known about, which creates a circular argument. The extent to which covert operations are publicly known about is a separate theme which is not the concern of this book). How then can the strategist today retain the utility of a pragmatic mindset in a more complex and fragmented political and information environment? This is the subject of the next two chapters, which look at strategic narrative: the tool which seeks to achieve cognitive coherence between an operational approach and its political context.

8

STRATEGIC NARRATIVE

The overnight insertion march from the helicopter drop-off point to the village of Lam in January 2008 was possibly the coldest night of the tour, with temperatures well below zero. There had been an insurgent meeting in this remote village the day before, but we had just missed them. In the event we spoke to the villagers, who spent most of the day crouched outside their mud houses to absorb heat from the sun. There was no water in the village, as the river was dry in winter; it had to be collected from a well a few miles away. These villagers truly had virtually nothing. Their concern was simply to survive the winter. In that context, wider political issues had little traction with them. Whether insurgents used the village as a transit point between Helmand and Kandahar Provinces was not their problem. In such circumstances our narrative, and indeed the insurgent narrative, held little of interest for them. Any strategic narrative, to be persuasive, must have emotional as well as rational purchase on an audience. This chapter considers the construction of strategic narrative in contemporary conflict; but first we must define its function.

'Strategic narrative' is a contemporary term, but is a formalisation of a concept that has been present in all conflicts. Strategic narrative is the explanation of actions. It can usually be detected chronologically before conflict starts, in some form, as the explanation for participation in, or initiation of, the conflict; strategic narrative also operates as the explanation of actions during and after conflict.

Figure 13: Gurkha patrol through snow in the village of Lam, North Kandahar Province, January 2008.

Strategy seeks to relate actions to policy. A policy outcome is ultimately an impression upon an audience. It can be a physical impression, which in war would typically be defined in terms of death and destruction. It can simultaneously be a psychological impression, typically defined in terms of an evolution in political alignment, not necessarily by consent. For strategy to connect actions to policy it must therefore invest them with a given meaning in relation to its audiences, both prospectively and retrospectively.

Policy starts as an abstract idea, because by logic it has not been achieved yet; policy finishes as a set of accomplished facts, the policy end-state, which in many cases may not meet the original intent, and may not represent a clear end point, as policy in a conflict merges into post-conflict policy. In this sense strategic narrative accompanies policy throughout the lifetime of the conflict (before, during and beyond the period of actual fighting): it explains policy in the context of the proposed set of actions in the abstract, and then explains those actions, having been executed, in terms of how they relate back to policy.

STRATEGIC NARRATIVE

Strategic narrative can be found in various forms which differ in accordance with the rhetorical context. The way the British Prime Minister justifies participation in Afghanistan to the British public differs in style and content from the narrative he might give to international audiences. A British soldier would explain the actions of his patrol to an Afghan audience differently depending a number of factors. Is he speaking to an individual or a group? Is the audience already familiar to him? If so, what is the nature of the existing relationship? What is the sociopolitical background of the audience? What are the operational circumstances of the discussion? The list goes on. Strategic narrative effectively proposes to its audience a structure through which to interpret actions. In another, intrinsically related, sense it is the expression of policy aims in narrative form. The last chapter, for example, set out how, by adjusting the strategic narrative of Britain's involvement in the Borneo Confrontation from a colonial to a Cold War context, the United States administration was persuaded to understand, or tolerate, Britain's actions in that conflict in a different way.

Strategic narrative should be adjusted to the audience. An Afghan peasant, for instance, is not particularly interested in who has power in Kabul; what the coalition and Afghan government are doing locally is far more important. Conversely, a provincial governor might be more concerned by national politics than the local situation in his province. For strategic narrative to vary is normal, in the same way that a salesperson pitches a product differently to resonate with a particular customer. The problem comes when a product is pitched so differently to different customers that it loses credibility because the versions are inconsistent. This is the challenge for strategic narrative today: the strategist has to consider how a narrative can gain purchase on audiences whose political persuasions vary widely, without coming apart. The model at Figure 14 illustrates an ideal form in which each narrative is 'nested' within a wider narrative, and is thus consistent.

General Stanley McChrystal stated in 2009 that counter-insurgency 'is about having a consistent conversation with the Afghan people'. In the context of national level strategic narrative, Captain Wayne Porter of the US navy and Colonel Mark Mykleby of the US marines have argued that the US needs to close the 'say-do gap': a convincing narrative means consistency in words and actions across the globe.[1] David

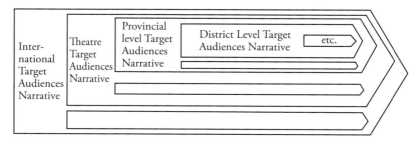

Figure 14: Idealised strategic narrative model (based on a fictional context): each narrative is nested.

Kilcullen has argued that it is important to 'exploit a single narrative' in his '28 Articles, Fundamentals of Company-level Counterinsurgency':

Since counter-insurgency is a competition to mobilise popular support, it pays to know how people are mobilised. In most societies there are opinion-makers … who set trends and influence public perceptions. This influence … including the pernicious influence of the insurgents—often takes the form of a 'single narrative': a simple, unifying, easily expressed story or explanation that organises people's experience and provides a framework for understanding events… To undercut their influence you must exploit an alternative narrative: or better yet, tap into an existing narrative that excludes the insurgents.[2]

This narrative should be realised in a coherent set of actions which give it expression. Figure 15 illustrates how strategic narrative binds together the various lines of operation in Afghanistan.

The diagram draws out how strategic narrative is not just concerned with audiences exterior to one's side, or coalition. One of its key functions is to achieve unity of effort, ideally to give coherent expression to that side's 'will', as Carl von Clausewitz would put it. In a 2010 lecture on the UK government's counter-terrorist strategy (named the 'Contest' strategy) Charles Farr, the head of its implementation at the Home Office, stated that: 'people work on Contest in High Commissions and Embassies around the world, in Departments in London, in local authorities, and in policing units up and down this country, they talk about the strategy and they refer to it'.[3]

The first part of this quotation exemplifies how strategic narrative is essential to overcome potentially fragmented and geographically disparate institutional boundaries on issues that require a cross-government

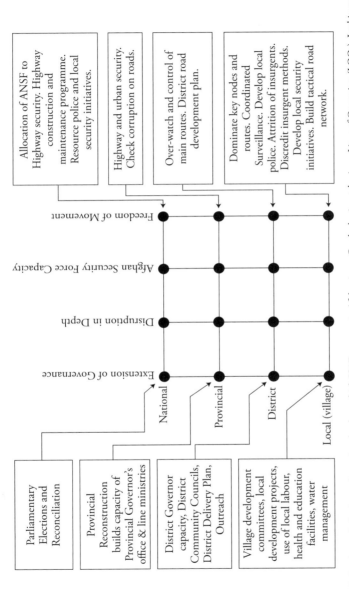

Figure 15: On the vertical axis are the various levels at which ISAF operates in Afghanistan. On the horizontal axis are Lines of Operation (LOOs). In this case the LOOs are drawn from the ISAF Regional Commander for Southern Afghanistan's priorities at the start of the summer of 2010. The actual substance of the horizontal and vertical axes is only used as an illustration; levels of operation and LOOs can be adjusted in number and substance as required. The boxes to the side show the types of action that are conducted at each level to support each LOO. Only two LOOs are expanded upon here for simplicity, and there would in reality be far more in each of the boxes. However, what this diagram illustrates is that lines of operation have to provide mutual support for one another, and activity at each level needs to be consistent with that above and below it. Strategic narrative plays a vital role in ensuring this coherence between actions, in the sense that it explains to people what is being done, so that people understand those actions in the manner intended by strategy. This includes achieving unity of effort among one's side, as well as explaining actions to other audiences. (ANSF, top right, signifies Afghan National Security Forces.)[4]

approach. The second part speaks to the importance that a strategy have purchase on those whom it seeks to direct. This may be common sense, but effective, unifying, strategic narratives that are alive in the minds of their protagonists, are less common than distant, bulky tomes that few people one one's side have actually read, and fewer still are inspired by. Third, this aspect of strategic narrative points to the fact that to draw a sharp distinction between strategy and strategic narrative is misguided: as the explanation of actions, strategic narrative is simply strategy expressed in narrative form.

In reality it is often impossible to satisfy every audience, just as politicians who try to please everybody may find themselves to be in pursuit of an incoherent agenda which actually pleases nobody. An essential variable in strategic success is how far strategy has managed to bind potentially conflicting narratives together into a coherent strategic narrative. In the traditional inter-state paradigm of war, the presence of an enemy whose intention is one's own destruction tends to concentrate minds; where there is not such an existential threat (a circumstance normal in contemporary conflict), political differences tend to come to the fore and frustrate coherent strategy. This chapter examines how strategic narrative can be constructed in the fragmented political environments that characterise contemporary conflict.

Strategy, meaning and rhetoric

In the film *Thirteen Days*, which is about the 1962 Cuban missile crisis, there is a great scene when Secretary of Defense Robert McNamara confronts Admiral Anderson, who is directing the naval blockade of Cuba.[5] President Kennedy has specifically ordered that there be no firing against Soviet transport ships without his permission. A star-shell (flare) has just been fired over one of the ships as a warning. Secretary McNamara is furious, thinking it was actual firing. He orders firing to stop, and then confronts the Admiral:

ADMIRAL ANDERSON: Get out of our way, Mr Secretary. The Navy has been running blockades since the days of John Paul Jones.

MCNAMARA: I believe the President made it clear that there would be no firing on ships without his express permission.

ADMIRAL ANDERSON: With all due respect, Mr Secretary, we were not firing on the ship. Firing on a ship means attacking the ship. We were not attacking the ship. We were firing over it.

MCNAMARA: This was not the President's intention when he gave that order. What if the Soviets don't see the distinction? What if they make the same mistake I just did? There will be no firing anything near any Soviet ships without my express permission, is that understood, Admiral?

ADMIRAL ANDERSON: Yes, sir.

MCNAMARA: And I will only issue such instructions when ordered to by the President. John Paul Jones ... you don't understand a thing, do you, Admiral? This isn't a blockade. This, all this [US tactical moves during the crisis], is language, a new vocabulary the likes of which the world has never seen. This is President Kennedy communicating with Secretary Khrushchev.

This exchange, though fictionalised, illustrates the importance of the interpretive structure through which people understand actions in conflict, as well as the instability of interpretive structures in situations which do not conform to more conventional templates of conflict, where improvisation is often necessary.

The essential variable governing the stability of a conflict's interpretive structure is the degree to which it depends upon the application of physical violence. Clausewitz's concept of the centre of gravity links physical action to a psychological, and essentially political, outcome (as Chapter 6 discusses). For Clausewitz, strategy's function is to identify the centre of gravity and orchestrate tactical action to strike against it. Victory by 'strategic manoeuvre' alone was for Clausewitz highly unstable; to call an enemy defeated because he has accepted the likelihood of actual physical defeat while his forces are largely intact may prove short-lived if he changes his mind.[6] Clausewitz placed a premium on tactical outcomes as the pegs on which strategic outcomes were hung. Tactics represented physical reality. Strategy was its exploitation, and represented the psychological component:

In strategy, there is no such thing as victory. Part of strategic success lies in timely preparation for a tactical victory... The rest of strategic success lies in the exploitation of a victory won.[7]

Tactical actions provided the building blocks for strategy to convert into a political end-state: 'the original means of strategy is victory—that is, tactical success; its ends, in the final analysis, are those objects that will lead directly to peace'.[8] Clausewitz wrote about how strategy is what invests the physical component of tactical victory with its psychological meaning: its 'sphere of influence'. Superiority in war was a combination of the two.[9]

Strategy was what gave meaning to tactical actions: 'we are dealing with one of the most fundamental principles of war. In strategy, the significance of an engagement is what really matters... That is why, strategically speaking, the difference between one battle and another can be so great that the two can no longer be considered the same instrument'.[10] The point he makes here is that significance can only be defined against something, which in this case is the result of the war as a whole, and it is strategy's role to propose and exaggerate that definition. It does this by orchestrating tactical actions and adjusting war itself as an interpretive tool, as Chapters 1–3 of this book set out. Thus, what Clausewitz is hypothetically arguing is that two battles could physically be identical, but as the result of a battle is only definable in relation to a given strategic context, this can vary, and therefore vary the results of the two battles.

In summary, Clausewitz stressed that the physical destruction provided by the engagement was the only advantage that permanently belonged to the victor.[11] The perceived meaning, and ultimately the policy outcome, that strategy invests in tactical actions can never itself be considered permanent.

Nonetheless, approaches to conflict which emphasise the perceived over the physical will often be more tempting, often for very sensible reasons, such as the fact that they require, at least if successful, less investment of physical resources. Military approaches have oscillated in terms of the degree to which they have exploited perception in war. Karl-Heinz Frieser's study of the German 1940 campaign in France argues that *Blitzkrieg* was not a formal concept at this stage, but the way in which the more imaginative and aggressive German generals operated was a revival in some ways of an older tradition of manoeuvre:[12]

The Blitzkrieg of 1940 at first seems like nothing other than the revival of the classic operational war of movement of men such as Moltke and Schlieffen. But that is only half the truth. The tie-in of traditional command principles with modern technology resulted in such a tremendous increase in speed during combat operations that there arose a dialectical turnabout, leading to a new, psychological quality. That is the essence of the revolution in the nature of war. The principle of psychological confusion replaced the old principle of physical annihilation... If at all possible, the German Panzers avoided all kinds of combat actions. After they had thrust deep into the enemy's rear areas, the enemy front collapsed by itself amid wild chaos.[13]

186

Karl-Heinz Frieser's argument indicates that massive reliance on the perceived component of actions in conflict (an idea associated today as much, if not more, with al-Qaeda and its franchise groups as state actors) is neither novel, nor out of place across the spectrum of conflict, including as here in the context of high-intensity, conventional, inter-state war. By the same token, the risks attendant on such an approach, which informed Clausewitz's scepticism about eighteenth-century warfare in his own post-Napoleonic era, are also neither novel, nor restricted to low-intensity warfare. Frieser argues that the German campaign of 1940 was, in its early stages, and contrary to popular perception, a very close run thing.

Great dependence on the perceived component of actions in conflict is therefore not new, nor are the risks of so doing. However, this dependence is undoubtedly driven and exaggerated by today's information revolution. There is a correlation here with Frieser's proposition that the successful German exploitation of perception in the 1940 campaign was also underpinned and enabled by agile exploitation of technological developments which irreversibly changed the nature of modern warfare. The *Wehrmacht's* spearhead Panzer groups were able to operate over long distances due to radio, and had command organisations which exploited the technology properly.

By contrast, Frieser offers an incredible vignette of the French supreme commander in the final stage of the campaign: Maxime Weygand, who at one point based himself in a headquarters in which there was no radio and only one telephone line, unavailable between midday and 2 p.m. as the telephone exchange girl insisted on her lunch![14] By analogy, liberal powers cannot opt out of today's information revolution for the purposes of armed conflict, as General Weygand did, even if that makes it incumbent upon us profoundly to adjust the way in which we consider contemporary conflict. Given that the effects of the information revolution are probably irreversible, at least in the visible future, the implication is that the experience of conflicts such as Afghanistan are not anomalous, but actually point to the future.

In contemporary conflict physical destruction tends to matter less to a conflict's outcome than how those actions are perceived (with certain exceptions). This is primarily because the outcome is defined against several audiences who are not the enemy, and therefore are beyond the range of physical violence. Moreover as various audiences frequently have significantly different interpretations of the conflict in which they are involved or are witnessing, it is much harder for strategy to invest physical actions with a meaning that corresponds with the desired policy outcome because there are so many possible interpretations of any tactical action.

David Kilcullen in *The Accidental Guerrilla* (2009) describes how the West tends to think about information operations as describing actions in war. Al-Qaeda and the Taliban, however, tend to act in order to convey a message. They are conducting 'an armed propaganda campaign. The informational side of AQ's operation is primary. The physical is merely the tool to achieve a propaganda result... Contrast this with our [the West's] approach: we typically design physical operations first, then craft supporting information operations to explain or justify our actions'.[15]

My view is that physical actions still matter, even if they are perhaps perceived badly at the time. An analogy might be made with a politician who introduces unpopular reforms which are only appreciated in retrospect. Moreover, the effects of campaigns thus fought are more durable, as Clausewitz argues. That said, the information revolution does not present liberal powers with such a convenient choice. Kilcullen is right to argue that liberal powers in many contemporary cases, such as in conflicts which are highly politicised at the tactical level, need to understand better how to orchestrate actions to achieve a given information effect. In these circumstances, the construction of strategic narrative approximates to the theory of rhetoric.

The construction of strategic narrative, like the construction of oratory, is designed to persuade people of something. The first question the rhetorician must consider is the relationship between the desired outcome and the audience. How does one break down the audience into segmented target groups? Does one seek broad approval from the audience or are certain sections of people targeted? How does one tailor one's narrative to resonate with each target audience without appearing inconsistent? Does one focus on timing parts of the speech to appeal to specific target audiences which may upset others, and if so, does one condition those who will be upset by appealing to them earlier on in the speech? Second, once the audience has been defined, the rhetorician considers how to convince his audience. In Aristotle's *Rhetoric*, he defines three rhetorical resources the orator could use to persuade: *logos* was appeal through rational argument, and thus referred to the speech itself (*logos* meant 'word', 'speech', 'account' or 'reason' in Greek); *pathos* was persuasion through emotional appeal, by putting the hearer in a certain frame of mind; *ethos* was persuasion through one's own moral standing.

Finally, how does one consider the length of time a meaning has to be impressed upon one's selected audience? If only short-term consent is intended or expected, rhetoricians may exaggerate the truth, lie, or construct arguments that have no basis in reality. Yet any effect gained upon an audience may quickly fall apart and damage one's future credibility.

Strategic narrative, as an expression of foreign policy, is often associated with rational propositions. I argue that in contemporary conflict strategic narrative needs to engage people in the domain of *logos*, the rational narrative, but also go beyond it by using *pathos* and *ethos*, in order to broaden its appeal and so gain purchase on politically disparate strategic audiences. This chapter looks at the function of and relationship between *logos* and *pathos* in particular; the next chapter examines the function of *ethos* in strategic narrative, and how all three require projection through confident vision.

Emotional and rational response: the centrifugal and centripetal forces in the narrative of war

'King George *saheb kasto hunu huncha?*' (How is King George?) Man Bahadur Ghimire asked me. We were in his farmstead perched on a steep ridge, a balcony facing the Himalayas, days from the nearest roadhead. I was on a duty trek as a Gurkha officer through the remote hill villages of eastern Nepal to check on our regiment's retired soldiers. It was thus that Man Bahadur Ghimire, former Rifleman in 9th Gurkha Rifles, and veteran of the battle of Monte Cassino, broke a natural pause in the conversation. He posed the question seriously, as if we were discussing a great matter of state in his goat pen. I suddenly felt that I must break the dreadful news to him. In fact, when told about Queen Elizabeth, he immediately absorbed her into his world, and indeed seemed apologetic for having asked, as if he had reminded me of a recent loss. However, he immediately recovered by asking enthusiastically how the Queen was. What struck me was that, although united by a common regimental tradition, we could have been from different worlds, and he was adjusting to me as much as me to him. What fascinated me was his memory of war.

Man Bahadur Ghimire had been shot in 1944 at the battle of Monte Cassino and showed me the scar. He remembered a few place names. Yet his relation of his experience of battle to me was exclusively aural. He re-created all the sounds from the mortar to the machine gun in detail, re-enacting ducking and diving to take cover. This was the common feature of many of the old soldiers I spoke to on that trek, most of whom had in fact fought not in Italy but in Burma. Thus former Rifleman Bom Bahadur Gurung remembered the names of the great battles he had fought in: 'Kohima, Arakan, Meiktktila'. He also described his experience by re-creating the sounds of battle. But above all what animated these accounts was the emotional recollection of battle: the chaos, fear, courage and death of friends. The names of the battles they fought in were only relevant as pegs on which were hung their human experiences of combat.

The worlds we inhabit profoundly shape the way we understand war. The old Gurkhas' narratives were distinctive precisely because they were so heavily situated in the emotional domain. They had little idea of the broader circumstances which created their war, and even of the logic of the battles in which they themselves fought. They could not tell you why their company was attacking the enemy, just that they were ordered forward, and then confronted the noisy chaos of combat. In a sense the old Gurkhas are for us an anomaly, a group who were in the war and fought in it but did not understand it in 'rational' terms. While that may be the case for many soldiers in battle, rationality can be imposed retrospectively through historical understanding. Yet as they have continued to live in a different world in the Himalayan foothills, even this retrospective rationality has bypassed them.

In *The Face of Battle* (1976) John Keegan argues that writing the history of a battle without the interpretive structure provided by war would be like trying to write the history of a wild party in terms of the impossibility of describing the chaotic.[16] This argument identifies how war is simply the definition one imposes on a series of human events. One does not need to use this definition. One can legitimately see chaos in what another would rationally define as a battle. A rational battle narrative can never claim to be definitive. Ahmed Rashid puts this in another way when he describes the conflict in Afghanistan:

'war is always a mixture of different, conflicting stories, depending on whether you are crouching in a ditch or sipping tea at the Presidential Palace. To have

Figure 16: Rifleman Bom Bahadur Gurung, wearing his medals, with the author, at his home in East Nepal, 2008.

dinner with Petraeus and then tea with President Karzai is a central part of the story, as is journeying to the edge of the city to the tiny, unlit, unheated flats, to talk to a former senior Taliban official'.[17]

War, however, is usually understood in exclusively rational terms. In this form of narrative, events are selected and interpreted in terms of how everything relates to a war's rationale. Rationality is a centripetal force, as it seeks to unify the narrative of war. A rational narrative would say that this is what happened in the Second World War and this is why it happened. It acknowledges sub-narratives, but they all fit into the 'big picture' according to war's interpretive hierarchy. So a company attack at the battle of Meiktila has its own story, but was part of the wider narrative of the Burma campaign, the War in the Pacific, and the Second World War. Emotional response is a centrifugal force. Emotional narratives of war are fragmentary. There are endless personal definitions of what the war was for an individual. It is a completely different mode of understanding from the rational narrative of war, but is just as legitimate. This applies to civilians as well as combatants. Who is anyone to argue that how a bereaved family understands war is not a legitimate interpretation: that is the war for them.

While there are evidently majority opinions regarding, say, the Second World War, and established historiographical trends, this should not be confused with the idea that there can be a singular definition of what it was. People, both in the singular and the plural sense, will differ in terms of their conception of the experience, be it direct or vicarious. The war 'was what it was' for the old Gurkhas. To assume that they 'don't understand' the war they fought in would be mistaken on two levels. First, the essence of war is violence and in that sense it would be perverse to deny their understanding of it. Second, to say that they do not understand the war is illegitimately to claim that 'the war' was a single, rationally defined event. War is a mosaic of individual experiences as much as the abstract phenomenon. For any individual, one's relationship to war in the abstract, its rationale, is mediated through that emotive experience.

How then are 'rational' and 'emotional' interpretations of war reconciled? Rational narratives are typically given preference by those for whom war has a function, from lance corporal to general to political leader: to understand the outcome of the fight they are in, rationality is required; a rational interpretation of events is required as a basis to plan how to influence them in the way one wants. For the historian, a rational interpretation of war can be required to link it to wider historical narratives. Emotional interpretations are not typically seen as functional. Beyond the domain of individual memory, emotional readings of war are typically found in art. This recognises the legitimacy of that mode of understanding without confusing it with functional understanding.

However, there exists an established tradition of strategic thought that recognises that, while war is planned using the rational mode of understanding, the political and military leader must also pay attention to the emotional mode. In this tradition, the relationship between the rational and emotional is not one of compartmentalisation: the emotional is precisely what legitimises the rational. The two are intrinsically bound together.

Clausewitz stressed that the human, emotional component was intrinsic to war's nature and formed the 'passionate' component of the trinity of war. Passion in the trinity was primarily associated with the people, one of the three components of the trinity's reflection in the state at war. The human passions unleashed in 1789 were for Clausewitz what caused the transformation of war during his lifetime: the emotional connection of the French citizen soldier with the state mobilised the entire resources of the nation to war.[18] Moreover, human passion also interacted with the other two parts of the trinity of war: policy (as represented by the government) and 'the play of probability and chance' (as represented by the army). Thus four elements make up the 'climate' of war: 'danger, exertion, uncertainty and chance'.[19] War is as much a test of emotional resistance as a rational execution of policy. The 'climate' of war produced 'friction': 'everything in war is very simple, but the simplest thing is difficult'.[20] In the light of this, the plan in the abstract, in war often thought of in terms of war on a map, had to be grounded in human reality, a concept which Clausewitz extended to strategic theory in general.

Clausewitz repeatedly stressed that the commander of the army must be attuned to moral factors as much as the plan in the abstract: 'military activity is never directed against material force alone; it is always aimed simultaneously at the moral forces which give it life, and the two cannot be separated'. The commander perceived the moral factors through his 'inner eye', his intuitive understanding of his men and the enemy, which combines the emotional and the rational: 'when all is said and done, it is really the commander's *coup d'oeil*, his ability to see things simply, to identify the whole business of war completely with himself, that is the essence of good generalship'.[21] By stressing that all the abstract, rational, theory of war had to be synthesised by a human being, the commander, who has to put it in its human context, Clausewitz presents a strong model for how the emotional and the rational are inseparable; by his account, they come together in instinct, the 'X factor' of a good commander.

Clausewitz's attention to the emotional component of war is illustrated in many passages, for example where he is at pains to describe the feeling of a defeated army: 'abstract concepts of this or that minor loss will never match the reality of a major defeat'.[22] Clausewitz was also obsessed with the personage of Napoleon himself, who symbolised for him the unity of reason and intuition.

A perusal of Napoleon's maxims of war draws attention to why Clausewitz might have considered Napoleon's style as a battlefield commander in terms of a unity of reason and intuition. In some maxims Napoleon is cold and rational: 'The first qualification in a general-in-chief is a cool head—that is, a head which receives just impressions, and estimates things and objects at their real value. He must not allow himself to be elated by good news, or depressed by bad'.[23] Yet a remarkable number of the maxims show that Napoleon was acutely aware of the psychology of the private solider, and the need for a commander to be attuned to this emotional element: 'The soldier is best when he bivouacs, because he sleeps with his feet to the fire, which speedily dries the ground on which he lies. A few planks, or a little straw, shelter him from the wind'.[24]

Napoleon has a realistic view of emotional intuition, in that continuous sensitivity to the issue is required of the commander, not sensationalism: 'It is not set speeches at the moment of battle that render soldiers brave. The veteran scarcely listens to them, and the recruit forgets them at the first discharge. If discourses and harangues are useful, it is during the campaign; to do away with unfavourable impressions, to correct false reports, to keep alive a proper spirit in the camp, and to furnish materials and amusement for the bivouac. All printed orders of the day should keep in view these objects';[25] alternatively: 'Every means should be taken to attach the soldier to his colours. This is best accomplished by showing consideration and respect to the old soldier'.[26]

Napoleon stresses that it is an emotional quality that he desires foremost in his soldiers: 'The first qualification of a soldier is fortitude under fatigue and privation. Courage is only the second; hardship, poverty, and want are the best school for the soldier'.[27] Perhaps this maxim summarises Napoleon's view: 'A good general, a well-organized system, good instructions, and severe discipline, aided by effective establishments, will always make good troops, independently of the cause for which they fight. At the same time, a love of country, a spirit of enthusiasm, a sense of national honour, and fanaticism will operate upon young soldiers with advantage'.[28]

Clausewitz viewed as vital the general's ability to make decisions which were 'promoted by strong emotions and by flashes of almost automatic intuition rather than being the product of a lengthy chain of reasoning ... after all, waging war is not merely an act of reason, nor is reasoning its foremost activity'.[29] To describe this quality Clausewitz used the word *geist*, which has no equivalent in English; the fact that it is usually translated as 'spirit' or 'intellect' reflects both the more emotional and more rational possibilities inherent in this concept.[30]

In summary, throughout *On War* we find Clausewitz stressing the unity of the rational and the emotional in war. Strategy had to unify both factors: 'we must allow for natural inertia, for all the friction of its [war's] parts, for all the inconsistency, imprecision, and timidity of man'.[31]

The necessity to unify the rational and the emotional has been recognised by military thought concerned with tactical effectiveness. The work of French officer Colonel Ardant du Picq, published posthumously in 1880, stressed the importance of the individual soldier's psychology to combat effectiveness.[32] He argued that fear was the natural response to battle, and that courage was a finite resource that would eventually be depleted. The key to overcome this was *esprit de corps*. The very language of *esprit*, 'spirit', recognises emotive motivation.

The idea of the *corps*, 'body', links the individual to his unit in a common emotive bond. This strand of thought developed in the French Army of the early twentieth century into the concept of *morale*, which is now employed far more widely. What has endured most in Du Picq's work is the training concept that tactics overcome fear through constant rehearsal and small unit cohesion. This is the idea that soldiers in combat fight primarily for each other rather than any wider cause. Moreover, tactical drills provide a default rational interpretation to understand the event. Thus getting shot at becomes 'a contact' in which there is a set procedure for dealing with that situation which ideally culminates in the defeat of the enemy. Professor Anthony King has described the outcome of such drills, or set procedures, as 'the repetition of an established choreography'.[33]

The unity of the rational and the emotional is today widely accepted at the tactical level. Recruit training seeks to instil a sense of ethos that will drive a soldier's combat motivation, regardless of how far the individual subscribes to the war's rationale. Clausewitz posited that: 'truth [the rational argument] is in itself rarely sufficient to make men act … the most powerful springs of action in man lie in his emotions'.[34] Emotions in war 'act as the essential breath which animates the inert mass'.[35] This argument applied beyond just the tactical domain. The political object of war had to have purchase on people's emotions for it to be successful:

The political object—the original motive for war—will thus determine both the military objective to be reached and the amount of effort it requires. The political object cannot, however, *in itself* [italics original] provide the standard of measurement. Since we are dealing with realities, not with abstractions, it can do so in the context only of the two states at war. The same political object can elicit differing reactions from different peoples, and even from the same people at different times. We can therefore take the political object as a standard only if we think of the influence it can exert on the forces it is meant to move.[36]

Any political rationale is interpreted through the prism of emotion, which varies depending on the audience. Plans cannot therefore be made in the abstract without consideration of how they will be interpreted by their intended human audience.

The unity of emotional and rational understanding is fundamentally articulated in the dialectic which informs legitimacy. This is legitimacy in the broad sense rather than any particular moral or legal definition. The synthesis between the rational and the emotional informs action. Thus it can apply to a soldier genuinely fighting for 'king and country' as much as to a mercenary who fights for money. In terms of audiences in general, it determines how far people subscribe to a strategic narrative, be it out of genuine ideological attachment, self-interest, 'subscribe' in the interest of self-preservation, or endless other reasons why people agree with a proposition.

The legitimisation of the rational narrative by emotional response is an idea already present in fields outside war. The American historian Bernard Bailyn has argued that memory's relation to the past 'is not a critical, sceptical reconstruction of what happened: It is the spontaneous, unquestioned, experience of the past … it is expressed in signs and symbols, images and mnemonic clues of all sorts. It shapes our awareness whether we like it or not, and it is ultimately emotional, not intellectual'.

As Gordon Wood writes in the *New York Review of Books*, Bailyn made remarks about history and memory at the conclusion of a 1998 conference on the Atlantic slave trade that had threatened to fall apart. Many black scholars and others had reacted to the presentations of the cold and statistically grounded papers dealing with the slave trade. Bailyn distinguished between history and memory to calm the conference. He argued that statistics helped, but that: 'memory of the slave trade cannot be reduced to an alien context; and it is not a critical, rational reconstruction; it is for us a living, immediate, if vicarious, experience'. While meaning may be shaped by history, 'so too may critical history be kept alive, made vivid, and constantly relevant and cogent by the living memory we have of it'. The point Bailyn eloquently made is this: a rational narrative that does not have purchase on the emotional substance of what it seeks to describe cannot claim legitimacy.[37]

The fragmentation of strategic narrative: when rational narrative is not legitimised by emotional response

The rational and emotional are of course rarely perfectly aligned. Irony tends to identify the gap between them, which is, to my mind, why it is so prominent in soldiers' humour. In *Memoirs of an Infantry Officer* (1930), Siegfried Sassoon starts with his withdrawal from the front to attend a course at an army school: 'my personal grievance against the Germans was interrupted for at least four weeks'. The lecturer on gas from general headquarters tells the audience of soldiers who have come from the front that gas is still in its infancy: 'most of us were either dead or disabled before gas had had time to grow up'. Another lecturer addresses them on 'the spirit of the bayonet': 'he spoke with homicidal eloquence'. Sassoon excoriates the lecturer with irony, noting how, as a colonel who had never fought, he was actually awarded a Distinguished Service Order 'for lecturing' (the DSO is properly awarded for exceptional leadership of a unit on operations).

Irony gives way to deep cynicism as the emotional and the rational are increasingly misaligned. One of Sassoon's men and a German sniper kill each other at the same time: 'he and Kendle had cancelled each other out in the process known as "the attrition of manpower"'. While 'a certain Prelate' states that every man who kills a German 'is performing a Christian Act', Sassoon talks of 'the silly stunt which the Bishops call the Great Adventure'. At one point he sees a dead English soldier and writes 'at the risk of being thought squeamish or even un-soldierly,

I still maintain that an ordinary human being has a right to be momentarily horrified by a mangled body seen on an afternoon walk'.

Now back in Britain training recruits in 1917: 'the War had become undisguisedly mechanical and inhuman. What in earlier days were droves of volunteers were now droves of victims. I was just beginning to become aware of this'. The emotional overturning of the rational is clear in his letter to his commanding officer, in which he refuses to take further part in the war (even though he was wounded and undeployable in any case): 'I have seen and endured the sufferings of the troops, and I can no longer be a party to prolong the sufferings for ends which I believe to be unjust'.

The distancing of the rational and emotional interpretations is clear when Sassoon deals with the issue of narrative itself with scathing irony: 'let the Staff write their own books about the Great War, say I. The Infantry were biased against them, and their authentic story will be read with interest'. 'The War' for Sassoon does not correspond with his experience of it. He agrees with another infantry officer that 'the front line is the only place where one can get away from "the War" because in the trenches "it is just one thing after another"'. A failed attack by his unit on 23 April 1917 results in four officers killed, nine wounded and forty other ranks killed: 'an episode typical of uncountable others, some of which now fill the pages of Regimental Histories. Such stories now look straightforward enough in print, twelve years later; but their reality remains hidden; even in the minds of old soldiers the harsh horror mellows and recedes'.

The process that Sassoon associates with the divergence of narratives is the abstraction of the pure experience, the 'emotional reality' into a rational narrative. 'The Second Battalion were wiped out 10 days ago because the Division General had ordered an impossible attack on a local objective. The phrase "local objective" sounded good and made me feel that I knew a hell of a lot about it'. Here Sassoon is highlighting the use of the word 'objective' precisely because it objectifies combat and sucks out the emotional component. He turns on newspapers for avoiding horror, and 'assuming that the dead are gloriously happy'.

However, Sassoon is more subtle in his treatment of abstraction than just using it to blame generals and journalists. He goes much further than that when he describes a man whose sons are fighting, who has no agenda in his desire to understand what is going on:

'the Gommecourt show had been nothing but a massacre of good troops. Probably he kept a war map with little flags on it; when Mametz Wood was reported as captured he moved a little flag on a map forward after breakfast. For him the Wood was a small green patch on a piece of paper. For the Welsh Division it had been a bloody nightmare'.

Sassoon is acknowledging here that abstraction is not necessarily malicious; it is a necessary function of rationality. The key point is that Sassoon is not saying that rationality is wrong in itself; that would be nonsense. He is saying that if a rational narrative is not underwritten by its associated emotional experience, the rational becomes divorced from reality. The legitimacy of the rational narrative is underwritten by its emotional basis.

The central importance of the rational-emotional tension is when their functional relationship is reversed. Strategic narrative has to align the rational and the emotional to persuade its audiences. Siegfried Sassoon's refusal to soldier had no significant impact on the British war effort at the time. However, the widespread mutinies in the French army in 1917 were a major threat to French strategy; they came after the Nivelle offensive, following from the battle of Verdun in 1916, in which the French sustained over 300,000 casualties. In such circumstances strategy has lost control of a strategic audience because the rational strategic narrative no longer has emotional legitimacy; the emotional response now produces a new rationale.

The illegitimate abstraction of emotional experience in the Vietnam War caused a loss of legitimacy in the rational narrative for large tranches of the US domestic population. Neil Sheehan's *Bright Shining Lie* (1989), an account of the war based on his extensive time as a journalist in Vietnam, cites such examples of illegitimate abstraction. For instance, the US air force in Vietnam when under General Anthis used to refer to all targets as 'structures', which implied some kind of Viet Cong installation.[38] The number of 'structures' destroyed by aerial bombing was used as a key metric of success. Many on the ground saw that most of these structures were just shacks and barns used by civilians, and their bombing was causing huge animosity among the peasantry, who had to witness the destruction of their villages and deaths of their relatives. Yet this emotion is not communicated by a set of statistics about structures. Sheehan also mentions that the refugees caused by the bombing were abstracted as 'long-term assets' by the US Embassy and military command, as they were under Saigon's 'control' in terms of their dependence on the South Vietnamese state.[39] When rational abstraction does not correspond to its underlying emotional basis it becomes a denial, not a distillation, of reality.

The photographs and television footage of the war contributed very significantly to shocking the US domestic population into recognition of the bombing campaign for what it was. These new mediums communicated the emotional dimension of war to the domestic population in a far more direct way than had previously been the case. In terms of US casualties, military strategy before Vietnam had generally been justified as an area of professional expertise which inevitably involved casualties. However, after the Tet Offensive and the 1968 Presidential election, the military logic of war started to become even more detached from the emotional response for large swathes of the US domestic public.

The Battle of Hamburger Hill in May 1969, for example, killed eighty-four and wounded 480 US soldiers for an objective that was evacuated days after it was taken.[40] The argument proposed by General Creighton Abrams, General Westmoreland's successor, was that 'we are not fighting for terrain as such. We are going after the enemy'. The 101st Airborne Division's commander, Major General Melvin Zais, argued along the same lines: 'that was where the enemy was, and that was where I attacked him'.[41] The rational military argument may well have made sense from a military perspective; at least 633 North Vietnamese troops were killed in the battle. However, this logic struggled to gain purchase with much of the US domestic population.

Neil Sheehan notes that, while more attritional battles earlier in the war had not caused such a political reaction, the fact that more US soldiers were dying per month in 1969 than in previous years created a particularly intense anti-war reaction to the battle. The US army itself by 1969 faced widespread ill-discipline and loss of belief among the ranks. Sheehan also remarks that it was at this stage that the notion that troops were not killed but were 'wasted' or 'blown away' became common US army slang.[42]

Strategic narrative and non-state audiences

Clausewitz writes that 'feelings' can 'act as a higher judgement': the emotional can trump the rational, and proposes a new rationale.[43] This distinction often serves more purpose as an analytical tool, since to distinguish between the two in actuality—to dissect an individual's sources of motivation for subscription to a given position—would be incredibly complicated. There is no clear distinction between rational and emotional sources of motivation at an individual level. Hence existential motivation for participation in war is often intertwined with, rather than distinct from, the war's political rationale. The endemic association of war with glory has meant that at some level most wars have an element of the existential. A similar argument might be made about armed humanitarian interventions, which are often justified in terms that satisfy an 'existential' emotive requirement, that are mixed in with geopolitical considerations.[44]

A primarily emotive rationale can, for instance, be an organising idea which sees war as the ultimate expression of national values, which could occur even in defeat. This has been termed 'existential' war. Hew Strachan identifies how the younger Clausewitz expresses this almost as a creed in manifestos he wrote in 1812. Here he extols the duty to defend the nation's liberty and values to the last drop of its blood:

Even the destruction of liberty after a bloody and honourable struggle assures the people's rebirth. It is the seed of life, which one day will bring forth a new, securely rooted tree.[45]

However, while Clausewitz acknowledged the existential dimension of war, both for the individual and the state participant, he assumed that his actors were within the state, and still bound by its rationale. Thus the general who made instinctive decisions was still in the service of state policy. By the same token, the people's role was critical: the 'condition and temper' of the civilian population mattered to strategy in terms of its ability to support a friendly army with supplies and information, or to deny this to an enemy army.[46] However, people's allegiances were fixed: they were friendly or enemy and, critically, were victorious or defeated with their state.[47] The state provided a vital common interpretive ground for the people, the army and the government to understand war in the same way and be defeated or victorious together.

For Clausewitz emotional dynamics underpin his concept of war. The polarity which defined the relationship of state opponents in war was grounded in emotional antagonism. This was not usually between individual soldiers, but between their states: 'modern wars are seldom fought without hatred between nations; this serves more or less as a substitute between individuals'.[48] Indeed the etymology of the word 'enemy' is from the Latin *in* + *amicus* (friend) giving *inimicus* (not friend). The distinction between oneself and the enemy is an emotional one; this sets up the antagonism which then determines when to demand recognition of legitimacy of one's strategic narrative through violence.[49]

Yet the total identification of strategic audiences with their state, which makes the enemy 'the' enemy (a single, unified, entity), is usually an idealised pole; this was so in Clausewitz's day too.[50] In contemporary conflict, the idea that there are audiences within the state who actively try to fight against the policies in war of their 'own' state is commonplace. British citizens have been known to fight as insurgents in Afghanistan and other parts of the world. The importance of identification with the state historically has been a matter of degree rather than a clear distinction.

When a strategic audience stops identifying with the state's strategic narrative, the inter-state paradigm of war starts to break down. This is one of the themes in *All Quiet on the Western Front*.[51] Paul Baümer is a patriotic German soldier who acts on the basis of his country's rationale for war. His own emotional understanding, however, comes to subvert that rationale. This process evolves predominantly as war's emotional reality imposes itself on its rationale: 'a hospital alone shows what war is'.[52]

As his experience of combat expands, Baümer and his comrades start to doubt their state's rationale for war. One of his comrades, Tjaden, responds to the suggestion that war starts 'by one country offending another': 'a country, I don't follow. A mountain in Germany can't offend a mountain in France. Or a river, or a wood, or a field of wheat'. This problem is brought out by another soldier in this discussion: 'it's queer when one thinks about it; we are here to protect our fatherland. The French are over there to protect their fatherland. Now, who's in the right?'[53] The deconstruction of the emotional antagonism between states prefigures Baümer's loss of hatred for his 'enemy' on an individual level. This is illustrated in a key passage in which he has just killed a French soldier:

But now, for the first time, I see you are a man like me. I thought of your hand-grenades, of your bayonet, of your rifle; now I see your wife and your face and our fellowship. Forgive me, comrade. We always see it too late. Why do they never tell us that you are poor devils like us, that your mothers are just as anxious as ours, and that we have the same fear of death, and the same dying and the same agony—Forgive me, comrade; how could you be my enemy?

Once Baümer distances himself from any personal enmity for the enemy, he begins to doubt the rational interpretation. Full realisation comes when his emotional response to killing a French soldier overcomes the purchase of the rational interpretation. His rationale is no longer aligned to the reasons for which he is being told to fight. The book's final paragraph portrays Baümer's death as the ultimate irony in its juxtaposition of the war's rational and emotion interpretations:

He fell in October 1918, on a day that was so quiet and still on the whole front, that the army report confined itself to the single sentence: All quiet on the Western Front. He had fallen forward and lay on the earth as though sleeping. Turning him over one saw that he could not have suffered long; his face had an expression of calm, as though almost glad the end had come.

Identification with the state in the paradigm of inter-state war is an important binding force which associates a rational narrative with a legitimating emotional response. Yet the paradigm of inter-state war does not easily comprehend situations in which people act according to emotional responses which derive from an identity not associated with that of a state party to conflict. Contemporary conflict is characterised by the proliferation of audiences beyond the enemy, as polarity gives way to politically kaleidoscopic conflict environments. These audiences always potentially existed, but were not audiences until the information revolution connected them to the conflict as audiences, hence their proliferation. A second, intrinsically associated trend is the proliferation of audiences beyond state parties as non-state audiences, or non-state actors (usually two statuses of the same entity, in that an action as an actor will probably be a function of interpretation as an audience).

For a state party's strategic narrative to gain purchase on these audiences it cannot assume pre-existing identification with the state, but neither can it persuade them by force. They are less likely to be persuaded by the rational component of a state party to the conflict's strategic narrative.

Because membership of a state is often a powerful emotional bond, people who identify with their state are more likely to subscribe to their state's strategic narrative, even if they may have their own reservations. Conversely, strategic audiences without affiliation to a state party involved in the conflict are more likely to assess the legitimacy of a strategic narrative based on their own emotional response, as they would usually have less reason to follow the rationale of a state which they do not identify with, especially if that state is acting in its self-interest. If these non-state audiences also lie beyond the enemy, neither can they be forced to subscribe to a strategic narrative. Hence the emotional response of non-state audiences becomes of paramount importance in order that those audiences see one's strategic narrative as legitimate.

The progressive inversion of the rational-emotional functionality is in many ways the leitmotif of the challenge to the paradigm of inter-state war. In contemporary conflict, the emotional aspect of strategic narrative comes increasingly to the fore as a persuasive device.

Where the emotional interpretation becomes functional for an audience, the 'identity' of the audience becomes a key factor because identity is usually the basis for emotional response. The massive expansion in the requirement for liberal powers and their militaries to understand the 'human terrain', a sort of conflict anthropology, bears witness to the revival of the importance of people's identities in contemporary conflict.

In Afghanistan, emotional responses by a range of actors of significantly diverse socio-political identities produce alternative rationales to that offered by the competing strategic narratives of the government of Afghanistan and the Taliban. The Wednesday Market Bombing is a practical example of this. On 31 March 2010 a bomb was planted by insurgents in the crowded weekly Wednesday bazaar of a rural part of Helmand Province. It was aimed at the Afghan police, who in the event were not there that day. Around thirteen civilians were killed and many more wounded. Reported on BBC news, the event was transmitted to global audiences, some of whom would have mattered more than others to the conflict's outcome (the 'strategic audiences'). All these audiences would probably have varied in their interpretations of the event's meaning. I arrived on the scene after the event, where the Coldstream Guards had been treating the injured in a nearby International Security and Assistance Force (ISAF) patrol base. This is an edited extract from a note I made at the time:

Shura [meeting] for returning dead bodies from IED this morning… Approx 40 injured/dead, all locals. Struck by dignity of scene: evening last light approaching, locals go out from shura to pray. What will be will be: '*inshallah…*' Rhythms and liturgies seem to channel their grief… The dead are buried the same day. Life goes on. One of our soldiers was speaking to a mullah: 'you (us and the Taliban) fight, we die'.

The BBC news story was fair but located the event in a wider government of Afghanistan/ISAF versus Taliban story.[54] That is indeed the story into which ISAF and the Taliban leadership tend to weave events. That is not necessarily illegitimate; the insurgents' intent in this case had been to kill the Afghan police; whether or not they had anticipated such a large blast and the civilian collateral damage is not known. There was another theory that traders from the Ishaqzai tribe wanted to destroy this popular bazaar in Barakzai heartland to shift economic activity in their direction. While I do not think this causal explanation is likely, the fact that locals were speaking in these terms, however conspiratorial, shows that they did not rely only on the polarised narrative to understand the conflict.

The ISAF-Taliban narrative of the war in relative terms is not, indeed, one that many farmers in Helmand care that much about. Unlike civilians in the paradigm of inter-state war, they are not strongly bound to state narratives (of either their official or shadow state). This emotional circumstance is fundamental to understanding the political positions of many Afghans. They do not have 'divided loyalties' as the paradigm of inter-state war would see it; they are loyal to their own interests. They are actors in their own right. Their emotional circumstance underpins the conflict's kaleidoscopic political configuration: this is the bridge to Clausewitz's ideas, for while Afghanistan is not an inter-state war, the emotional texture of the conflict is the legitimising base of any presentation of its rational, abstracted, form.

When the Afghan conflict is understood in terms of war, war provides a fragmented, rather than a stable, interpretive structure because the war means so many different things to so many different people. This subverts the relationship between the rational and the emotional in the inter-state paradigm of war. In the inter-state paradigm the rational mode of understanding is a centripetal force which unifies events into a single narrative: the 'big picture'. It is on the basis of this rational 'big picture' that strategists can make sense of events and make plans. Conversely, the emotional mode of understanding is a centrifugal force in which what the war means to an individual has endless variation. It is recognised as legitimate but not a basis on which to plan. When the emotional mode becomes functional it acts against the rational by suggesting a new rationale. This is dangerous for the rational interpretation: it begins to fragment as it is pulled by the centrifugal force of emotional interpretation. As globalisation reworks identity both in terms of unifying and dividing people, the rationale for any war will find it hard to gain purchase on every potential strategic audience.

This presents strategic narrative with a problem. An appeal exclusively to *logos* risks the marginalisation of certain strategic audiences (which policy may well accept as a risk), as arguments based exclusively on national interests may not have a sufficiently broad emotional appeal to audiences beyond one's state. Conversely, appeal to *pathos* is inherently unstable, as it encourages strategic narrative to latch onto utilitarian and supposedly universal concepts such as 'freedom' to bind together strategic audiences (this is discussed in the next chapter). Problems occur when it becomes clear that national interest starts to compete with these more idealistic propositions when choices about campaign resourcing and achievability of aims need to be made. Yet a connection between *logos* and *pathos* is nonetheless required in any strategic narrative to achieve legitimacy. The next chapter examines how to stabilise their relationship, particularly with reference to the last of Aristotle's rhetorical resources: *ethos*.

9

ETHOS, VISION AND CONFIDENCE
IN STRATEGIC NARRATIVE

If war loses its integrity as a common interpretive structure for strategic narrative to rely upon, actions in conflict may well be subject to significantly differing interpretations. This establishes a tension at the core of the strategic narrative that can pull it apart: for strategic narrative to be legitimate in the eyes of a strategic audience, its rational argument needs to find resonance with the identity of that audience in human, emotional terms; emotional interpretation legitimises the rational narrative.

Yet as the differences in socio-political identity between strategic audiences proliferate in an ever more interconnected world, no single narrative can usually satisfy everyone. That is, to define victory absolutely would mean universally to convince strategic audiences of victory, or success, in one's own terms, which is generally impossible. This chapter examines how to stabilise the relationship between the rational and emotive components of strategic narrative—*logos* and *pathos*—in order to generate a sense of legitimacy and to gain purchase on strategic audiences.

Three themes are suggested: the centrality of the moral component, or *ethos*; the power of historical association; and the necessity for liberal powers to avoid literalism in their arguments with fundamentalists, and instead present a strategic vision confident in its own values.

207

Strategic narrative and ethos

The First World War came to be justified by several participants through explanations that went beyond national interest. President Woodrow Wilson in his speech announcing the US Declaration of War on Germany on 2 April 1917 appealed to universal motives:

> It is a war against all nations... It is a challenge to all mankind... Our motive will not be revenge or the victorious assertion of the physical might of the nation, but only the vindication of right, of human right, of which we are only a single champion... Our object now, as then, is to vindicate the principles of peace and justice in the life of the world as against selfish and autocratic power and to set up among the really free and self-governed peoples of the world such a concert of purpose and of action as will henceforth insure the observance of those principles.

While such justifications make apparently powerful appeals to domestic and worldwide audiences, the idea of fighting for universal values is clearly a paradox since there would be no enemy if those values were genuinely universal. Given the scale of destruction in the First World War, an ironic dimension can be detected in the post-war label of a 'war to end all wars'. The need to bind people together through narratives that appeal to 'universal' values, which are more heavily located in the emotional than the rational rhetorical domain, is at odds with the inherent fragility of such universal claims. This is a difficult tension that often finds expression in contemporary conflict.

In a highly interconnected world, rational strategic narratives based on national interest, which might equate to Aristotle's *logos*, are less able in a conflict scenario to gain broad traction, as strategic audiences beyond the enemy, and beyond the state, proliferate in their diversity. This is common sense. Why would Afghan civilians, for example, support coalition efforts (or even be passive) in Afghanistan if the coalition was purely there for its own interests, and not for the well-being of Afghans? Strategists delve increasingly into the emotional domain, *pathos*, to gain purchase on target audiences beyond the enemy and the state. Thus 'freedom', for example, becomes a strategic aim. President Bush in November 2003 spoke about the 'forward strategy of freedom' at a speech in London.[1] In terms of rhetoric, fighting for freedom suggests an experience which can be universally shared by the target audiences and thus bind them together.

The experience of applying a forward strategy of freedom suggests that emotionally-based narratives are highly problematic. Many audiences did not interpret freedom in the same way as President Bush. The key tension in strategic narrative in the context of contemporary globalisation is between universal themes, which tend to be situated in the emotional domain, and themes based on particular political agendas, which tend to be defined in rational terms. Strategy has to keep them in an uneasy relationship to maintain coherence.

The difficulty of so doing can be illustrated with reference to coalition aims in Afghanistan. Over the course of the conflict the following sets of objectives, which have all appeared at various points, have often competed and clashed with one another rather than be mutually reinforcing: democracy, development, drug eradication, women's rights, the removal of the Taliban, the denial of Afghanistan to al-Qaeda and its associated syndicates, the credibility of NATO, regional stability, the denial of a safe haven to the Pakistani Taliban, the commitment to the Afghan people.

To deal with the problem of universality of appeal versus national interests, other countries have opted for a simple, and sometimes brutal, alternative: to define their strategic audiences far more narrowly. This is the equivalent of a political approach in domestic politics that focuses on the satisfaction of a narrow part of the electorate without concern for the alienation of other audiences. Russia, for example, has in a sense succeeded in securing Chechnya in two wars. The Sri Lankan government forces also seem to have succeeded in their war against the Tamil Tigers. However, the definition of success in both of these instances is partial. The extent of human rights violations committed in these cases qualifies the recognition of victory in the eyes of much of the international community. To operate in this way is to make a Faustian pact, as the resentment which such methods inevitably will arouse may come to compromise the stability of any strategic effect achieved in the short-term. The use by liberal powers of extraordinary rendition is another example of such practice. The moral high ground, once evacuated, is very hard to regain.[2]

How can this problem be resolved, or at least mitigated? Strategy needs to pay attention to the third rhetorical resource: *ethos*. *Ethos* stabilises and insulates strategic effect, which otherwise can be over-exposed to the conflicting relationship between rational and emotional narrative, which, in terms of Aristotle's understanding of rhetoric, can broadly be equated with *logos* and *pathos*.

Strategic narrative is permanently aspirational. Strategy is necessarily arrogant in the sense that it seeks to impose a permanence of meaning against the challenge of future interpretation.

The Pyrrhic victory is an extreme example. In fact the outcomes of most wars have evolved, as their consequences mesh with the future and people interpret the outcome—the meaning—of the war differently. The two world wars of the twentieth century were seen as victories for Britain by the majority of British people at the time; they also, however, broke the British Empire, a result that will itself be read differently by various constituencies. Vietnam could legitimately have been interpreted as a partial American success, or at least a draw, when President Richard Nixon declared that the 1973 Paris peace agreement brought 'peace with honour in Vietnam and South East Asia'. That view was re-interpreted after the fall of Saigon in 1975.

The Soviet withdrawal from Afghanistan in 1989 was, to my mind legitimately, not considered a failure by the USSR at the time (and Western analysis has been heavily distorted by a victor's view of the Cold War's end); the USSR had handed power over to a relatively stable Afghan state headed by President Najibullah. Although his army suffered reverses, it stabilised the situation and decisively defeated the Mujahideen at the battle of Jalalabad in 1989. (The most dangerous moment for an insurgency is often when it has to convert to a conventional force finally to topple the state forces; since conventional high-intensity battle is far more complex and resource-intensive than guerrilla warfare, insurgencies often fail at this point. The Mujahideen here are not the only example of this; note the same phenomenon with the Tamil Tigers. This factor will, I think, come to play a role in the current Afghan conflict too.)

The more genuine reason for the collapse of the Najibullah regime is fairly obvious: the collapse of the USSR itself in 1991, which had been funding the Afghan government. However, for the USSR, a perception of having at least forced a stalemate in 1989 was seen as a failure once the Mujahideen entered Kabul. As Clausewitz himself recognised: 'in war the result is never final'.[3] The requirement to maintain the narrative—perpetually to win the argument—is enduring, not finite.

One deduction is that where the meaning of war is not compartmentalised by a common interpretive structure, strategic effect is often based on how future interpreters perceive the moral component of a strategic narrative. The British policy of appeasement in the 1930s is remembered with shame less because it was strategically unsuccessful than because it was cowardly; in one analysis Hitler's perception of moral weakness was a key factor in the strategy's failure from the British perspective, so the two factors were linked at the time too, not just in retrospect. In *Unfinest Hour* (2002) Brendan Simms documents how British policy during the Bosnian War of the 1990s was plagued by a morally questionable foreign policy.[4] There may be rational reasons why Dutch troops failed to act to prevent a massacre at the Srebrenica enclave in 1995, but they have little purchase on most audiences. Troops at another safe area in Gorazde in 1994–5 were under largely the same authority and successfully prevented a massacre by taking on Serbian soldiers.

The Second World War, although globally more damaging in human terms than the First, is remembered as more purposeful because questions of right and wrong were far more distinct. The original supporters of the Iraq War today often focus on Saddam Hussein's removal as a positive fact, despite the subsequent narrative of the conflict. Even many of those who did not support the war would agree that Saddam Hussein's removal, in itself, was a good thing. Conversely, many of the rational reasons, such as weapon of mass destruction (WMD), or the emotional reasons, such as the general, confident, mood of 'what next' in the US administration after the 2001 Afghanistan success, have long since evaporated. At the time of writing it is unclear how things in Iraq will progress. However, depending on the outcome, those earlier rational reasons may be rehabilitated, or not, while Saddam Hussein's removal is permanent. The point is that rational and emotional reasons oscillate; moral reasons are more stable.

There are some important caveats to this argument. First, one cannot construct foreign policy exclusively on the basis of moral imperative. The danger would be that it is very hard to limit moral arguments, and limitation of conflict is critical to wider international stability. State sovereignty, for example, needs to be taken into consideration. In short, there also have to be other forms of strategic rationale. Yet to gain traction on a politically diverse range of target audiences, strategic narrative in contemporary conflict may struggle if it appeals purely to national interest, which might be associated with more *logos*-type rational arguments; the narrative may also struggle if over-exposed to fragile universal claims more associated with the emotional domain of *pathos*. Appeal to *ethos* is a powerful binding force. However, used on its own it is also a destabilising force, as it has no obvious limit. The alternative approach is to try not to have wide appeal in the first place and to ignore wider strategic audiences, for which the Russian approach in Chechnya provides an example, but this evidently brings problems of its own.

Counter-insurgency theory stresses living among people to develop human relationships, and thereby persuading people to see the counter-insurgent in a different light. There are several instances in Afghanistan where a local inhabitant may not agree with the presence of British forces in his area, but has told a soldier he has got to know personally of an improvised explosive device (IED) ahead. The effect of living among people in the context of counter-insurgency has an extraordinary effect, which is hard to quantify in rational terms.

As a Gurkha battlegroup in Central Helmand during the summer of 2010, we found that the single greatest shift in popular perceptions of us came when we started to live among people. This meant getting out of our forward operating bases and actually permanently living in the villages in much smaller fortified compounds. The people then got to know us as other human beings. Greeting people on patrol by name makes a massive difference. Sergeant Govinda Gurung, who commanded a checkpoint, was actually clapped out by villagers, who lined the streets, when his multiple left the village at the end of their tour. The fact that this side of the narrative in Afghanistan is consistently pushed back by the more sensational emotional appeal of violent activity, even if the latter may be less prevalent in a given area, accounts for much of the quality of perceptions of contemporary conflicts.

Conversely, I often thought when I was a platoon commander that turning up to a remote village for the first time, despite our best efforts to adopt a soft posture, and despite explaining that we were here to hand out medical supplies, was, from the villagers' perspective, rather odd. They may well have been grateful for the medical care but they were suspicious about its context. Doctors in the UK don't typically turn up with an armed entourage! It is far easier to communicate intention if one feels at ease and trusts one's interlocutor.

Living among the people in small outposts was also one of the key success stories of the surge in Baghdad. General Lamb in his commander's guidance for counter-insurgency writes that 'your morality defines your legitimacy', and advances an association between 'minimum force' and 'moral force'.[5] In short, humanity often cuts across prejudice. In an information age in which public diplomacy is as important as traditional diplomatic activity, engagement with whole peoples on a human level becomes ever more necessary as a form of persuasion.

As war fuses with politics, humanitarian considerations can become the lowest common denominating cognitive unit among very diverse audiences. As time progresses, the perceived moral component of strategic narrative becomes increasingly important in the stability of strategic effect: a perceived victory does not suddenly appear as a defeat. In the longer term, strategy convinces less through Aristotle's *logos*, the rational component of narrative, and *pathos*, emotional appeals, but more through *ethos*, the moral component of narrative. Moreover a strategic narrative which neglects ethos completely is in danger of finding itself illegitimate in the longer term.

Strategic narrative and history

The construction of an interpretive framework is critical to give meaning to actions in order to achieve a policy outcome. During the global financial crisis of 2008 the world looked to the US government's actions in order to decipher the 'pathology' of the crisis against which to act.[6] This was a combination of how the US government acted in terms of its support (or absence of support) to financial institutions and in terms of how that behaviour was situated in a broader historical framework. In Andrew Ross Sorkin's account of the crisis, *Too Big to Fail* (2009), he relates an answer which Ben Bernanke, the chairman of the Federal Reserve, gave in response to a question asking whether this would be a second Great Depression, or another 'lost decade', as Japan had experienced: 'No. Because we've learnt so much about them that we won't have either'.[7]

In the summer of 2010 in one of the villages that our battlegroup patrolled, an old mud-walled stables is still known as the 'British fort'. British forces occupied Gereshk and its outskirts during both the First and Second Afghan Wars, and the outpost probably dates from one of these interventions. In both cases the British backed the Barakzai tribe of central Helmand, who were traditional enemies of the Alizais in the north of the province, and in both cases provoked a fierce Alizai reaction.[8] The second time the Alizais actually made common cause with the Barakzai and chased the British out of Gereshk; this led to the destruction of a British brigade at the battle of Maiwand in 1880. In 2006 British forces were drawn into the key towns of northern Helmand: Sangin, Nowzad and Musa Qala. The Alizais reacted in the same way, especially as the British deployment had been preceded by the removal of Sher Mohammed Akhundzada, the Alizai provincial governor. Mike Martin has argued that, in 2006, following his dismissal due to British pressure:

Sher Mohammad, the excluded powerbrokers and the cross-border elements simply played to the Helmandi feeling that the British were historical enemies and that the deployment was 'revenge for Maiwand'. In a scenario that could have happened 170 years earlier, the British had managed to align previously antagonistic groups again, and the uneducated population did not know any better than the narrative that 'They [the British] have come to oppress your wives, they are infidels', with religion being used to sharpen grievances felt.[9]

History matters. Strategic narrative, which effectively provides the interpretive structure that seeks to give particular meaning to tactical actions, must take this into account. The British did not do so in 2006 and suffered, when many Helmandis, especially in the north of the province, came to see what Britain genuinely intended to be a reconstruction mission as a rehearsal of older grievances. If history is 'a dialogue between the past and the present', the ability to tap into, and channel, historical currents, is important in the construction of effective strategy. The power of how people perceive history can be a powerful 'force multiplier', or can alternatively be a huge drain on resources where strategy tries to swim upstream against historical perception.[10]

This theme is more familiar in the context of domestic politics. Competition over the interpretation of American history (in rhetoric which, for example, stresses the intentions of the founding fathers, and the polarisation of responses to movements such as the Tea Party, whose very name claims a particular interpretation of US history) is at the heart of current US political competition.[11] Political messaging in a domestic context is aware of popular perceptions of history and is attuned accordingly.

In Afghanistan the Taliban make frequent appeal to historical analogy: 'Are you a son of Shah Shuja or Dost Mohammed?' is one of their recruiting slogans. Shah Shuja was the ruler of Afghanistan installed by the British following the First Afghan War who ruled 1839–42; he is remembered in Afghanistan as a weak and effeminate ruler. Dost Mohammed was the great ruler of Afghanistan who overthrew Shah Shuja and ruled 1826–39 and 1843–63. The intention of this slogan today seeks to connect the comparison of Shah Shuja and Dost Mohammed to that between President Karzai and Mullah Omar. Virtually every aspiring Afghan political group since Dost Mohammed has tried to associate itself with him. Mullah Omar himself in April 1996 wore the cloak of Mohammed in Kandahar and professed himself leader of all Muslims, the *Amir-al-Mu'minin*. The last man to have performed this act was Dost Mohammed in 1834, who used it as a rallying call for war against the Sikhs.

Historic claims are often highly subjective. The banter between the Afghan police and the Taliban over unsecure radio offers an amusing insight into the subjective nature of historic claims. Both groups claim that they are the true Afghans, and that they are the ones continuing the struggle against foreigners for which the 1980s Mujahideen fought. The Taliban call the Afghan police 'American slaves', to which the Afghan police usually reply that the Taliban are the 'Pakistani slaves'; the same historical figures and anecdotes, as well as a choice selection of insults, are thrown in by both sides to communicate the opposite meaning.

History is a powerful spring of emotion; the strategist who can construct his narrative to tap into that well gains access to its power. The malleability of history is in part due to the instability of 'national' histories. For example, the oft-recited argument that Britain actually achieved its strategic objectives in the First and Second Afghan War despite some tactical defeats may well be a legitimate interpretation of the historical record. However, it has no purchase for Afghans, whose belief in the defeat of the British is an idea ingrained in their national history.

Yet neither is there any such thing as a universal 'Afghan' view of history. This was made evident to me in March 2008 when my company was sent to Maiwand, a small town on the road between Helmand and Kandahar. We were the first coalition troops to have spent any length of time in the area since the start of the war in 2001. We had been briefed that Maiwand was the site of a famous British defeat mentioned above, and that villagers might comment on this. Moreover, the Taliban had actually been spreading rumours in Helmand that the 'real' reason the British were there was to avenge the battle of Maiwand. During the first patrol in the town my platoon sergeant, Bel Gurung, was earnestly asked by some of the villagers if he was Russian, followed by 'I didn't realise you people were still here'. This was all the more odd since he is Nepali! (To be fair, a lot of the Soviet troops in the 1980s were from the Asiatic parts of the USSR, and perhaps it was I who had the wrong pre-conceptions).

In another case, at a place called Hyderabad in the Upper Gereshk Valley, I remember one of the villagers asking why the American army had come, even though all the troops were in British uniform. For them, at that time, we were all much the same. The point is that it is perhaps too simplistic to extrapolate clear ideas about how people in rural southern Afghanistan make political judgements based on a particular oral historical tradition. I cannot claim to understand how exactly we fitted into the historical traditions at play in southern Afghanistan; it would have been a complex web of historical anecdote, conspiracy, current news, actual human interaction and mutual miscomprehension.

Because history is not stable, strategy can work with it and weave its narrative into its tapestry. Strategy can use the flow of history as an emotional current upon which to float its rational narrative. Leo Tolstoy wrote in the second epilogue to *War and Peace* (1869):

In historic events, the so-called great men are labels giving names to events, and like labels they have but the smallest connection with the event itself. Every act of theirs, which appears to them an act of their own will, is in an historical sense involuntary and is related to the whole course of history and predestined from eternity.[12]

A common metaphor for Tolstoy's theory is that of the shepherd looking at his flock from a hill. All the sheep are acting of their own free will and the flock moves around in different directions. The sheep at the head of the flock is seen to be the leader at that point in time, although his position is really a function of the particular alignment of the flock at that time; the leader is a label for events.

Although Tolstoy's view is an extreme position, the idea that we can associate strategic effect by aligning ourselves with the currents of history is an important consideration. For example, what was effectively regime change in Libya, going with the current of the Arab Spring, generated much less opposition than in Iraq. In an alternative example, in an analysis of President Truman's foreign policy, Nick Cullather argues that the idea of 'development' was forged in the context of the conflict against the Soviet Union to further US strategic interests. Yet by situating development in a particular historical framework, US strategy was able to avoid the anti-colonial opprobrium for an idea which closely resembled colonial practice:

When President Harry S. Truman announced a 'bold new program ... for the improvement of underdeveloped areas'[13] in January 1949, the global response was startling. Truman 'hit the jackpot of the world's political emotions', *Fortune* [Magazine] noted.[14] National delegations lined up to receive assistance that a few years earlier would have been seen as a colonial intrusion. Development inserted a new problematic into international relations, and a new concept of time, asserting that all nations followed a common historical path and that those in the lead had a moral duty to those who followed... Leaders of newly independent states, such as Zahir Shah of Afghanistan and Jawaharlal Nehru of India, accepted these terms, merging their own governmental mandates into the stream of nations moving toward modernity. Development was not only the best, but the only course: 'There is only one-way traffic in Time',[15] Nehru observed.[16]

Cullather's article exemplifies how the United States was able to exercise far more strategic influence by situating its strategic narrative within a powerful historical discourse, to which US strategy contributed by channelling that discourse towards its own interest. Cullather also argues that development as an abstract idea did not work very well on the ground in Helmand. The Helmand Valley Development Project, which tried to settle immigrants from all over Afghanistan on land reclaimed from the desert through irrigation, caused as many problems as it addressed. The events in the Middle East today show the importance (and difficulty) of being on the 'right' side of history. Yet, like the actual conduct of development, the difficulty for strategy is to balance what gains purchase on a wide audience with what that entails on the ground.

The issue of strategy and the flow of historical narrative plays out in Helmand today. The main Soviet forces withdrew from Helmand in 1988, leaving garrisons of the Soviet Afghan Army in the main cities. Subsequently, the remaining political actors, including the then local government, the army and the Mujahideen factions, fought each other in a vicious struggle for power which had been building throughout the

217

1980s (under the surface of the two-dimensional Soviets-versus-Muja-hideen narrative). The eventual outcome was colonisation of much of Helmand by the most successful Mujahideen group, which was effectively a tribal-based faction run by the Akhundzada family.

When one looks under the bonnet of the conflict today, local power-brokers (most of whom lived through the 1980s conflict) often talk of the fighting in terms of an extension of the same conflict—making reference to which Mujahideen party/communist faction an actor belongs/belonged to, and generally trying to figure out who will be sitting in what chairs when the music stops (or at least changes records). Moreover in Helmand the rural farmers' perception of the Afghan National Army is historically informed. As locals sometimes remind us, the Taliban used to conscript men from their villages to fight Ahmed Shah Massoud's predominantly Tajik group in the north of Afghanistan in the 1990s. The Afghan National Army today is largely composed of northerners. On the other hand, Taliban conscription was very unpopular, and the Afghan National Army in other areas is seen positively because it is more impartial in the factional disputes of the south.

The competition between strategic narrative and historical experience is as much a problem for the Taliban leadership as it is for the coalition. The Mujahideen split up after the Soviets left in the 1980s and fought among themselves. The Taliban leadership know that and, more to the point, the Taliban leadership must know that everyone else knows that too. The Taliban has a weak political identity because it means different things to different people. Many Taliban fighting groups themselves do not even follow orders from their leadership in any formal sense, and often ignore direction.

How does the Taliban leadership deal with this? Given their lack of a solid corporate identity, how do they communicate a strategic narrative that is remarkably effective? They attach labels to stories. They seek to transform anything into an information effect. Any coalition actions are 'spun' by the Taliban to communicate a certain message. Several actions are invented, and the Taliban invariably blame the coalition publicly for civilians killed by their IEDs (even though the statistics show that, at least since 2009, the insurgency has caused far, far more civilian casualties than the coalition).

In a strategic sense, their campaign plan is not to lose: 'you have the watches, we have the time' is the standard expression of this. History is what is remembered. The Taliban leadership hopes to claim victory by placing a label on a narrative before it has even happened, which is a good strategy if you have nothing to lose. By staking out a claim to future victory the Taliban leadership takes credit for the actions of those who are within its franchise, who may in reality be fighting for personal gain rather than any wider cause.

Is this strategic narrative effective? On the one hand, yes: by placing an overwhelming emphasis on perception and communication, the Taliban are able to persuade people faster than the coalition can. On the other hand, to base one's entire strategy on perception rather than on the reality that lies beneath it is highly unstable. In the aftermath of the global financial crisis, it is clear that strategies which depend massively on perception without a base in physical reality are very dangerous!

The Taliban leadership looks powerful, but in claiming small successes illegitimately they are giving themselves far more authority than they really have. At some point people might see that the emperor is naked. That point may come about in negotiations with the Taliban, as it becomes clear that either they will not negotiate, or that they will not agree on anything, because the groups they claim to command may well ignore them and they would lose all credibility. While they are merely negotiating, however, they appear to represent all of the Taliban, which improves their stature. To use a financial analogy, the Taliban leadership may well be creating a bubble in their own stock price.

In a broader sense, both the coalition-Afghan government and the Taliban are anti-historical in their treatment of historical experience. Both wish to ignore the 1980s war in Afghanistan, despite it being the most powerful lens through which many Afghans understand the present. The process of transition to Afghan forces was relatively successful for the Soviets, but the Afghan army really only controlled the roads and cities after the Soviet withdrawal. This is an important memory for much of Afghanistan's rural population, especially in the south. Conversely, for the Taliban, the Mujahideen split up and fought among one another after the Soviet withdrawal, and many of them had no problem joining the government because their fight had been against foreigners, not Afghans.[17]

People are not a clean slate on which a strategic narrative can be imposed. The situation in sixteenth-century England during the Reformation provides an unusual, but useful, analogy.[18] In the 1520s and early 1530s Thomas More argued that individual readers were not passive *tabulae rasae*, 'clean slates', who receive the self-contained literal meaning of the Biblical text without mediation of any kind. On the contrary, More contested the notion of a 'literalist' interpretation of the Bible, since, he argued, readers inevitably come to the text with presuppositions as to probable meanings from beyond the text.[19] Without such presuppositions, interpretive communities fragment and fall to internecine dispute.

This is by analogy the position that the international coalition, and indeed the Taliban leadership, find themselves in today; by treating people as a-historical personages, competition over the meaning of most events in the conflict involves tearing apart their factual stability, as 'facts' are put on a pedestal, over the broader context of what each side is trying to do. When there are an endless number of potentially significant events, as there are in mosaic conflicts, the effect is a loss of overall meaning; ISAF investigations of 'what happened' compete with insurgent counter-claims amid all sorts of alternative views presented by other actors, from Afghan villagers to internet bloggers: this produces not a comprehensible Roman mosaic but a postmodern jumble with no discernible story.

The result of the dynamic is that audiences latch on to stories that have some kind of linear thread, which can range from casualty figures to number of girls in schools, which ultimately generate eccentric, partial, and incoherent comprehensions of conflict. Indeed, one of General Petraeus' successes as commander of ISAF was to set out a clear story of how transition would occur, a structure through which audiences could make some sense of an eclectic range of facts available to them that might relate to the conflict.

Fighting fundamentalists on literalist battlefields is a terrain as tedious as it is dangerous for liberal powers. Liberal powers should be confident about the values that underpin their title. Those values should be expressed in terms of strategic vision that beats fundamentalists because they have nothing to offer in the longer term, apart from a sort of puritanical, purgatorial, stasis (take the Taliban rule in the 1990s for example). Liberal powers have failed to present a convincing vision of their role in the world in the first decade of this century. Engaging fundamentalists on a literalist plane is the corollary of this loss of strategic self-confidence: if people had confidence in what liberal powers stood for they would have some faith in what we are trying to do in Afghanistan, and interpret our actions more sympathetically.

Strategic narrative and strategic vision

The importance of vision in strategic narrative, in the sense of an aspirational proposition, was brought home to me by a remarkable encounter I had in Nepal in 2008. I was in the west of the country in a town called Tamghas, which suffered in the Maoist civil war. The town was racked by the troubles which result from the polarisation of political affiliations that civil wars encourage. I met a local teacher who was also one of the wealthier peasants, and one of the few moderates left. He was fairly despondent about the situation. The moment of complete surprise for me came when he started talking about '1215 Magna Carta', which, since we were speaking Nepali, I initially thought was some kind of technical Nepali term. It turned out that he listened to the BBC World Service and, incredibly, was familiar with this episode of English legal history.

He said I was lucky to live in the UK, even though to him the UK was more of an imagined community than a real place. This informed the entire way in which he conceived the work of the British government in Nepal, namely the good work that the Gurkha Welfare Scheme did in the town. This kind of narrative is essential; the Maoists could all too easily dress up what the Gurkha Welfare Scheme does in anti-imperialistic terms. Vision and confidence in one's values is today at the core of strategy. Vision provides stability to the interpretive structure proposed by strategic narrative, because it offers a way for people to understand confused situations on the basis of their belief in that vision; this is superior to dependency on an exclusively literal understanding of 'what happened', which can be unclear and often invented in the competition in conflict to persuade people of a particular agenda. Vision of strategic narrative is therefore of little value if not accompanied by confidence in that vision.

The construction of strategic narratives in fragmented political environments often generates a paradox for the strategist. On the one hand, the orchestration of actions directly to target people's perceptions is an immensely powerful strategic tool; on the other hand, it is a dangerous drug which can encourage huge instability by forgetting that there should be a physical reality underpinning perceived reality. How does the strategist deal with this? Ultimately strategy faces a rhetorical question: how do we combine actions with the perception of those actions in order to persuade an audience over a period of time?

When strategy operates in a stable interpretive structure, such as when the inter-state paradigm of war is used symmetrically by both sides, the meaning of actions only makes sense as part of a larger whole. When that interpretive constraint is removed, as is often the case in contemporary conflict, the meaning of every action can be contested. The way in which actions are contested on a global scale in the Long War and in Afghanistan between the coalition-Afghan government and the Taliban is typical of a literalist, unstable, interpretive environment, unconstrained by agreed presuppositions. Virtually every action is challenged by and within either side.

At the local level, if there is a civilian killed, the Taliban will always blame it on the coalition; the reality is usually that they have accidently trodden on an IED. If there is any fire-fight, the Taliban will claim that there was damage to civilian property or casualties. If the coalition arrests anybody, a crowd of locals will turn up at the gate of the patrol base insisting that the man is innocent; it can be hard to distinguish genuine argument from those that are forced by the Taliban to complain to the coalition. Indeed on one occasion in 2010 a village elder harangued us for hours about how two people whom we had detained were innocent. At the end of the meeting when he was out of earshot he said privately and discreetly that the men were guilty but that there were Taliban spies in the meeting who had told him what to say.

This type of situation is commonplace. Every coalition action is woven into conspiracy theories of what is 'really' going on. I remember how many villagers I met in 2007–8 genuinely thought that my platoon had arrived to spy on their women. The idea that the coalition 'really' supports the Taliban to prolong the struggle to control resources is but one of innumerable conspiracies which, disappointingly, are rife.[20] The outcome is that every action has to be contested and explained, as there is no stability to its meaning. For strategic audiences, this resembles a vicious, never-ending argument about who did what, which is never resolved, and ultimately provides no stable basis for a strategic narrative to persuade them.

The *Daily Telegraph's* information campaign during the 2009 British parliamentary expenses scandal illustrates how the speed of information in a fragmented story makes actual fact less important than the overall impression. On one day, the paper would run with the accusations against an MP on the front page and present a short explanatory statement from the MP which he or she would have had little time to work up. The next day, by which time the MP would have had time to investigate and present a proper response, the caravan had moved on and another MP was under scrutiny, and responses from the previous day were old news. Thus the reality of whether the accused MPs were guilty, and all of the mitigating circumstances, were far less important than the initial perception.[21] This offers an analogy with events in Afghanistan. The endless argument over the facts of individual events is less significant than the overall impression. The overall impression in turn is far more related to people's pre-existing prejudices than attention to individual facts.

This kind of situation, where sides argue tooth and nail over the meaning of every point or action, is typical of unstable interpretive environments, and those environments are in turn produced when people are insecure about who they are, and what they are about. Returning to the analogy of sixteenth-century England, we find that a parallel situation would be the debate over the interpretation of the English translation of the Bible in the 1520s and 1530s. The translators of the Bible into the vernacular claimed that it would allow every person to read it individually without the distorting intervention of Catholic doctrine. The immediate result was that every word was contested, as people disagreed over precise literal meanings, since there is clearly no such thing as an incontrovertible 'literal' meaning.

Texts mean different things to different readers, according to the presuppositions they bring to the text in the first place. The Protestants of the 1520s and 1530s courageously translated the Bible into the vernacular; once the project was completed, however, Protestants vehemently disagreed both with Catholics and with other Protestants over all kinds of meanings; every word became a battlefield. Hence key ideas were contested on the basis of technical philological points (that is, not on the basis of the overall direction of the text's meaning), until Protestant traditions formed that stabilised scriptural meanings with the establishment of alternative presuppositions.

As has been argued in *Burning to Read: English Fundamentalism and its Reformation Opponents* (2007), in such unstable interpretive circumstances the authority of the philologist, the expert on the translation and meaning of words, replaced the authority of the Church; now the text was 'not property of the reader and interpreters but its translators', thus creating 'new frontiers for confusion'.[22] The role of the philologist provides a neat parallel with the role of the media today. There are essentially two rhetorical responses to such a problem. The first is to state that some people will always understand the 'real' meaning, and that these are the people one is trying to persuade. Thus one Protestant reaction in the 1530s was to claim that the elect (those predestined by God to go to heaven) had the real meaning of the Bible 'written on the heart', and would always interpret a text correctly.[23]

This is similar to propositions which claim to act on the basis of universal values, such as the persistent rehearsal by President George W. Bush of the argument that the United States was engaged in a war with those who 'hated freedom'. The argument is essentially that it is the 'other' which irrationally does not understand something that is universal. This rhetorical approach imposes blame not on the text, or in the context (here the strategic narrative), but on the reader, or the strategic audience. Thus the sixteenth-century culture of blaming the 'bad reader' who missed the point of a text whose meaning should be literal finds resonance today in the frequent assertions that audiences domestic and foreign 'don't understand' what the coalition is doing in Afghanistan. This suggests that the problem is one of communication for which the audience is responsible, rather than the issue itself.

The other, more positive, rhetorical response to an unstable interpretive environment is to persuade people of the overall intention, as opposed to becoming trapped in an endless 'who did what' argument about each action. In terms of our Biblical analogy, this is a tradition strongly associated with Augustine (354–430 ACE). His key argument was that people should read the Bible with a general sense of the text's overall meaning and direction, which was elucidated by non-textual elements of the wider Christian tradition. The theme of charity, for example, provided an essential interpretive guide to understand obscure passages. That Augustine stressed confidence in vision and the overall message, while living at a moment of profound self-doubt for the Roman Empire, with barbarians at its gate and the fall of its western half approaching, makes his views particularly resonant today. Augustine's is a very different, and more stable, interpretive tradition than the simplistic idea that words, or actions, can speak for themselves if the right person interprets them. Essentially it privileges intention over specific content.

An alternative and perhaps more familiar example would be the debate about how British judges interpret the law. One of the key issues is how far they should understand the intention of Parliament in the literal words of the statute, or look beyond the text to other sources. The late Lord Denning, who was judge in a 1950 case, stated controversially that 'we do not sit here to pull the language of Parliament and of Ministers to pieces and make nonsense of it... We sit here to find out the intention of Parliament and of Ministers and carry it out, and we do this better by filling in the gaps and making sense of the enactment than by opening it up to destructive analysis'.[24]

Nor were Augustine or Lord Denning's views so different from the way the British army today emphasises the need for 'mission command' in battle: that commanders should be clear about what their commander wants to achieve and select the best route to get there; this is a much more stable way of communicating meaning than describing in detail exactly what to do, which would unnecessarily have people debate whether to go left or right around a hill if it hasn't been exactly specified.

The acknowledgement of the centrality of vision in strategy is certainly not new. It seems at present, however, that the literalist approach is in the ascendancy. For actions in contemporary conflict to have political utility—to be in support of an idea—strategy needs to understand that the role of strategic narrative is to convince people; in imitation of the good orator, that requires effectively binding *logos, ethos* and *pathos* together. President Abraham Lincoln's Gettysburg Address or President John F. Kennedy's inauguration speech are both classic examples of highly successful presentations of strategic narrative. They blend rational argument with passion, history and vision; they are essentially persuasive in terms of all three of Aristotle's rhetorical resources. From a strategic perspective, they set conditions for future actions to be understood in a particular context which encourages people to see those actions in terms of what they were driving at, rather than in terms of the action itself.

An episode related by General Sir Graeme Lamb captures the effective matching of words, actions and vision. He speaks about the issue of General Stanley McChrystal's effort to reduce civilian casualties on taking command in 2009:

[The insurgents] operate in the communication space incredibly better than we do. It is the area in which we are horribly deficient. It was important therefore that we change the dynamic through the ways people drove [road traffic accidents, and a perception of coalition arrogance by defensive driving, had been a big problem]—so it was how we were perceived by the population—and how we tried to reduce the casualties in the use of force and other ways.

Hobbes world is a grim old place. Both sides are getting broken up, killed and damaged in the process of this, and people apply the Surrey [an English county] map to it, which just doesn't work. Trying to reduce those casualties is recognised by the people. There was an incident in the North, in Kunduz ... when a tanker was blown up and a number of locals who had been told by the Taliban to get the fuel were killed. McChrystal went straight there, and a lot of people said, 'What are you doing? We haven't had the inquiry yet, and Germany are upset about this'. The bush net [informal communication] of Afghanistan is every bit as good as the bush nets you will find in other parts of the third and second world. It is often far better than where we have a clever communication space. It went around the country that he was someone who was genuinely trying to reduce civilian casualties, and the vast majority of Afghans got that. So McChrystal was seen as somebody who was in charge of ISAF and the coalition forces, who was genuinely aware of Afghans. That is not how they had perceived it before.[25]

The dry, banal, bureaucratic language and legalese of official justifications for a conflict, or the endless announcement of 'investigations' into who did what in relation to allegations of wrongdoing, characterise the West's strategic narratives today (President Obama's speeches, or General McChrystal's actions, are perhaps exceptions which prove the rule). This is not just a case of finding it hard to persuade people because we are boring; by engaging fundamentalists on the battlefield of literal interpretation, we fight on ground that favours them, because their messages are simplistic and work better in that environment. Moreover, the Taliban are able to exploit the fact that the coalition is honest; the Taliban continuously gain political advantage by lying and making up stories. To shift the interpretive environment by emphasising ultimate intentions plays to the West's strengths, because fundamentalism has nothing to offer in the long-term.

CONCLUSION

CONTEMPORARY STRATEGIC THOUGHT

I first met insurgents when I taught at a school in a hill village in eastern Nepal in 2002. The Maoist insurgency was taking off in this part of the country. The 'Maobadi' arrived for the first time one night; I woke up to find a band of around platoon size sleeping in the house of the family I was staying with. There was mutual surprise in the morning! They were not expecting a Westerner to turn up at breakfast and nor was I expecting them. I got to know them as they came and went from the village over the next few months. What struck me was the need to understand insurgents on their own terms. Most were very young, between 13 and 18; many were girls; they were virtually all illiterate; they were mainly poor, low-caste Nepalis; few wore uniform; they were not from the local area; their weapons were a mix of old rifles, which they cleaned assiduously, and quite sophisticated improvised explosive devices (IEDs) manufactured from pressure cookers.

These were indeed real guerrillas who had left their families and were ideologically motivated: they were sworn to fight to the death, at least in their boasts to me. Their commander, not much older than me, even gave me a particularly enthusiastic and largely incorrect presentation on Marxism, including an eccentric and obsessive emphasis on the Paris Commune (which I must say was a rather bizarre, but entertaining, experience in this rural Himalayan village!). He felt that he was part of a wider and energetic historical movement. That his genuine idealism should have been channelled in this way was somewhat tragic.

227

The brief outline of circumstances described above indicates that any counter-insurgent would have to deal here with a very particular political problem. To have understood Nepal's civil war in generic military terms as 'insurgent' versus 'government', in isolation of its actual political and social context, would have been overly simplistic. Yet fixation with these generic doctrinal categories has proved to be problematic in the coalition campaign in Afghanistan, particularly in the earlier phase of the campaign, as well as more broadly in the 'Long War', which the 'War on Terror' seems to have become. This is what happens when an operational approach is upscaled to the level of strategy, or policy: when operational ideas, which demand a political context, are not adequately provided with one, they move up to fill the vacuum. This in turn produces a danger that the campaign is not understood on its own terms, but rather aims at generic military metrics that are largely self-referencing, and distort comprehension of the conflict. In Afghanistan, this has led people to see counter-insurgency as a strategy in itself, which it is not, and to criticise it on that basis; the irony being that counter-insurgency is a perfectly sensible operational approach.

The examination of war from an exclusively military perspective, isolated from its social and political context, leads to false conclusions and poor strategy. Carl von Clausewitz's *On War* was partly a response to his experience of the Napoleonic Wars, which he saw as the product of the French Revolution: 'very few of the manifestations in war can be ascribed to new inventions or new departures in ideas. They result mainly from the transformation of society and new social conditions'.[1]

War today is in the process of undergoing another evolution in response to social and political conditions, namely the speed and interconnectivity associated with contemporary globalisation and the information revolution. However, strategy, particularly in the West, still tends to be constructed with two basic assumptions which derive from inter-state war, even for conflicts which are not inter-state: first, that competitors in war are essentially polarised; second, that the core strategic audiences of the conflict are to be found within the sides themselves.

The information revolution connects new audiences to contemporary conflicts, accelerating the proliferation of potential strategic audiences beyond the enemy (people against whom a conflict's outcome is defined other than the enemy), and beyond the state (people who do not identify with one of the state parties to a conflict); these categories often overlap. Those beyond the enemy are out of range of force, the traditional, coercive means by which hostile audiences come to subscribe (by forced consent) to the legitimacy of one's strategic narrative; they are more likely to interpret actions in directly political terms, outside the interpretive structure offered by war. Those beyond the state, 'non-state audiences' (who include citizens who refuse to identify with their 'own' state, or at least have strong multiple identities), are more likely than citizens of a state party to be persuaded through their emotional and moral responses, given that the state rationales of national interest may have less or no purchase on them.

Although audiences beyond the parties to a conflict have always been recognised, victory and defeat in the inter-state paradigm relate to effects upon these core audiences, who identify with their state to the extent that they are defeated or are victorious with it, typically as a result of the defeat of their army on the battlefield. This latent inter-state mentality often extends to circumstances in which the enemy is not a state, in the sense that the enemy is essentially considered unitary. The presentation of the 9/11 attacks in terms of an 'act of war' against the United States by President Bush in his 20 September 2001 address to Congress suggests such a default association of organised violence with the concept of war. He asserted that 'either you are with us, or you are with the terrorists'; this reaches to the heart of a conception of war's function as the resolution of an issue between polarised sides.[2]

This conception needs re-evaluation in the light of recent experience. In Afghanistan there is a central tension between the government and the insurgency. However, these sides are better characterised as franchises that do not clearly align many of the conflict's actors. These actors tend to manoeuvre to gain political advantage vis-à-vis one another. This is significantly different from the polarised, two-way conflict of inter-state war; although that conceptual premise is immediately suggested when people speak of the Afghan conflict in terms of 'war'.

To speak about the actions of 'the insurgency' in Afghanistan is accurate only insofar as it is recognised that the insurgency is a franchise movement that comprehends many factions and interests, including some who are close to, or also part of, the government 'franchise'. Moreover, the umbrella term is convenient because it is often not clear which part of the insurgency is responsible for an action. However, this should not be confused with the notion that 'the Taliban' are a unitary enemy whose leadership exerts direct control over the whole insurgency down to the tactical level.

What are the consequences in contemporary conflict of utilising as a default the inter-state paradigm of war, even for conflicts which are not inter-state? If that paradigm were merely a label to describe war, typically industrial war, between states, 'conventional warfare' would be merely an inaccurate qualification for it, since it has been the exception in terms of the conflicts fought by Western states since 1945. Yet the durability of conventional war as the basic analytical structure of war goes far beyond semantic inaccuracy; it frustrates the need to re-define conflicts which are not 'conventional', such as Afghanistan, so that they can be prosecuted successfully.

There is a contemporary requirement to be more precise about what we mean by military activity in terms of distinguishing between the use of force and the use of war. I have argued that the term 'means', in Clausewitz's dictum that war is an extension of policy by other means, has a twofold signification, both meanings being intertwined. The first meaning refers to the actual use of force, the second to war as an interpretive structure which makes war 'itself' a particular political instrument. War offers an interpretive template which can be used by strategy to persuade audiences to understand actions in a conflict in a given 'military' way (just as the words of a barrister are understood through the interpretive context of court advocacy; outside of court, the same words might be interpreted in significantly different ways). Strategic thought, notably in popularised public debates preceding conflicts, tends to focus intensively on the former (the actual use of force) and to neglect the latter (war itself as a political instrument).

The question 'should we intervene militarily in country X?' is common, and rarely semantically challenged. Such phrasing would imply that the use of military means for military ends is indistinguishable. Yet the difference between military means and military ends corresponds to the distinction between the two significations available in Clausewitz's dictum: the military apply armed force, but military ends are traditionally defined through the concept of war. While the two may well be inseparable in certain circumstances, especially in conventional war, military means can be, and are in many contemporary conflicts, used independently of military ends the more they directly seek a political goal.

The converse is a grey area: would a state on state attack without traditionally defined military means, using cyber alone for example (which has happened already: Russia's three week cyber-attack on Estonia in 2007, which was described in the press as 'cyberwar', being the most notorious), be said to make use of the interpretive framework of war?[3]

When war fails clearly to separate the military and the political, organised violence in human affairs is not contained. Take the Long War for example. Such a redefinition of the 'War on Terror' exemplifies that, if a war's mechanism cannot provide a military outcome, it does not end. The Long War may not be absolute war in the sense of huge armies clashing, but it clearly approaches an abstract conception of absolute war because the use of force is unrestrained by policy: how can policy regulate force if force is a direct extension of policy?

'Absolute war' in contemporary conflict can subvert Clausewitz's own definition of the same term. For Clausewitz, *ganze Krieg* is the ultimate form of decisiveness, not war without end. Moreover, in contemporary conflict, combat is not, as it was for Clausewitz, the 'only means of war'. In the Long War, force is used across whole regions of the world, and sometimes in minuscule quantities in terms of firepower, in conjunction with other means (economic, legal, cyber, media-related, for example), to achieve political results more directly. In the Long War, therefore, 'war' does not clearly contain violence within an interpretive structure. On the contrary, war is expanded to incorporate all means which deliver political effect: violence is mixed into other political activity, so that there is a severe erosion of the interpretive difference between military and political activity; war and peace.

In reality, the complete fusion of military and political activity is an abstract pole, which contemporary conflict may have moved towards, but elements of war as more traditionally defined remain in place. Indeed 'military' activity remains a useful and legitimate term in contemporary conflict. In terms of distinguishing means, it can describe the activity of armed forces—the military—as opposed to their civilian counterparts. Even in terms of the ends which armed forces seek to achieve, the boundary between when soldiers seek 'military' or 'political' objectives, especially at the tactical level, is blurred and subjective. There are many people trying to kill coalition soldiers in Afghanistan; they can legitimately be considered an enemy, at minimum in a temporary sense.

The extent to which they can then be dealt with militarily is where the possibilities of defining military activity in terms of its means, ends, or both are blurred.

Military activity in the traditional inter-state paradigm sense of setting conditions for a political solution, in a sequential manner, is by no means redundant either. Enemies can be dealt with militarily by killing or capturing them, as in Sri Lanka's recent destruction of the Tamil Tigers.[4] If conventional war thinking is applied in this extreme sense in contemporary conflict, the military might well set military conditions for a political solution in a literal sense. Yet the West, to my mind entirely correctly, does not engage in such practices, because they normally represent an evacuation of the moral high ground, which exaggerate rather than resolve the conflict in the long-term. Contemporary globalisation challenges the idea of war as a compartmentalised military domain, where decisions are reached on the battlefield, is compromised in most situations other than those where unrestrained physical force is used.

Thus most strategic audiences, including most insurgents, need to be persuaded of a strategic narrative while often being beyond the range of armed force, so cannot be 'forced' to subscribe to a given narrative, as in the inter-state paradigm. Indeed the metrics that tend to be used to evaluate progress in the Long War are far more about global opinion than they are about any military balance, and as much about the control of political as physical space. General Stanley McChrystal, for example, attempted to reduce the use of indirect ordnance and air-delivered bombs in the Afghan War, not because they are not effective in military terms; they are. However, their political effect is often more harmful than their military value. As the use of force is often interpreted in direct political terms by audiences, the concept of 'war' struggles to bind its audiences into recognition of a military outcome that sets conditions for a political solution. War moves towards becoming a direct extension of political activity.

The dynamics of contemporary conflicts can often be clarified, by way of analogy, in terms of what liberal powers would understand as normal political activity in a domestic context. When liberal powers base their strategic narratives on the template of inter-state war, they define expectations (in the conventional military sense) in relation to an enemy (which implies more absolute expectations of victory or defeat) before political aims can be considered. In domestic politics, political aims are defined primarily against one's political constituencies rather than the opposition party (the 'enemy'). Hence whether success in domestic politics involves cooperation with, or defeat of, the opposition is secondary.

The enemy therefore plays a very different function in these two conceptions: in the first, he is an obstacle to be fought before any outcome can occur; in the second, he is an inconvenience who, one has to accept, will permanently frustrate one's goals. Confusion of these two modes of understanding can encourage a belligerent to seek absolute outcomes to problems that might be better understood as part of the normal fabric of international politics. That is, in the context of domestic politics, nobody expects even the most successful government to persuade everyone, especially their opponents' 'home base' political constituencies; that is unrealistic. Yet these false, decisive expectations are encouraged when a paradigm of 'war' is employed to conceptualise conflicts that actually are a lot closer functioning according to the dynamics of domestic politics.

This mismatch between expectation and possibility has placed huge strain on liberal powers to explain what they are doing, and drawn attention to the role of strategic narrative in contemporary conflict. Strategy is a two-way bridge between policy on one side and action on the other, both violent and non-violent. Strategic narrative expresses strategy as a story, to explain one's actions. Different people may tell the story differently, to persuade different audiences, and perhaps place particular emphasis on different goals. That is fine, so long as the different versions of the story remain consistent.

A coherent strategic narrative not only enables one to convince different audiences according to the ends of policy, but also to bind together one's team across levels of authority and function: the diplomatic head of mission, the army company commander, the aid specialist, the politician working from a domestic capital, for instance. Effective solutions in contemporary conflict emphasise pragmatic combinations of means synchronised in time and space to achieve common objectives. Conversely, the language of 'the diplomatic solution…' or 'the military solution' as strategic alternatives is increasingly frustrated.

Liberal democracies are today not particularly effective in the configuration of strategic narrative. Part of this is to do with the Cold War legacy of rigid civil-military relations, in which those executing policy on the ground are largely sealed off from those making it. This still makes constitutional sense, but no longer makes strategic sense.

In summary, the conception of war today is paradoxical. The West still understands war's mechanism essentially in terms of a paradigm of inter-state war, conceptualised so influentially by Clausewitz; yet in another sense, war, in this paradigm as employed today, often subverts Clausewitz's conception of war's political utility. Clausewitzian war still works if its two prerequisites are generally satisfied: polarity and the containment of strategic audiences within the opposing sides. The irony today is that we blame the failure of the Clausewitzian inter-state paradigm on the mechanism itself rather than on the contemporary circumstances in which it is used, and in which these two prerequisites are typically compromised.

Strategy today can to an extent shape war to ensure that the preconditions which give Clausewitzian war political utility are sufficiently satisfied. War in its Clausewitzian conception regulates violence in the world by confining organised violence (the use of armed force) within an interpretive structure (the battlefield, where outcomes are defined in military terms) in which it is regulated by policy. This idea contributed to the Weinberger doctrine of 1984 (slightly adapted by General Colin Powell's version of the doctrine before the First Gulf War) which rehabilitated US strategic thought after Vietnam. It worked. The limited and successful use of force in the 1991 Gulf War is a classic example.[5]

Conversely, twenty years on from the First Gulf War, one might argue whether any potential enemy will take on the US military in conventional battle in the near to medium term. Moreover, the inter-connectedness enhanced by contemporary globalisation has changed the world in the intervening two decades; strategic audiences beyond the polarised sides are likely to remain a key feature of future conflict. Reversion to a Weinberger-Powell type doctrine might be sensible for wider international stability, but such a reversion would also require refusal to intervene in many cases where genuine national interests were at stake.

This is a hard choice. The consequences of not paying attention to such a choice are essentially to get the worst of both possibilities: failure in the Long War and wider international instability. However, this book has argued for a pragmatic mentality in the formulation of strategy; part of this involves trying not to see strategic choices in absolute terms. Hence the choice outlined above offers a dialectic tool of strategic analysis, rather than an absolute prescription to choose one or the other. This tool is available to consider the consequences and opportunities available in each, unique, conflict situation; such consequences, positive and negative, will be less visible if both forms are confused within a single conception of war.

War in the Clausewitzian paradigm is not the use of force for directly political outcomes. Clausewitzian war contains violence in human affairs; it has clear limits. The relevant international law is constructed on the basis that one can define specific 'military' targets. Yet the idea that one can distinguish between 'military' and 'political' targets, when strategy uses force directly for political effect, is problematic: the definition of military activity in terms of its means rather than its ends is perhaps overly privileged.[6]

However, to challenge the practice of using force outside the paradigm of war for directly political ends on the basis of wider international stability raises its own concerns. Such practice is highly effective in operational terms, and the imperative to succeed in conflict obviously remains. Counter-insurgency opens up the operational option to use force for directly political advantage. If in a given conflict the policy choice has been to commit military forces to achieve an outcome in a country in which the enemy refuses conventional battle and lives among the people, counter-insurgency, properly resourced, and in a realistic political context, can be highly effective. There is a particular imperative to be operationally effective in less extreme forms of armed conflict: to avoid escalation to extreme forms that 'work'. However, counter-insurgency should not be elevated to the level of global strategy. That would remove its limits, and compromise the boundary between war and peace.

Western liberal powers have genuine security concerns in many parts of the world, which are operationally most effectively addressed through the use of force more directly for political ends. However, the conflict generated when force is used more for directly political, rather than military, outcomes is not war in the Clausewitzian sense, but effectively a continuation of normal political activity, which is endless.

Clausewitzian war is brutal, decisive and finite. When liberal democracies fail to make such a distinction they contaminate the clear boundaries in which violence operates in Clausewitzian war. Because liberal democracies have generally failed to make such a distinction, the result has been a proliferation of violence in the world which has the potential to drag the West into endless conflicts that go beyond political utility, not least in terms of their human and financial cost. The use of force as a direct extension of policy may be operationally effective, but it is a very dangerous game when unbounded by a clear strategic construct, the risks of which are masked by the idea that it is war.

One danger of the way in which liberal powers deal with contemporary conflict is the failure to distinguish between what is temporary and what is permanent. In his seminal study of Soviet strategic culture in 1977, Jack Snyder argued that Soviet nuclear strategy had achieved a state of semi-permanence that could be understood now to represent a culturally informed position, rather than mere policy. The boundary between culture and policy is primarily one of choice, in that policy implies a deliberate, as opposed to a default, strategic option.[7] To take another example, in republican Rome the citizens could elect a dictator to rule with absolute power for a specified period in order to deal with a military crisis. This system was effective, but it was a policy of choice, distinct from the culture of absolute authority that later characterised the imperial period.

If liberal democracies become intoxicated with the idea that their contemporary conflicts represent the future of war, the result will be a challenge to the liberal tradition: we seem to forget that war should ultimately be about peace. Conversely, as was indicated in earlier chapters, the conflicts of the first decade of this century do not seem anomalous, and may point to the future, because the information revolution is likely to make many of the characteristics they exhibit irreversible. The challenge for the West is therefore to deal with the inevitable aspects of change, but also to recognise where there is room to manoeuvre.[8]

To summarise, there is a basic strategic question apparent in contemporary conflict, specifically the West's 'Long War'. This question has two related parts: first, in strategic terms, should liberal powers aggregate their conflicts into one 'global counter-insurgency' or disaggregate them, treating each discretely and on its own terms; second, in operational terms, should liberal powers only fight conflicts in which they can defeat the enemy in conventional battle (which would often mean to refuse battle with an enemy who does not present himself, and so take risk on legitimate security concerns), or beat the enemy at his own game through armed political activity?

CONCLUSION

I have suggested here two responses. First, that the nature of contemporary globalisation blurs the line considerably between these choices at the strategic and operational levels; in contemporary conflicts short of absolute war there does not exist a sealed military domain. However, that does not mean that thinking in terms of such a choice is not an important tool of strategic analysis. The consequences of not thinking in such terms are clear: operational areas become ill defined, and there is a real risk that operational approaches are elevated to become strategies in themselves, which look inwardly to their own metrics rather than connecting to policy.

Second, counter-insurgency, understood as a broad and flexible set of doctrinal ideas underpinned by the idea of armed political activity, remains a highly effective operational approach when faced with insurgents. However, the relative operational effectiveness of armed political activity should as far as possible be boxed by clear strategic boundaries.

A failure to think in terms of such a choice, and raise what is an operational concept to a policy, which creates wider international instability, or not to engage at all, and not contest insurgencies, are two paths to the same destination anyway: a world full of insurgencies is unstable. So either way, proper attention to the question is needed.

To answer this strategic question adequately, and to facilitate the application of the two responses set out, this book has sought to draw attention to particular modes of strategic thought. This represents largely an effort to rehabilitate older traditions rather than anything new. These modes can be summarised as follows. At the policy level, genuine political choices, based on strategic dialogue that often needs to extend right down to the tactical level, are required to provide a workable political context for an operational approach to function. Operational approaches need to be constructed pragmatically, adapting doctrine to particular problems, not being its slave.

To enable these approaches to both policy and operational issues, liberal powers need to move on from thinking about military activity (and its civilian operational equivalent) as a one-way, unquestioning execution of policy, to incorporate it as part of a two-way dialogue; the aim of such an evolution is to produce sound strategy through continuous reconciliation of what is desired and what is possible. Finally, strategic narrative as an interpretive framework needs to establish its boundaries through vision, and its credibility through confidence. Only then can a narrative convince disparate strategic audiences in a fragmented political environment, and so avoid literalist debates with religious fundamentalists. In this context, the art of strategy can approximate by analogy to the classical art of rhetoric in its attempt to convince people of an idea through a combination of rational argument (*logos*), emotional appeal (*pathos*) and moral standing (*ethos*).

The interaction in war between policy and operational approaches, and the interpretive quality of war itself as a medium between military and political outcomes, are modes of strategic thought that originate from the ideas of Carl von Clausewitz. The notion that contemporary conflict has more to do with people, and their persuasion, as the boundaries between the political and military are blurred, may seem at odds with Clausewitzian thought, in which war does provide a clear military domain. However, people in war did matter to Clausewitz; the recognition that war is a human activity is essential to understanding his strategic ideas.

Clausewitz comprehended war in terms of the interactions between the three elements that make up the 'one' of his trinity of war: policy, passion and war itself. Clausewitz saw a tendency in the logic of war itself to encourage war to move to extremes: 'war is an act of force and there is no logical limit to the application of that force. Each side, therefore, compels his opponent to follow suit; a reciprocal action is started which must lead, in theory, to extremes'.[9]

Yet in reality, as opposed to in theory, human factors prevented war from operating in this manner: 'concern, prudence and fear of excessive risks find reason to assert themselves and to tame the elemental fury of war'.[10] So 'the vast array of factors, forces and conditions in national affairs that are affected by war' act as a 'non-conducting medium': 'logic comes to a stop in this labyrinth'.[11] Thus while the 'grammar of war' in theory, through reciprocal violence, would tend to drive war to extremes, in reality 'war is not the kind that explodes in a single discharge… War is a pulsation of violence'. While war's grammar is subordinate to policy, policy itself is, in the final analysis, dependent on passion. Human passion is the oxygen whose presence animates combat (or whose absence stifles it), be it for the soldier on the battlefield, the population at home, or the politician in government.

The human element was what differentiated real war, as Clausewitz had experienced it, from war in the abstract, played out on a map. He was keen that *On War* should aid strategists to prosecute the former, not the latter. Thus Clausewitz stressed the human, emotional, passionate aspect of war in the first chapter of *On War*:

It would be a fallacy to imagine war between civilised people as resulting merely from a rational act on behalf of their governments, and to conceive of war as gradually ridding itself of passion, so that in the end one would never have to use the physical impact of the fighting forces—comparative figures of their strength would be enough. This would be a kind of war by algebra...Theorists were already beginning to think along such lines when the recent wars [the Napoleonic Wars] taught them a lesson. If war is an act of force, the emotions cannot fail to be involved.[12]

Clausewitz's recognition of the human aspect of war informs his understanding of war's military domain in terms of its political and cultural context, which provides its overarching logic. He reminds us that as much as one may like to blame 'war' itself for its inhumanity, war is a human activity. For liberal powers to blame 'war' rather than themselves for the problems they are facing is illusory.

Clausewitz's strategic ideas were based on his understanding of the nature of war. The titles of the first three books of *On War* reflect this supposition: 'On the Nature of War'; 'On the Theory of War'; 'On Strategy in General'. Strategy had to balance the three elements of war's trinity 'like an object suspended between three magnets'.[13] Policy, the rational component, had to be kept in line with human passion, the human component. Strategy also had to remain agile to keep its actions related to the aim of policy, and not allow war's logic to drive itself, through escalation, beyond the point of political utility. The reason why Clausewitz frequently uses dialectics in *On War* is, to my mind, to stress the need for balance in strategy, as if strategic answers are never finite, but kept valid through perpetual motion, like a tightrope artist keeping steady. Today this balance can be understood in terms of strategic dialogue.

This conception of strategy is intimately associated with the dialogue between theory and experience which Clausewitz repeatedly stresses in *On War*. Theory is necessary in the sense that it transmits what has worked in the past in distilled form; it is a bridge to access historical experience vicariously. Yet theory is really only a springboard of ideas which should be grounded in the experience of a particular situation.

The dialectics proposed in *On War* between the abstract and the practical, reason and intuition, theory and experience, desire and possibility, history and the present day, are parallel tensions which run throughout the work; they go to the heart of the way in which Clausewitz thought about strategy in terms of balance.

Contemporary strategic thought is overly weighted towards one side of Clausewitz's dialectic tightrope. The abstract is not sufficiently kept in check by the practical, reason by intuition, theory by experience, desire by possibility, and contemporary issues by history. Effective strategy is formed when these factors are kept in balance. To privilege one part of a pair over its counterpart is to over-emphasise a 'top-down' or 'bottom-up' approach. In reality, neither can work without being properly situated in the other. Clausewitz himself summarises this best:

> Should theory [of war] go on elaborating absolute conclusions and prescriptions? Then it would be of no use at all in real life. No, it must also take the human factor into account, and find room for courage, boldness, and even foolhardiness. The art of war deals with living and moral forces. Consequently, it can never reach the absolute, or certainty.[14]

Clausewitz's work offered a counter-argument to a tradition of overly rational and unrealistic strategic thought, in particular the eighteenth-century emphasis on mathematics and algebra in the study of strategy.[15] Daniel Moran has argued that in this context 'strategy would not merely organise the violence of war, it would replace it'. He notes the eighteenth-century connection between the 'flourishing of strategic rationalism' and a new literature on perpetual peace. Both of these themes were probably more idealistic than realistic given the expansion of war's intensity that characterised the start of the nineteenth century in Europe.[16]

In contemporary conflict and public discussion in general, policy justifications which stress rationality are normal, and often make sense. However, preference for rational concepts which do not find resonance in the human, emotional reality of the world encourages policy to privilege overly abstract ideas. War is a human activity as much as an inanimate tool of policy. However, the abstractive process that rationalises reality can suck out its emotional content: when people are statistics, and soldiers are military formations, war can truly resemble the board game 'Risk'. For Clausewitz, the human element is what gives theory (and policy) a broader base than just rational argument in the abstract, which prevents the abstract from the prescription of definite (and typically extreme) concepts: 'the probabilities of real life replace the extreme and absolute required by theory'.[17]

CONCLUSION

The application of abstract doctrine is a prominent feature of contemporary conflict which typically occurs when operational ideas are confused with strategy and are scaled up to the level of policy. For those on the ground it can be clear that there is a disconnect between the strategic narrative and how people respond to it. If, for example, a commander in Helmand tells the local population that their opium crops will not be burned, he is going against Afghan government policy, but may need to do this to avoid totally alienating people.

In one personal example, typical of many others, an Afghan police commander was told to eradicate some opium fields. In front of an angry crowd protesting against the (legal) destruction of their livelihoods, he drove 5 metres into the field, in his red government-issued opium-crushing tractor, then stopped and lit up a cigarette. That was his opium eradication effort for that year. Neither is it uncommon for farmers to invite insurgents, whom they otherwise really tend to dislike, to place IEDs in their fields to deter opium eradication. Disconnections in strategic dialogue put commanders, both ISAF and Afghan, in such a position in the first place.

Strategies that are situated in the abstract encourage extreme prescriptions because they are not proscribed by the reality of human behaviour and the unpredictability of war. One cannot apply abstract templates of what has worked in the past and hope that they will produce the same results in wholly different social and political contexts. Yet that is what is done when counter-insurgency is thought to be a strategy in itself. Counter-insurgency is itself not the problem, indeed it is a legitimate and necessary set of conceptual tools which should be used in Afghanistan given current policy goals, but within a realistic political context. Problems arise when the political context, which any abstract doctrine has to assume as a hypothetical starting point (in this case: government versus insurgency), replaces the actual political context. This was in particular a problem with the earlier phase of the Afghan campaign. The campaign in Afghanistan has gone better since 2009, despite public perception, and part of this is due to a far more realistic association of policy goals and operational possibility. Whether this adjustment came too late remains to be seen.

Overly abstract thought can also distort national strategy. In the UK, for example, the 2010 UK National Security Strategy alludes to the 'world of 2030' and the security threats of the next 20 years.[18] From one perspective this makes sense. To consider broad global trends is no doubt of value. However, any expectations situated so far into an abstract future should at least be tempered by today's concerns. Abstract assumptions can be upset when the real world, with its human passions and uncertainties, such as the Arab Spring, comes to knock at the door. The UK Labour opposition at the time called for a revision to the Strategic Defence Review on this basis.[19] A distant-horizon gazing approach to strategy can leave one reacting to distant and fragile shadows that may vanish as one approaches them: the fact that major world events, which change the course of history, from the fall of the Berlin Wall, to 9/11, to the financial crisis of 2008, are typically not anticipated by mainstream policy should be a warning about any attempts too prescriptively to game twenty years ahead.

The UK Parliament's own report on UK National Strategy, published in October 2010, advances the proposition that: 'we have found little evidence of sustained strategic thinking or a clear mechanism for analysis and assessment. This leads to a culture of fire-fighting rather than long-term planning'.[20] The distinction between long-term planning and fire-fighting is important. The irony is that fire-fighting can be the consequence of overly abstract long-term planning: while looking into the distance too much, the realities of the present day can creep up and ambush you!

The point here is again not an absolute one. To deny the value of long-term planning, which is of obvious utility, would not make sense. The argument here is about balance: the correct identification of the UK's strategy-making problems should not by default be solved by craning one's neck to look even further ahead, which might exaggerate the problem identified. In other words, to gaze far into the future is usually an unreliable strategic guide, but staring even harder into the crystal ball is often the well-intentioned, but misguided, default reaction to a loss of strategic self-confidence. National strategy does require long-term planning, but primarily on the basis of analysis not of an abstract construction set far in the future, but of one's present situation, and assessment of one's vulnerabilities that others, it can safely be assumed, will exploit.

A pragmatic mentality can facilitate the association of abstract ideas and practical reality. However, pragmatism means little in itself, as it is a human quality that has to be expressed by a real person. A pragmatic mentality can, however, encourage the requirement for balance in strat-

CONCLUSION

egy. It can also be an aid to resolve an apparent contradiction in strategy between the requirements for vision and agility. Vision is necessary to energise strategic narrative with a genuine sense of purpose. Yet agile adjustment of strategic narrative is necessary to maintain a balance between what is desired by policy and what is realistically possible on the ground.

The strategic dialogue which evaluates and adjusts the relationship between desire and possibility may well generate conclusions which significantly challenge the strategic vision. The question then arises as to which to privilege, and which audiences to satisfy. While such questions may be taken by military and civilian strategists alike, elected or une-lected, at various levels of authority, the question is essentially of a political nature. The commander him-, or herself, and the human personalities of the audience, become critical at this point. Clausewitz emphasised the commander's intuition as a key factor in war. The same is true today: the personality of the human decision-maker, and the ability to understand an audience in human terms, remain of fundamental importance. Clausewitz's emphasis on balance in strategic dialogue, between people, policy and the play of probability and chance that war itself generates, still makes sense today.

The speed and extent of inter-connectivity brought about by the information revolution is fundamentally changing the world, and war too. People, individuals and communities, fragment in each other's image: the intertwining of all kinds of cultures has huge power to unite people through common understanding; conversely, the endless disa-greement over the meaning of an event becomes more common, as world audiences are so diverse.

War From The Ground Up has suggested a way to forge effective strat-egy in order to approach conflict in this contemporary environment. However, as liberal democracies seem to sleepwalk into the fusion of war and routine international politics, they do not seem not to grasp that, if encouraged, this profoundly unstable evolution of 'war' will challenge core aspects of the liberal tradition in its broad sense as the tradition which underpins liberal democracies. War is just as much the IED-mangled body, the icon of early twenty-first-century combat, as it is a tool of policy; its proliferation is undesirable. War as war serves a legiti-mate function and this is not an anti-war book. However, war is cur-rently not compartmentalised as it should be. By increasingly merging it with regular political activity, and investing in operational ideas a policy-like quality, we are confronted with policy as an extension of war; that used to be the wrong way round.

NOTES

INTRODUCTION

1. David Kilcullen, 'Counter-Insurgency in Iraq, Theory and Practice' (2007), PowerPoint presentation, available at http://smallwarsjournal.com/, slide 45.
2. Technically the strategic distinction is between ends (aims), means (resources) and ways (the application of resources in a plan). A full discussion of the function of all three aspects of strategy is at Chapter 5.
3. Robert Haddick, 'Nagl and Gentile Are Both Right, So What Do We Do Now?' *Small Wars Journal* op-ed (November 2008).
4. Paul Brister, William H. Natter III and Robert R. Tomes, *Hybrid Warfare and Transnational Threats: Perspectives for an Era of Persistent Conflict* (New York: Council for Emerging National Security Affairs), February 2011.
5. This debate has primarily been driven in journal articles by the question of how the US should configure its military post-Afghanistan. The two positions have been characterised in debates between Lieutenant Colonel (retired) John Nagl and Colonel Gian P. Gentile. See Shawn Brimley, 'Mediating Between Crusaders and Conservatives', *Small Wars Journal* op-ed (October 2008).
6. For a summary of the concept, see Frank G. Hoffman, *Conflict in the 21ˢᵗ Century: The Rise of Hybrid Wars* (Arlington, VA: Potomac Institute for Policy Studies, December 2007).

1. THE LANGUAGE OF WAR

1. Antulio J. Echevarria II, *Preparing for One War and Getting Another?* (US Army Strategic Studies Institute, Advancing Strategic Thought Series, September 2010), p. 26.

2. The operation involved several other units on the British side, especially a company from the Royal Welsh Regiment, and other nationalities, particularly Dutch, Australian and United States, as well as Afghan army and police units.

3. This phrase was coined by Paul Watzlawick; see Paul Watzlawick, John Weakland, Richard Fisch, *Change: Principles of Problem Formation and Problem Resolution* (New York: W. W. Norton, 1974). This Book drew on work by Gregory Bateson, *Steps to an Ecology of Mind* (Chicago: University of Chicago Press, 1972).

4. Dr Conrad Crane, US Army War College, Counterinsurgency Workshop held at Merton College, Oxford, 26 May 2011. The Counterinsurgency Field Manual referred to is the *Unites States US Marine Corps and US Army Field Manual 3–24*.

5. Carl von Clausewitz, *On War*, Book 1, ch. 1, trans. Michael Howard and Peter Paret (Princeton: Princeton University Press, 1976), p. 87.

6. Ibid., Book 2, ch. 1, p. 126.

7. George MacDonald Fraser, *Quartered Safe Out Here: A Recollection of the War in Burma*, (London: Harper Collins, 1995; first published by Harvill, 1992), p. 49.

8. See Hew Strachan, 'The British Way in Warfare', ch. 19 in *The Oxford History of the British Army*, ed. David Chandler and Ian Beckett (Oxford: Oxford University Press, 1994), p. 402.

9. The US strategic concept of 'limited war', which developed in response to concern over escalation to nuclear war, exemplifies the very real influence that 'war' can exert on policy as a future possibility rather than an actual event. Such a concept was expressed most prominently by the post-war theories of 'Limited War' (coined by Robert Osgood in his Book *Limited War*), in which war is used as a regulated political instrument without escalation to absolute (nuclear) war. See Robert E. Osgood, *Limited War: The Challenge to American Strategy* (Chicago: University of Chicago Press, 1957).

10. Clausewitz, *On War*, Book 2, ch. 1, p. 127; also Book 6, ch. 1, p. 357.

11. Ibid., Book 4, ch. 11, p. 260.

12. Ibid., Book 8, ch. 6B, p. 605. Andreas Herberg-Rothe notes that the explicit connection that Clausewitz makes in this passage between war and language is located in the way in which grammar was conceptually understood at the time. Herberg-Rothe argues that much of the content of Clausewitz's conceptualisation of war can be found in an article on grammar in the *Enzyklopädie der Wissenschaften und Künste* (Encyclopaedia of the Sciences and the Arts, ed. Ersch and Gruber, First Section A-G ed. H. Brockhaus (Leipzig, 1865), pp. 1–80), if one substitutes 'language' for 'war'. Thus just as the speech or writing of thought (the equivalent of political intention)

are regulated by grammar, so too is war. Herberg-Rothe argues that for Clausewitz the concept of grammar 'illustrates both war's unity with a greater whole and its relative autonomy' (Andreas Herberg-Rothe, *Clausewitz's Puzzle*, Oxford: Oxford University Press: 2007, p. 151). He notes the fact that the treatment of grammar in this encyclopaedia required an entry of almost 80 pages. Hardly any other concepts are examined so comprehensively. This indicates the significance of the concept at the time.

13. See, for example, John Cantile, 'Upper Gereshk: The Helmand plan meets tough reality', *BBC News Online*, 2 October 2011, http://www.bbc.co.uk/news/magazine-14897977.

14. Declan Walsh, 'Video of girl's flogging as Taliban hand out justice', *Guardian Online*, 2 April 2009, http://www.guardian.co.uk/world/2009/apr/02/taliban-pakistan-justice-women-flogging.

15. This analogy specifically relates to the study of hermeneutics in a theological sense. I have used the term 'interpretive' rather than 'hermeneutic' throughout the Book for simplicity and accessibility.

16. See James Simpson, *Burning to Read, English Fundamentalism and its Reformation Opponents* (Cambridge, MA: Harvard University Press, 2007).

17. Clausewitz, *On War*, Book 3, ch. 1, p. 182.

18. Chancellor Angela Merkel first referred to German troops being involved in 'combat operations' in September 2009. This represented a gradual progression of the German conception of the mission. Before German involvement in Kunduz Province (North Afghanistan) in 2007, the German Ministry of Defence referred to soldiers who 'died' in Afghanistan; post 2007 they 'fell'. This acknowledged that the mission was more than just reconstruction, but it was not 'combat' until 2009. Dr Timo Noetzel, University of Konstanz, lecture at the Oxford University Changing Character of War Programme, 22 February 2011. See also Timo Noetzel, 'The German Politics of War: Kunduz and the War in Afghanistan', *International Affairs*, vol. 87, issue 2 (March 2011), pp. 397–417,

19. Hew Strachan, 'Strategy and the Limitation of War', *Survival*, vol. 50, no. 1 (Feb.-March 2008), pp. 31–54.

20. Ibid., p. 35.

21. Ibid., p. 35.

22. Rupert Smith, *The Utility of Force* (London: Penguin, 2006; first published by Allen Lane, 2005), p. 302.

23. Although even in wars of this type the boundaries are only ever essentially the same. The controversy over the sinking of the *General Belgrano* (whether it was within the 'war zone') illustrates this point in the case of the Falklands. Moreover, the Falklands War of 1982 was not the start or the end of the conflict in the wider sense: for example, there had been a possibility of

an Argentinian operation during the Callaghan government; Argentinian reconnaissance patrols on the Islands have occasionally been reported post the 1982 war; the Argentinian government still uses the issue to gain political leverage in domestic politics. The basic political problems remain unresolved today.

24. *'Quintili Vare, legiones redde!'* Suetonius, *Vita Divi Augusti*, 23.49.
25. Harry Kreisler and Thomas G. Barnes, 'Military Strategy: Conversation with Colonel Harry G. Summers Jr', interview held on 6 March 1996. Full citation can be found at http://globetrotter.berkeley.edu/conversations/Summers/summers2.html.

2. CLAUSEWITZIAN WAR AND CONTEMPORARY CONFLICT

1. Museum of Military History, Vienna. Copyright 2012.
2. The Gurkha platoon commander was Lieutenant Paul Hollingshead, who was awarded a Mention in Dispatches for leading a counter-attack in this ambush.
3. House of Commons Foreign Affairs Committee, Eighth Report on Global Security, 'Afghanistan and Pakistan' (21 July 2009), ch. 6, paragraph 245.
4. Damien McElroy, 'Afghan governor turned 3,000 men over to Taliban', *Daily Telegraph*, 20 November 2009.
5. Antonio Giustozzi and Noor Ullah, 'Tribes and Warlords in Southern Afghanistan 1980–2005' (London School of Economics Crisis States Research Centre Working Paper, 2006), pp. 12–13.
6. Sher Mohammed Akhundzada comes from the Hassanzai sub-tribe of the Alizai tribe. While Provincial Governor of Helmand he also oppressed Alizais from other sub-tribes (Pirzai and Khalozai). His affiliation with the Alizai tribe is used here in the broad sense for simplicity.
7. The National Directorate of Security (NDS) is the Afghan equivalent of MI5.
8. Mike Martin, *A Brief History of Helmand* (British Army Publication by the Afghan COIN Centre, August 2011), p. 49. Martin cites Sarah Chayes, *The Punishment of Virtue: Inside Afghanistan after the Taliban* (London: Portobello Books, 2007, first published by Penguin, 2006), pp. 274–9.
9. Pajhwok Afghan News, 'Dozens of insurgents killed, 60 rounded up in Helmand' (11 September 2005), http://www.pajhwok.com/en/2005/09/11/dozens-insurgents-killed-60-rounded-helmand. See Martin, *A Brief History of Helmand*, pp. 47–51 for a much broader discussion of this theme.
10. Mike Martin, *A Brief History of Helmand*. Martin cites International Crisis Group, 'Afghanistan: The problem of Pashtun Alienation' (*Asia Report* no. 62, 2003), p. 18; Joel Hafvenstein, *Opium Season, A Year on the Afghan*

Frontier (Lyons Press, 2007), p. 132; Economist Intelligence Unit, 'Country Reports—Afghanistan' (Q2/3003), p. 9; Ali A. Jalali, 'Afghanistan in 2002: The Struggle to Win the Peace', *Asian Survey* (2003), p. 183; Sarah Chayes, *The Punishment of Virtue* (London: Portobello Books, 2007), pp. 273–4.

11. Sarah Chayes, *The Punishment of Virtue.*
12. Antonio Giustozzi, *Koran, Kalashnikov and Laptop: The Neo-Taliban Insurgency in Afghanistan 2002–2007* (Columbia University Press, 2008), p. 60.
13. Stephen Carter and Kate Clark, 'No Shortcut to Stability: Justice, Politics and Insurgency in Afghanistan' (Chatham House Paper, December 2010), p. 18.
14. General Sir Peter Wall, evidence to House of Commons Defence Committee, Fourth Report, *Operations in Afghanistan* (17 July 2011), pp. Ev 145, Q 676.
15. David Kilcullen, *The Accidental Guerrilla: Fighting Small Wars in the Midst of a Big One* (London: Hurst, 2009).
16. The district governor of Nad Ali in this case was Habibullah. I am grateful to Mike Martin for this observation.
17. House of Commons Foreign Affairs Committee, Eighth Report on Global Security, 'Afghanistan and Pakistan' (21 July 2009), ch. 6, paragraph 230.
18. House of Commons Foreign Affairs Committee, Fourth Report, *The UK's foreign policy approach to Afghanistan and Pakistan* (February 2011), paragraph 103.
19. Anthony King, 'A private war Britain must settle if it is to win in Helmand', *Parliamentary Brief Magazine* (28 April 2011).
20. House of Commons Defence Committee, Fourth Report, *Operations in Afghanistan* (17 July 2011).
21. Ibid., pp. Ev 144–5, Q 674.
22. For narrative simplicity I have not mentioned the other international coalition partners who operated in Helmand in 2006, most notably US, Canadian, Danish, and Estonian troops.
23. Clausewitz, *On War*, Book 3, ch. 12, Howard and Paret, p. 205.
24. Ibid., Book1, ch. 1, p. 75. Andreas Herberg-Rothe has argued that: 'This assumption of symmetry in the concept of the duel has far reaching consequences. Clausewitz's argument here reflects the political theory of the eighteenth century, according to which every state had the right to wage war. This concept differed from the medieval idea of 'just war' by assuming that the right to wage war was an aspect of every state's sovereignty. This symmetry brings with it a tendency to justify wars, but it has other consequences as well. It includes a recognition in principle that one's opponent is *iustus hostis*—an equal—so the enemy is no longer considered a crimi-

nal. This assumption that enemies in war are equal is the basic precondition of respect for the laws of war'. Andreas Herberg-Rothe, *Clausewitz's Puzzle*, p. 106. Herberg-Rothe cites Carl Schmitt, *Der Begriff des Politischen*, 6th edn (Berlin, 1996), p. 29.

25. Clausewitz had intended to write a separate chapter on the principle of polarity. In an article written shortly before he died, he stated that: 'the whole of physical and intellectual nature' is kept in balance by means of antitheses. Clausewitz, *On War*, p. 83. On the article written before his death, see Andreas Herberg-Rothe, *Clausewitz's Puzzle*, p. 119. Herberg-Rothe cites Clausewitz, *Die Verhältnisse Europas seit der Teilung Polens*, in Karl Schwartz, *Leben des Generals Carl von Clausewitz und der Frau Marie von Clausewitz geb. Gräfin Brühl*, 2 vols. (Berlin, 1878), pp. 401–17.

26. There is debate about the translation of *ganze Krieg*. Alternative translations have used total war, ideal war, or pure war. There are two tensions at play. First, does one mean absolute political goals or absolute use of violence? Second, is absolute war a theoretical pole which war in the abstract can be analysed by, or is it a real event? While both ideas are problematic, the definition I would use stresses the absoluteness of political goals over violence, although the latter is no doubt central to defining the quality of the conflict; it is hard to argue that combat in any context is not absolute for the individual. The key seems to be the correlation between political goals in terms of their proximity to absolute political objectives and the extent to which they remove qualitative restraints upon the means by which violence is applied. I also take absolute war to be a theoretical pole which has been closely approached, but not actually reached, because all wars have ultimately ended. (A full-scale nuclear exchange might well be absolute war in reality.)

27. Clausewitz, *On War*, Book 6, ch. 28, pp. 488–9.
28. Ibid., Book 6, ch. 7, p. 377.
29. Ibid., Book 7, ch. 1, p. 523.
30. Ibid., Book 7, ch. 7, pp. 530–31.
31. Ibid., Book 1, ch. 1, p. 84.
32. Ibid., Book 1, ch. 1, p. 83.
33. What is meant by attack and defence here is 'the attacker' and 'the defender'. Ibid., Book 7, ch. 22, p. 566.
34. J. C. Wylie, *Military Strategy: A General Theory of Power Control* (New York: Rutgers, 1967), p. 85.
35. Tacitus, *Agricola*, ch. 30.
36. Ibid., Book 1, ch. 2, p. 90.
37. *Gladiator* (2000).
38. Clausewitz, *On War*, Book 1, ch. 1, p. 77.

39. Field Marshal Viscount William Slim, *Defeat into Victory* (London: Pan Books, 2009; first published by Cassell, 1956), pp. 609–10.
40. Clausewitz, *On War*, Book 7, ch. 5, p. 528.
41. Wolfgang Schivelbusch, *The Culture of Defeat: On National Trauma, Mourning, and Recovery*, trans. Jefferson Chase (London: Granta, 2003).
42. Both Rifleman Padam and Corporal Basanta were awarded the UK Chief of Joint Operation's Commander's Commendation for their part in this action.
43. Major Shaun Chandler was awarded a Mention in Dispatches as a Company Commander on this tour.
44. Ibid., Book1, ch. 1, p. 88.
45. General Raymond Odierno, quoted in Steven Lee Myers and Thom Shanker, 'General Works to Salvage Iraq Legacy', *New York Times* (24 March 2010). Cited by Hew Strachan, 'Strategy or Alibi? Obama, McChrystal and the Operational Level of War', *Survival*, 52:5, p. 176.
46. Clausewitz, *On War*, Book 1, ch. 2, p. 95.
47. Ibid., Book 1, ch. 2, p. 98.
48. Daniel Moran has argued that this was very much Clausewitz's view. There is a strong argument that eighteenth-century wars were just as vicious, and were by no means a game, but that commanders were logistically constrained from the exploitation of a victory to crush the enemy completely. In the Seven Years War (1756–63), for example, all of the great battles took place in the first four years, but the war dragged on and ultimately ended not on the battlefield but through mutual exhaustion. By comparison, Moran points out that the Austerlitz campaign of 1806, which was a decisive and massive victory for Napoleon, was over in three weeks. See Daniel Moran, *Strategic Theory and the History of War* (US Naval Postgraduate School, 2001), p. 6.
49. Clausewitz, *On War*, Book 8, ch. 8, trans. O. J. Matthijs Jolles (New York: Random House, 1943), p. 570.
50. Hew Strachan, *Clausewitz's On War: A Biography* (London: Atlantic Books, 2007), p. 61.
51. Clausewitz, *On War*, Book 8, ch. 8A, Howard and Paret, p. 593.
52. Ibid., Book 8, ch. 8A, pp. 583–4; Book 8, ch. 2, p. 581.
53. Ibid., Book 8, ch.3A, pp. 583–4.

3. GLOBALISATION AND CONTEMPORARY CONFLICT

1. Rupert Smith, *The Utility of Force: The Art of War in the Modern World* (London: Allen Lane, 2005), p. 1.
2. Patrick Porter, *Military Orientalism: Eastern War Through Western Eyes* (Columbia University Press/Hurst, 2009), pp. 173–4.

3. Patrick Porter, *Military Orientalism*, p. 174.
4. Ibid., p. 174.
5. Dan Halutz, 'Airpower as a Variable of Hachraah', in 'Ben Hachra'ah L'nitzachon (Between Decision and Victory)': A Joint Seminar between the Center for Study of National Defense, Haifa University and the National Defense College, IDF, 28 January 2001 (Haifa: University of Haifa, 2001), p. 96.
6. Dan Halutz, 'Airpower as a Variable of Hachraah', p. 98.
7. Patrick Porter, *Military Orientalism*, p. 184.
8. US Army/Marine Corps Field Manual 3–24, *Counter-Insurgency*.
9. Lieutenant General (retired) Sir Graeme Lamb, direction issued as Commander Field Army, *Counter-Insurgency Commander's Guidance*, May 2009.
10. Such as Tehrik-i Taliban Pakistan (TTP), Lashkar-i Tayyiba (LT), Tehrik-i-Nifaz-i-Shariat-i-Muhammadi (TNSM), Harakat-ul-Jihad-al-Islami (HuJI), the Qari Zia Group (QZG), Lashkar-i-Islami (LI), Lashkar-i-Jhangvi, the Islamic Movement of Uzbekistan (IMU), the Islamic Jihad Union (IJU). See Gretchen Peters, 'Crime and Insurgency in the Tribal Areas of Afghanistan and Pakistan', The Combating Terrorism Center at West Point, October 2010; Peters' list at p. 5 is particularly helpful.
11. This is well encapsulated by the term 'accidental guerrilla', coined by David Kilcullen and referred to in *The Accidental Guerrilla: Fighting Small Wars in the Midst of a Big One* (London: Hurst, 2009).
12. Martine van Bijlert, 'Unruly Commanders and Violent Power Struggles: Taliban Networks in Uruzgan', ch. 7 in Antonio Giustozzi (ed.), *Decoding the New Taliban: Insights from the Afghan Field*, (London: Hurst, 2009), pp. 160–61.
13. Ibid., p. 160. Bernt Glatzer as cited in Robert D. Crews, 'Moderate Taliban?', in Robert D. Crews and Amin Tarzi (eds), *The Taliban and the Crisis of Afghanistan* (Cambridge, MA.: Harvard University Press, 2008), p. 242.
14. Adam Holloway, *In Blood Stepp'd In Too Far: Towards A Realistic Policy for Afghanistan* (Centre for Policy Studies, October 2009), p. 14.
15. Daniel Marston, 'Realizing the Extent of Our Errors and Forging the Road Ahead: Afghanistan 2001–10', in Daniel Marston and Carter Malkasian (eds), *Counterinsurgency in Modern Warfare*, (Oxford: Osprey Publishing, 2010).
16. Ahmed Rashid, 'The Way Out of Afghanistan', *New York Review of Books* (13 January 2011), quoted in House of Commons Foreign Affairs Committee, Fourth Report, *The UK's foreign policy approach to Afghanistan and Pakistan* (February 2011), paragraph 85.
17. The Revolutionary United Front, for instance, were heavily involved in the

destabilisation of Sierra Leone that led to the successful British intervention 2000. They were a 'franchise' of different militia groups held together
by their commander. He kept control over them through a number of methods that resembled a franchise, such as retaining control over the distribution of logistics, especially ammunition. He would personally hold the key
to the ammunition store and distribute it. Brigadier Richard Iron, *Expert
Military Witness Report into the Revolutionary United Front*, written for the
Special Court of Sierra Leone. Note on relationship between logistics and
command at p.C-51; report dated 15 April 2005.

18. Patrick Porter, *Military Orientalism*, p. 156.
19. Antonio Giustozzi, 'Armed Politics and Political Competition in Afghani-
    stan', Chr. Michelsen Institute (CMI) Working Paper, 2011.
20. Antonio Giustozzi, 'Armed Politics and Political Competition in Afghani-
    stan', p. 19. Giustozzi cites as his sources: local notables, administration
    staff, Afghan intellectuals, UN officials. Map by Sebastian Ballard.
21. Antonio Giustozzi, 'Armed Politics and Political Competition in Afghani-
    stan', p. 22. Giustozzi notes that MPs with a past in *Hizb-i Islami*, but cur-
    rently affiliated with other groups, have been excluded. He cites as his
    sources interviews with former and current members of *Hizb-i Islami*, Kabul,
    London, Jalalabad 2006–7; his personal communications with UN and
    diplomatic staff. Map by Sebastian Ballard.
22. Clausewitz, *On War*, Book 1, ch. 1, Howard and Paret, p. 89. It has been
    argued that association of policy with 'government' in the state at war can
    be understood more broadly than 'government'. Clausewitz uses the word
    der Regierung which can imply regimen, or governing authority, as well as
    government. In this reading reason, or policy, can be associated with the
    'cohesive' element which provides the unifying rationale within any 'polit-
    ical community' (the state in the broad sense). This reading would imply
    that Clausewitz's intention was to resist tying his theory exclusively to the
    nation-state, or at least that Clausewitz's theory of war has legitimacy beyond
    the nation-state. See Andreas Herberg-Rothe, *Clausewitz's Puzzle: The Polit-
    ical Theory of War*, (London: OUP, 2007). pp. 99, 141–2 and 164. More-
    over, the term 'state' has been understood more metaphorically in terms of
    the representative parts of an individual, or a 'body' of men more gener-
    ally: the rational mind (reason/policy); one's emotions (passion); the abil-
    ity to fight (to deal with violence). Whether Clausewitz himself allowed for
    the possibility of his paradigm being literally, rather than metaphorically,
    applied to political communities that were not nation-states is debatable.
    Clausewitz, *On War*, Book1, ch. 1, p. 88; Book 8, ch. 6, pp. 606–7.
23. Clausewitz, *On War*, Book 2, ch. 2, Howard and Paret, p. 138.
24. Tacitus, *Histories*, Book 1–39. This phrase is used by Tacitus in the context
    of plotting during the Roman Civil War of 68 to 69 ACE.

25. Stathis N. Kalyvas, *The Logic of Violence in Civil War* (New York: Cambridge University Press, 2006). See in particular ch. 11, 'Cleavage and Agency', pp. 364–87.
26. Ibid., p. 364.
27. Ibid., p. 389.
28. Ibid., p. 387.
29. David Loyn, *Butcher and Bolt: Two Hundred Years of Foreign Engagement in Afghanistan* (London: Hutchinson, 2008), p. 89.
30. Ibid. pp. 143–162.
31. Ibid. pp. 88–94.
32. Ibid. p. 121.
33. Ibid. p. 146.
34. Ibid. p. 161.
35. John Masters, *Bugles and a Tiger*, (New York: The Viking Press, 1956), p. 191.

4. STRATEGIC DIALOGUE AND POLITICAL CHOICE

1. Dr Conrad Crane was the editor of the *Unites States US Marine Corps and US Army Field Manual 3–24*.
2. I am grateful to Dr Conrad Crane of the US Army War College for these illustrations, from a presentation given by Lieutenant General David Petraeus at Fort Leavenworth in February 2006.
3. Colonel Joseph Felter, US Army, Royal United Services Institute Conference on Counterinsurgency Tactics, London, 8–9 December 2010.
4. Admiral J. C. Wylie, *Military Strategy: A General Theory of Power Control* (Annapolis, MD: Naval Institute Press, 1967).
5. Frederick Spencer Chapman, *The Jungle is Neutral* (London: Chatto and Windus,1949).
6. Bob Woodward, *Obama's Wars*, ch. 30, p. 350.
7. House of Commons Defence Committee, Fourth Report, *Operations in Afghanistan* (17 July 2011), pp. Ev 67, Q 295.
8. David Kilcullen, *Counter-Insurgency in Iraq, Theory and Practice 2007*, PowerPoint presentation, available on the *Small Wars Journal* website, slide 26.
9. Antonio Giustozzi, 'Armed Politics and Political Competition in Afghanistan', in Astri Suhrke and Mats Berdal (eds), *The Peace In Between: Post-War Violence and Peacebuilding* (London: Routledge, 2011).
10. Lieutenant General Sir Graeme Lamb, *Counter-Insurgency Commander's Guidance*, British Army internal unclassified publication (May 2009).
11. William S. Lind, Colonel Keith Nightengale, Captain John F. Schmitt, Colonel Joseph W. Sutton, and Lieutenant Colonel Gary I. Wilson, *The*

Changing Face of War: Into the Fourth Generation, Marine Corps *Gazette* (October 1989), pp. 22–6; 'Bin Laden Lieutenant Admits to Sept. 11 and Explains Al-Qa'ida's Combat Doctrine', Middle East Media and Research Institute, Special Dispatch 344 (10 February 2002); cited by Patrick Porter, *Military Orientalism*, p. 63.

12. Neil Sheehan, *A Bright Shining Lie* (London: Pimlico, 1998; first published by Jonathan Cape 1989), p. 67.

13. 'Remembering the Vietnam War, Conversations with Neil Sheehan' (14 November 1988), part of 'Conversations with History', University of California, http://globetrotter.berkeley.edu/conversations/Sheehan/sheehan-con6.html

14. Neil Sheehan, *Bright Shining Lie*, p. 317.

15. Ibid., p. 697.

16. General Sir Frank Kitson, *Low Intensity Operations: Subversion, Insurgency, Peace-keeping* (London: Faber and Faber, 1971), p. 72. Kitson set out very clearly thirty years ago many of the lessons that have taken the British Army eight years to re-learn in Afghanistan. Kitson advertises as a model the US military, which by 1970 had become in his eyes a highly effective counter-insurgency force in Vietnam; the irony being that this experience was subsequently largely jettisoned by the US military, forcing them to (successfully) re-learn their older lessons in Iraq and Afghanistan. Kitson also criticises the widely held view among army officers on both sides of the Atlantic (of his time, but which is also to be found today) that the army should get back to 'proper soldiering' (conventional conflict), and that 'a fit solider with a rifle' can accomplish any task. He points out that this is simply not true. Subversion and counter-insurgency are professional specialisations which any force will struggle to improvise. History repeats itself. (pp. 199–200).

5. LIBERAL POWERS AND STRATEGIC DIALOGUE

1. There is an issue of translation here. See Clausewitz, *On War*, Howard and Paret, p. 608 footnote 1.

2. Clausewitz, *On War*, Book 8, ch. 9, Howard and Paret, p.633.

3. Samuel Huntington, *The Soldier and the State* (Cambridge, MA: Harvard Belknap Press, 1957).

4. The historical roots of this idea lie more with Jomini (1779–1869), the Swiss-born theorist of warfare, than with Clausewitz. John Shy in his essay on Jomini argues that it was he who popularised the idea that 'interference' by strategically naïve political leaders led to military failure. Jomini used the example of Austria, which lost many major campaigns between 1756 and

1815, by comparison with the success of Frederick the Great or Napoleon, who united the political and military in one man. Shy notes that: 'these difficulties were a central theme of *On War*, but soldiers managed to read even Clausewitz in ways that twisted his meanings back into comfortable formulae'. John Shy, 'Jomini', in Peter Paret (ed.), *Makers of Modern Strategy* (Princeton: Princeton University Press, 1986), p. 161.

5. Clausewitz, *On War*, Book 8, ch. 6, Howard and Paret, p. 608.
6. Huntington, *The Soldier and the State*, p. 100.
7. Ibid., p. 73.
8. Ibid., p. 74.
9. Ibid., p. 308. Huntington cites Command and General Staff School, *Principles of Strategy*, pp. 19–20; USNIP, XLVI (1920), pp. 1615–16.
10. Ibid., pp. 322–5.
11. Ibid., p. 329.
12. Ibid., p. 336; Huntington cites *Hearings before the Senate Committee on Military Affairs* on S.84, 79th Cong., 1st Sess. (1945), p. 521.
13. Ibid., p. 344.
14. Ibid., p. 456.
15. Ibid., pp. 465–6.
16. This conception of strategy can be found in Clausewitz, although in its modern form it is associated with the work of Arthur F. Lykke. See 'Towards an Understanding of Military Strategy' in the US Army War College *Guide to Strategy* (2001), ch. 13, p. 179.
17. Harry R. Yarger, *Strategic Theory for the 21st Century: The Little Book on Big Strategy*, US Army War College (February 2006), p. 1.
18. J. C. Wylie, *Military Strategy*, p. 78.
19. Clausewitz, *On War*, Book 8, ch. 6B, pp. 606–7.
20. Ibid., Book 2, ch. 4, p. 152.
21. Ibid., Book 2, ch.1, p. 128.
22. Hew Strachan, 'The Lost Meaning of Strategy', *Survival*, vol. 47, no. 3 (Autumn 2005), p. 35.
23. Loc. cit.
24. Harry R. Yarger, *Strategic Theory for the 21st Century: The Little Book on Big Strategy*, p. 12, reproduced with permission of the author.
25. 'Military experts, not political amateurs, should decide whether we go to war', Oxford University debate, 2010. http://www.ox.ac.uk/oxford_debates/past_debates/hilary_2010_war/index.html
26. International Security and Assistance Force website (ISAF): http://www.isaf.nato.int/mission.html
27. See COMISAF's Initial Assessment to the Secretary of Defense (30 August 2009), obtained by the *Washington Post*. http://media.washingtonpost.com/wp-srv/politics/documents/Assessment_Redacted_092109.pdf

28. Prime Minister Gordon Brown, speech on 13 December 2008.
29. See for example Adam Holloway MP, 'In Blood Stepp'd In Too Far: Towards a Realistic Policy for Afghanistan', paper for the Centre for Policy Studies (October 2009), p. 5: He challenges a statement from the British Ministry of Defence in 2009 that 'our commitment is first and foremost about Britain's national security interest. Put starkly, the choice is between fighting the AQ insurgents in Afghanistan, and fighting them on the streets of UK towns'. Holloway's response is: 'this statement from the MoD is nonsense. Put starkly, our current situation is working against the West's security interest and is making attacks on the streets of Britain more, not less, likely'.
30. Woodward, *Obama's Wars*, pp. 271, 239.
31. NATO OPLAN 10302 (Revise 1), Unclassified version released December 2005, p. 1, paragraph d. See also Lt.Col. Steve Beckman '*From Assumption to Expansion: Planning and Executing NATO's First Year in Afghanistan at the Strategic Level*' (Carlisle, PA: US Army War College, 2005).
32. Ibid., p. 2, paragraph 2.
33. Ibid., p. A-2, paragraph b.
34. Adam Holloway MP, *Hansard* vol. 477, Part 112. UK Parliament Westminster Hall Debate, 17 June 2009.
35. Clausewitz, *On War*, Book 1, ch. 1, p. 77.
36. Ibid., Book 1, ch. 1, p. 87. Note that Clausewitz used the word *Politik*, which does not differentiate between policy and politics.
37. Ibid., Book 8, ch. 6B, p. 605.
38. J. C. Wylie, *Military Strategy*, p. 80.
39. 'The aims a belligerent adopts, and the resources he employs, must be governed by the particular characteristics of his own position; but they will also conform to the general spirit of the age and to its general character. Finally, they must always be governed by the general conclusions to be drawn from the nature of war itself'. Clausewitz, *On War*, Book 8, ch. 3, p. 594.

6. PRAGMATISM AND OPERATIONAL THOUGHT

1. Clausewitz, *On War*, Book 2, ch. 1, Howard and Paret, p. 128.
2. A doctrinal distinction between centre of gravity and decisive point can also be made.
3. Ibid., Book 8, ch. 4, p. 596.
4. 'War can be a matter of degree. Theory must concede all this; but it has the duty to give priority to the absolute form of war and to make that form a general point of reference, so that he who wants to learn from theory becomes accustomed to keeping that point in view constantly, to measuring all his hopes and fears by it, and to approximating it *when he can*, or *when he must* [italics original]… Without the cautionary examples of the destructive power

of war unleashed, theory would preach to deaf ears. No one would have believed possible what has now been experienced by all'. Clausewitz here is referring to the huge expansion in scale and lethality in war that European states experienced during the Napoleonic Wars. Clausewitz, *On War*, Book 8, ch. 2, Howard and Paret, p. 581.

5. Ibid., Book 4, ch. 9, p. 248. Clausewitz has been criticised, perhaps legitimately, for advocating methods that stressed, sometimes obsessively, the imperative to seek physical destruction of the enemy. To ignore aspects of Clausewitz that are largely unpalatable today is to be partial. We should not brush over the brutality of aspects of his argument. There is undoubtedly an element of obsession with the destruction of the enemy that one can read in many parts of the work. He states that 'the price of battle is blood', and that if a general 'blunts his sword in the name of humanity', eventually somebody would 'come along with a sharp sword and hack off our arms' (Ibid., Book 4, ch. 11, pp. 259–60). While apparently brutal, Clausewitz does not seem to make a fetish of war's brutality; that was war as he had experienced it. Indeed in some ways he is more honest about war than accounts that keep their distance from actual description of the battlefield. One of the most striking and original parts of *On War* is the short series of chapters at the end of Book 1 which vividly describe actual battlefield experience (Ibid., Book 1, ch. 4,5,6,7, pp. 113–21). While this argument had purchase at the time in which Clausewitz wrote, it would not today, especially in the context of nuclear warfare and a very different ethical and legal environment. Furthermore, one of Clausewitz's intentions was for *On War* to be of practical value to soldiers in war. In that context, he was trying to come to terms with the problem of how to deal with a potential enemy who would use Napoleonic methods. To that end, the last chapter of *On War* is a long description of how to fight a hypothetical war against France. In the context of Europe immediately after the Napoleonic Wars, it would have made sense for Clausewitz in *On War* to have suggested operational methods which had been proven as effective by Napoleon: 'our conviction that only a great battle can produce a major decision is founded not on an abstract concept of war alone, but also on experience' (Ibid., Book 4, ch. 11, p. 260). Indeed, it was by imitating his methods that his opponents had ultimately defeated Napoleon.

6. Ibid., Book 4, ch. 11, p. 260.

7. Andreas Herberg-Rothe, *Clausewitz's Puzzle*, p. 32. Herberg-Rothe cites Carl von Clausewitz, *The Campaign of 1815. Strategic Overview*, p. 89, translated and edited by Daniel Moran, unpublished manuscript (Monterey: 2005).

8. Clausewitz, *On War*, Book 6, ch. 30, p. 501.

9. Ibid., *On War*, Book 8, ch. 3, p. 582.

10. Ibid., *On War*, Book 3, ch.16, p. 218.
11. Ibid., *On War*, Book 6, ch. 30, p. 516.
12. Ibid., *On War*, Book 8, ch.4, p. 597.
13. Clausewitz, *Two Letters on Strategy* (1827), edited and translated by Peter Paret and Daniel Moran (1984). http://www.clausewitz.com/readings/TwoLetters/TwoLetters.htm
14. Clausewitz's views evolved as he was writing *On War*, which was an unfinished Book at the time of his death. In many places he can legitimately be seen to be obsessed with the destruction of the enemy, and advocates this as the default operational method. Yet in the books he revised towards the end of his life, namely Book 1 and Book 8, the mature Clausewitz offers a far more nuanced analysis which recognises the primacy of policy and the need of an operational approach to satisfy political objectives.
15. Clausewitz, *On War*, Book 6, ch. 30, p. 516.
16. Clausewitz's work only came to real prominence in Europe following Prussia's successes in the wars of German unification (1866–71).
17. Both Jomini and Clausewitz drew upon, and challenged, the work of a retired Prussian Officer, Heinrich von Bülow (1757–1807). Bülow's conception of strategy conformed to its 'traditional' location, between tactics and policy; strategy was defined as: 'all military movements within the enemy's cannon range or range of vision', tactics was 'all movements within this range'. What distinguished Clausewitz and Jomini's works in relation to Bülow's was their reaction to his advocacy of universal military principles. Peter Paret, the American military historian and Clausewitz specialist, has argued that Jomini agreed with Bülow's approach, but disagreed with his conclusions, replacing Bülow's universal principles with his own. Peter Paret, *The Cognitive Challenge of War, Prussia 1806* (Princeton: Princeton University Press, 2009), pp. 111–12.
18. This was the concluding 35th chapter of the 3rd volume of his *Traité de grande tactique*.
19. Peter Paret, *The Cognitive Challenge of War, Prussia 1806* (Princeton: Princeton University Press, 2009), pp. 111–12; see footnote 6 on p. 111 for discussion of publication dates of the *Résumé*.
20. Clausewitz criticised General von Bülow and Antoine-Henri Jomini for looking for set rules that applied universally in war. This is perhaps an unfair criticism given that their views were in fact very similar to his; the key difference is the distinction as to the context in which they are applied. See for example the extensive footnote in *On War*, Book 6, ch. 3, p. 363; also Book 6, ch. 30, p. 516.
21. Peter Paret, *The Cognitive Challenge of War*, pp. 112 and 129.
22. John Shy stresses how Jomini's view was that irregular warfare was not the

business of regular armies; he rejected civil wars and religious wars as 'wars of opinion' that were ill suited to rigorous analysis; Antoine-Henry Jomini, *Précis de l'art de la guerre*, new edn, 2 vols. (Paris, 1855; reprinted Osnabrück, 1973), 1:83. Jomini found guerrilla warfare morally repugnant; he did not think it was the business of regular armies. He wrote that soldiers prefer war *'loyale et chevaleresque'*. Jomini had for example written about the horrors of the French experience of guerrilla warfare in Spain. Jomini advanced that if armies were forced to engage in such conflict the principles of conventional war did not apply. Rather than striking a decisive point, a mobile force should be created, while other territorial 'divisions' garrisoned each conquered district; commanders of such forces should be *'instruit'* (politically attuned). Antoine-Henry Jomini, *Traité des grandes opérations militaires, contenant l'histoire des campagnes de Frédéric II, comparés à celles de l'empereur Napoléon; avec un recueil des principes généraux de l'art de la guerre*, 2nd edn, 4 vols. (Paris, 1811), 4: 284–85n; John Shy, 'Jomini', in Peter Paret (ed.), *Makers of Modern Strategy* (Princeton: Princeton University Press, 1986), pp. 170–71.

23. Shy, 'Jomini', pp. 179–84. The 'six principles' of the American Thayer Mahan's very influential *The Influence of Sea Power upon History 1660–1783* (1890), for example, popularised Jominian method in naval context. Giulio Douhet's *The Command of the Air* (1921) anticipated the notion of 'air power' and its associated principles.

24. Daniel Moran, *Strategic Theory and the History of War* (US Naval Postgraduate School, 2001), p. 7.

25. Karl-Heinz Frieser, *The Blitzkrieg Legend: The 1940 Campaign in the West*, translated by John T. Greenwood (Annapolis, MD: Naval Institute Press, 2005); first published as Karl-Heinz Frieser, *Blitzkrieg-Legende. Der Westfeldzug 1940* (Munich: Oldenbourg Verlag, 1995).

26. Ibid., cited in Hew Strachan, *The Lost Meaning of Strategy*, p. 46.

27. Hew Strachan, Clausewitz's *On War, A Biography*, p. 17.

28. Eric Ludendorff, *Kriegführung und Politik* (Berlin: E. S. Mittler, 1922), pp. 320–42. Cited in Hew Strachan, *The Lost Meaning of Strategy*, p. 45.

29. Neil Sheehan, *A Bright Shining Lie*, p. 637; this is the father of the General Krulak associated with the 'three block war' concept. See also Lieutenant Colonel John Nagl, 'Counter-insurgency in Vietnam', in Daniel Marston and Carter Malkasian (eds), *Counterinsurgency in Modern Warfare* (London: Osprey, 2008), p. 139.

30. Brian M. Jenkins, *The Unchangeable War*, RM-6278–2-ARPA (Santa Monica, CA: RAND, 1970), p. 3. The speaker is not identified by name.

31. Hew Strachan, 'Strategy or Alibi? Obama, McChrystal, and the Operational Level of War', *Survival*, 52:5 (2010),pp. 157–82.

32. Ibid., p. 160.
33. Strachan cites Tommy Franks, *American Soldier* (New York: Regan Books, 2004), p. 440.
34. Ibid., p. 166.
35. Edward Luttwak, *Strategy: The Logic of War and Peace* (Cambridge, MA: Belknap Harvard, revised enlarged edn 2002), p. 111. The same argument relates to the distinction between 'strategic' and 'tactical' nuclear weapons.
36. Shy, 'Jomini', p. 154.
37. Shy notes that this term had already been used by Henry Lloyd and the Prussian Colonel Fredrick von Tempelhoff.
38. 'Security and Stabilisation: The Military Contribution', Joint Doctrine Publication 3–40 (London: Ministry of Defence, 2009), pp. 4–24.
39. Susan L. Woodward, 'The Paradox of "State Failure", States Matter; Take Them Seriously', *Enjeux Internationaux* (Brussels), special issue on state failure edited by Jean-Paul Marthoz, no. 11, 2006, http://www.statesandsecurity.org/_pdfs/enjeuxintle.pdf
40. Gian P. Gentile, 'A Strategy of Tactics, Population Centric COIN and the Army', US Army War College *Parameters* magazine (Autumn 2009).
41. Edward Luttwak, 'Dead End: Counter-insurgency Warfare as Military Malpractice', *Harper's Magazine* (February 2007), pp. 33–42.
42. Daniel Dombey and Matthew Green, 'US shifts Afghan tactics to target Taliban', *Financial Times* (17 March 2011).
43. See particularly US DOD *Joint Force Quarterly* 52 (1st quarter 2009); 58 (3rd quarter 2009); two op-eds of *Small Wars Journal* in particular comment on the issue: Shawn Brimley, 'Mediating Between Crusaders and Conservatives' (October 2008), and Robert Haddick, 'Nagl and Gentile Are Both Right, So What Do We Do Now?' (November 2008).
44. Nagl has also argued for the creation of a corps of advisers to conduct low-level counter-insurgency-type missions worldwide in partnership with local forces to deal with potential conflicts before they become bigger problems.
45. John Nagl, *Learning to Eat Soup with a Knife: counterinsurgency lessons from Malaya and Vietnam* (Chicago: University of Chicago Press, 2005, reprint of an earlier thesis).
46. Brigadier General H. R. McMaster, 'On War: Lessons to be Learned', *Survival* (February-March 2008); cited by John Nagl, 'Let's Win the Wars We're In', US DOD Joint Force Quarterly 52 (1st quarter 2009), p. 23.
47. Bob Woodward, *Obama's Wars*, ch. 8, p. 83.
48. Ibid., Glossary, p. 381.
49. Colonel Gian P. Gentile, 'Freeing the Army from the Counter-insurgency Straitjacket', US DoD *Joint Force Quarterly* 58 (3rd quarter 2010), p. 121.

50. Colonel Gian P. Gentile, 'A Strategy of Tactics: Population Centric COIN and the Army', p. 6.
51. Plutarch, *Life of Pompey*, 10, 7.
52. John Paul Vann quoted in Neil Sheenan, *A Bright Shining Lie* (London: Jonathan Cape, 1988), p. 67.
53. General Sir Frank Kitson, *Low Intensity Operations: Subversion, Insurgency, Peace-keeping* (London: Faber and Faber, 1971), p. 199.
54. See for example *A New Way Forward, re-thinking US Strategy in Afghanistan*, A Report of the Afghanistan Study Group (August 2010).
55. Although most obviously associated with Malaya, the term 'hearts and minds' was possibly coined by Sir Robert Sandeman, a British official associated with the campaigns in South Baluchistan in the 1870s. See David Loyn, *Butcher and Bolt: Two Hundred Years of Foreign Engagement in Afghanistan* (London: Hutchinson, 2008), p. 162.
56. Alex Marshall, 'Imperial nostalgia, the liberal lie, and the perils of post-modern counter-insurgency', *Small Wars and Insurgencies Journal* 21:2 (2010), pp. 233–58. His argument concludes by criticising policy-makers in the context of Afghanistan for not having provided a political context in which counter-insurgency as an operational concept can have political utility, if the counter-insurgent is not the sovereign power. I would not go this far, as counter-insurgency was highly effective in Iraq, and has so far achieved localised effects in Afghanistan. However, I agree with Marshall's broader point about the critical association of political context and operational method.
57. Neil Sheehan, *Bright Shining Lie*, pp. 365, 373.
58. Ibid., p. 374.
59. British Army Training Team (BATT) notes on the raising and training of irregular forces in Dhofar, p. 65, paragraphs 4 and 12, document from the Middle East Centre, St Anthony's College, Oxford. I am grateful to the Counterinsurgency Scholars Programme at the US Command and General Staff College, Fort Leavenworth, run by Professor Daniel Marston, for this document.
60. Many of the observations for the Dhofar section were presented by veterans of the Oman Sultan's Armed Forces (SAF) at a conference in Oxford run by members of the US Army Counterinsurgency Scholars Programme, US Command and General Staff College, Fort Leavenworth. The SAF veterans present were: Ian Gordon, Mike Lobb MBE, Knobby Reid OBE, John McKeown. I am grateful to Lt. Col. (retired) McKeown for his unpublished Masters dissertation, *Britain and Oman: The Dhofar War and its Significance* (submitted to the University of Cambridge, 1981). See also Ian Gardiner, *In the Service of the Sultan, A First Hand Account of the Dhofar*

Insurgency (London: Pen and Sword, 2007). Also General Sir John Akehurst, *We Won a War* (Salisbury: Michael Russell, 1982); Peter Thwaites, *Muscat Command: The Muscat Regiment in Oman in 1967* (Combined Books, 1995).

61. Major Shaun Chandler and Captain Emile Simpson, 'The Shade-Shift Approach to Operations', *British Army Review*, no. 150 (Winter 2010/2011).

62. Emile Simpson, 'Gaining the Influence Initiative: Why Kinetic Operations are Central to Influence in Southern Afghanistan', *British Army Review*, no. 147 (Summer 2009).

63. I am not sure who coined this. I have tried and failed to find the source.

7. BRITISH STRATEGY IN THE BORNEO CONFRONTATION 1962–6

1. A good account of the diplomatic aspects of the Commonwealth position is presented in John Subritzky, *Confronting Sukarno* (London: Macmillan, 2000); the military contribution of Australian and New Zealand forces in particular is well covered in Peter Dennis and Jeffrey Grey, *Emergency and Confrontation: Australian Military Operations in Malaya and Borneo 1950–1966* (St Leonard's, NSW: Allen and Unwin, 1996); and Christopher Pugsley, *From Emergency to Confrontation: The New Zealand Armed Forces in Malaya and Borneo 1949–1966* (Oxford: Oxford University Press, 2003).

2. Denis Healey to the House of Commons, 27 November 1967, in General Sir Walter Walker, 'How Borneo Was Won', *The Round Table* (January 1969), p. 395.

3. J. A. C. Mackie, *Konfrontasi: The Indonesi-Malaysia Dispute 1963–1966* (London: Oxford University Press, 1974), p. 125.

4. Leifer notes how Dr Subandrio, in the same speech of 20 January 1963, 'reasserted the primacy in political life of Nasakom (the acronym which endorsed a harmonious integration of nationalist, religious and communist forces), without which Indonesia's unity was said to be impossible'. Michael Leifer, *Indonesia's Foreign Policy* (London: George Allen and Unwin, 1983), pp. 62, 79–82.

5. This period is well covered in Matthew Jones, *Conflict and Confrontation in South East Asia, 1961–65* (Cambridge: Cambridge University Press, 2002). Chapters 2 and 3 deal with the formation of Malaysia prior to Malaysia Day on 16 September 1963.

6. Matthew Jones offers an amusing vignette here. Major Roderick Walker, the assistant British military attaché in Jakarta and SAS officer, marched around the embassy in uniform playing the bagpipes while the crowd threw a bar-

rage of stones in 'a bizarre example of late imperial gusto'. Jones, *Conflict and Confrontation*, p. 196.

7. Ibid., pp. 34–7.
8. Jones, *Conflict and Confrontation*, p. 60.
9. 'Policy towards Indonesia', 6 January 1964, PRO: CP(64)5 CAB/129/116.
10. The Anglo-Malaysian Defence Agreement of 1957 allowed Britain to station troops on Malaysian soil.
11. 'Policy towards Indonesia', 6 January 1964, PRO: CP(64)5 CAB/129/116, p. 3727.
12. Although Labour won the October 1964 General Election, they continued with the same policy with regard to the Indonesian Confrontation, at least until the withdrawal east of Suez.
13. John Subritzky, *Confronting Sukarno* (London: Macmillan, 2000), ch.5, pp. 95–114.
14. Cabinet meeting, 18 February 1964, PRO: CM(64)12, CAB128/38.
15. Subritzky, *Confronting Sukarno*, p. 104.
16. Jones, *Conflict and Confrontation*, p. 293.
17. Walker, 'How Borneo Was Won', p. 1.
18. Note from Edward Peck, Assistant Under-secretary of State at Foreign Office 1961–6, note to Secretary of State, 19 October 1964, PRO: FO371/176484, IM 1192/15. See also 'British Policy towards Indonesia', April 1965, PRO: FO371/176484, IM 1051/7.
19. Paper from British High Commissioner in Malaysia to the Secretary of State for Commonwealth Relations entitled 'Malaysia: Confrontation', 11 December 1963, PRO: FO371/175065, p. 99.
20. Walter Walker, *Fighting On* (London: New Millennium,1997), p. 112.
21. Telephone interview with Lord Denis Healey (2005); he was the Minister of Defence during the Wilson government. Note that Walker was appointed during the previous administration, but continued to serve under the Labour government.
22. Walker, 'How Borneo Was Won', p. 3.
23. Tom Pockock, *Fighting General* (London: Collins, 1973), p. 173.
24. Walker, *Fighting On*, p. 150.
25. Walker, *Fighting On*, p. 164.
26. Interview with Brigadier (retired) Christopher Bullock, then curator of the Gurkha Museum, 1 July 2004.
27. Walker, 'How Borneo Was Won', p. 387.
28. Interview with General (retired) Gareth Johnson, Gurkha company commander during Confrontation, 2 July 2004.
29. Interview with the late Lt. Col. (retired) John Woodhouse, commander of 22 SAS during the Indonesian Confrontation, 7 January 2005.

30. Walker, *Fighting On*, p. 148.
31. Pockock, *Fighting General*, p. 196–7.
32. Note from Secretary of Defence to the Prime Minister, 2 November 1964, PRO: FO371/176484, IM1192/25–7.
33. Major General George Lea quoted in Peter Dickens, *SAS: The Jungle Frontier: 22 Special Air Service in the Borneo Campaign 1963–66* (London: Arms and Armour Press, 1983), p. 194.
34. Interview with Brigadier (retired) Christopher Bullock.
35. Records of the 10ᵗʰ Gurkha Rifles, Gurkha Museum, Winchester.
36. Records of the 2ⁿᵈ Gurkha Rifles, Gurkha Museum, Winchester.
37. Christopher Bullock, *Journeys Hazardous: Gurkha Clandestine Operations in Borneo 1965* (Eastbourne: Antony Rowe, 1994).
38. 2/2 Gurkha Rifles Battalion Records 1964–6, Gurkha Museum, Winchester. Sketch by Sebastian Ballard.
39. Note from Colonel N. H. N. Wild to the Foreign Office on requirements for the Indonesian Confrontation identified by the Chiefs of Staff Committee on 29 September 1964, PRO: FO371/176484, IM1192/7.
40. Note from the Chiefs of Staff Committee to the Secretary of Defence, 'Dispatch of V-Bombers to Far East', 27 November 1963, PRO: DEFE7/2374.
41. Circular paper from Peck, 23 October 1964, PRO FO 371/176484 IM 1192/20.
42. Plan 'Mason' was formerly known as plan 'Shalstone'.
43. Defence and Oversees Policy Committee minutes, 16 November 1964, PRO: FO371/176484, IM1192/37. See also letter from A. A. Golds on plans Addington and Mason dated 3 December 1964, where he details how to synchronise the political action associated with Mason: PRO: FO371/176485, IM1192/62.
44. Paper by Peck, October 1964, PRO: FO371/176484, IM1192/15, p. 8.
45. *Daily Mirror*, 9 November 1964; *The Times*, 8 November 1964.
46. Jones, *Conflict and Confrontation*, p. 246.
47. Walter Walker, 'How Borneo Was Won'.
48. Robert Osgood, *Limited War* (Chicago: University of Chicago Press, 1957).
49. Christopher Tuck, 'Borneo, Counter-Insurgency and War Termination', *Defence Studies*, vol. 10, Issue 1–2 (March–June 2010), pp. 106–25.

8. STRATEGIC NARRATIVE

1. Captain Wayne Porter, USN, and Colonel Mark Mykleby, USMC, with a Preface by Anne-Marie Slaughter, *A National Strategic Narrative* (Woodrow Wilson International Center for Scholars paper, 2011), p. 10.

2. David Kilcullen, 'Twenty-Eight Articles, Fundamentals of Company-level Counterinsurgency', *Small Wars Journal* (Edn 1, 2006), p. 7, paragraph 21.

3. Charles Farr, 'Counter Terrorism Strategy in the UK: Are We Winning?', Lecture given at the Global Strategy Forum, London, 6 July 2011.

4. I am grateful to Lt. Col. Gerald Strickland for this illustration, a version of which he presented at the Royal United Services Institute conference on Counter-Insurgency Tactics, London, 8–9 December 2010.

5. *Thirteen Days* (2000), based on the Book by Ernest R. May and Philip D. Zelikow (eds), *The Kennedy Tapes—Inside the White House During the Cuban Missile Crisis* (Cambridge, MA: Harvard University Press, 1997).

6. Clausewitz argued that the eighteenth-century emphasis on 'strategic manoeuvre' was overly dependent on the psychological component at the expense of its underlying physical reality: 'A general such as Bonaparte could ruthlessly cut through all his enemies' strategic plans in search of battle'. Clausewitz, *On War*, Book 6, ch. 8, Howard and Paret, p. 386.

7. Ibid., Book 6, ch. 3, p. 363.

8. Ibid., Book 2, ch. 2, p. 143.

9. Ibid., Book 6, ch. 29, p. 499.

10. Ibid., Book 6, ch. 30, pp. 509–10. This idea is similar that of the highly influential naval theorist, Alfred Thayer Mahan, who wrote at the turn of the nineteenth and twentieth centuries. He argued in his work on sea power that in naval warfare when opposing forces are in contact, that is 'tactical'; everything else is 'strategic'.

11. Ibid., Book 4, ch. 4, p. 232.

12. Namely Heinz Guderian and Erwin Rommel, who were following an idea that Frieser suggests was originally Erich von Manstein's.

13. Karl-Heinz Frieser, *The Blitzkrieg Legend: The 1940 Campaign in the West*, translated by John T. Greenwood (Annapolis, MD: Naval Institute Press, 2005), p. 344.

14. Karl-Heinz Frieser, *The Blitzkrieg Legend*, p. 326.

15. David Kilcullen, *The Accidental Guerrilla: Fighting Small Wars in the Midst of a Big One* (London: Hurst, 2009), pp. 299–300.

16. John Keegan, *The Face of Battle* (London: Jonathan Cape, 1976).

17. Ahmed Rashid, 'The Way Out of Afghanistan', *New York Times Review of Books*, vol. LVIII, no. 1 (January-February 2011), p. 19.

18. Clausewitz, *On War*, Book 3, ch. 17, p. 220.

19. Clausewitz, *On War*, Book 1, ch. 3, p. 104.

20. Ibid., Book 1, ch. 3, p. 119.

21. Ibid., Book 2, ch. 2, p. 137; Book 8, ch. 1, p. 578.

22. Ibid., Book 4, ch. 10, p. 254.

23. *Napoleon's Maxims of War, With Notes by General Burnod,* first published 1827, translated by Lieutenant General Sir G. C. D'Aguilar (Philadelphia: David McKay, 1902), Maxim 73.
24. Ibid., Maxim 62.
25. Ibid., Maxim 61.
26. Ibid., Maxim 60.
27. Ibid., Maxim 58.
28. Ibid., Maxim 56.
29. Clausewitz, *On War,* Book 6, ch. 30, Howard and Paret, p. 514.
30. On *geist* in Clausewitz, see Hew Strachan, *On War, A Biography,* p. 127. Peter Paret writes that in one of the manuscripts Clausewitz wrote in 1812, next to a comment on the need to understand the character of supreme command, Clausewitz had himself noted: 'Wallenstein. Schiller'. (Peter Paret, *The Cognitive Challenge of War,* p. 54. Paret cites Clausewitz, *Schriften-Aufsätze-Studien-Briefe,* ed. Werner Hahlweg (Göttingen, 1966), 1:1700.) This makes an overt connection to what Paret sees as linkages inherent in Clausewitz's works between factors that are present in war, but have justification beyond it. This is one of the themes of Friedrich von Schiller's *Wallenstein* trilogy of plays (which Schiller had started writing in 1794); one of the protagonist's quotations from this play is, for example: 'even in war, what ultimately matters is not war'; another line from the same character is: 'for if war does not already cease in war, from where should peace return?' (Peter Paret, *The Cognitive Challenge of War,* p. 53. Paret cites Schiller, *Die Piccolomini,* act 1, scene 4.) Paret emphasises the connections between Clausewitz's writings and more broadly the 'new emphasis in the arts on character, temperament and feeling', reflected in Clausewitz's works in the need 'to bring emotional factors far beyond such matters as the soldiers' discipline and morale into the structural analysis of war'. (Ibid., pp. 56–63. Paret cites, for example, linkages with Franz von Kleist's play *Prinz Friedrich von Homburg,* written between 1809 and 1811.) Clausewitz experienced war first hand and was attuned to its reception in not just political but also in cultural terms. Hence his use of contemporary cultural reference points to inform his analysis of war is paralleled by the stress in his work in locating war not just in its political context, but in its cultural context.
31. Clausewitz, *On War,* Book 8, ch. 2, p. 580.
32. Ardant Du Picq, *Etudes sur le combat: Combat antique et moderne.* Translated into English as *Battle Studies* from the 8th edn in French by John Greely and Robert C. Cotton (New York: Macmillan, 1920). Cited by Hew Strachan, keynote paper at the Oxford University Changing Character of War Programme conference on *Post-Heroic Warfare,* March 2011.

33. Anthony King, paper on 'Cohesion in the Armed Forces' at the Oxford University Changing Character of War Programme conference on *Post-Heroic Warfare*, March 2011.
34. Clausewitz, *On War*, Book 1, ch. 3, p. 112.
35. Ibid., Book 1, ch. 3, p. 105. See also Book 3, ch. 16, p. 217.
36. Ibid., Book 1, ch. 1, p. 81.
37. Bernard Bailyn, quoted in Gordon S. Wood, 'No Thanks for the Memories', a review of *The Whites of Their Eyes* by Jill Lepore, *New York Times Review of Books*, vol. LVIII, no. 1 (January-February 2011), p. 42.
38. General Anthis served in Vietnam 1961–4. It is somewhat ironic in retrospect that he was the first recipient of the US Air Force Association's Citation of Honor Award for outstanding work in counter-insurgency in South East Asia.
39. Neil Sheehan, *Bright Shining Lie*, p. 541.
40. The exact number is not clear; this is *Time Magazine's* figure.
41. Colonel Harry G. Summers, Jr. Hamburger Hill proved to be the telling battle of the Vietnam War, as Pork Chop Hill was for the Korean War. *Vietnam Magazine*, June 1999. See also Neil Sheehan, *Bright Shining Lie*, p. 742; and 'The Battle for Hamburger Hill', *Time Magazine*, 30 May 1969.
42. Neil Sheehan, *Bright Shining Lie*, p. 742.
43. Clausewitz, *On War*, Book 1, ch. 5, p. 116.
44. See Brendan Simms and D. J. B. Trim (ed.), *Humanitarian Intervention: A History* (Cambridge: Cambridge University Press, 2011).
45. Clausewitz's style in 1812 was not that of the more mature author of *On War*, started in 1816, and still unfinished by 1830. Hew Strachan argues that Clausewitz most clearly subscribed to an 'existential' view of war in the years 1809–12. His later views, which we find in *On War*, are far more balanced and incorporate the idea of 'instrumental' war. The two forms are reconciled by a broad definition of policy. Clausewitz, *Historical and Political Writings*, edited and translated by Peter Paret and Daniel Moran (Princeton: Princeton University Press, 1992), p. 290. In Hew Strachan, *Clausewitz's On War, A Biography*, pp. 53–4.
46. Clausewitz, *On War*, Book 5, ch. 16, p. 345; Book 6, ch. 3, p. 365; Book 6, ch. 6, p. 373.
47. Hew Strachan in his biography of *On War* argues that even Clausewitz's treatment of insurrections is framed in terms of an extension of state on state warfare, where the people continue the state struggle through unconventional means. As a Prussian officer, Clausewitz drew up contingency plans in 1811 for a possible insurrection in Silesia against France. He argued that not just Prussia but the German nation should rise up. Hew Strachan, *Clausewitz's On War, A Biography*, p. 182.

48. Clausewitz, *On War*, Book 2, ch. 2, p. 138.
49. The term 'ally' also has an emotional implication. It comes from the Latin *alligare* (to bind to); in medieval English 'ally' was used as a verb to mean 'to join in marriage' (late thirteenth century), and subsequently as a noun to mean 'relative' or 'kinsman' (late fourteenth century).
50. Peter Paret notes that even in 1806, at the time of Clausewitz's experiences of warfare, despite the emergence of ideas of the 'German Nation', there were widely different political reactions to the Prussian defeat at Jena by the other German states and principalities. Some felt admiration for French reforms, which Paret argues was not inconsistent with broader German patriotism. Peter Paret, *The Cognitive Challenge of War*, p. 38.
51. Erich Maria Remarque, *All Quiet on the Western Front*, originally published in *Vossische Zeitung* (1929), translated by A. H. Wheen (London: Putnam, 1930).
52. Ibid., p. 287.
53. Ibid., pp. 222–3.
54. 'Afghanistan bombing kills 13 in busy Helmand market', BBC News Online, 31 March 2010. http://news.bbc.co.uk/1/hi/8596312.stm

9. ETHOS, VISION AND CONFIDENCE IN STRATEGIC NARRATIVE

1. Quoted in Hew Strachan, 'The Lost Meaning of Strategy', *Survival* 47:3, 33–54 (2005), pp. 33–4.
2. I am grateful to Ian Gordon for this expression. He is a former Gurkha officer who himself uses this expression in relation to his experience of the Dhofar War of the 1970s.
3. Clausewitz, *On War*, Book 1, ch. 1, Howard and Paret, p. 80.
4. Brendan Simms, *Unfinest Hour: Britain and the Destruction of Bosnia* (London: Penguin, 2002).
5. General Graeme Lamb, 'Counter-insurgency Commander's Guidance' (British Army internal unclassified publication, May 2009).
6. Andrew Ross Sorkin, *Too Big to Fail* (Allen Lane, 2009) p. 432.
7. Ibid., p. 223.
8. Northern Helmand used to be called Zamindabar. The province of Helmand was only created in 1960 and was called Gereshk Province from 1960–64 when the provincial capital moved to Lashkar Gah. See Mike Martin, *A Brief History of Helmand* (British Army publication, 2011).
9. Mike Martin, *A Brief History of Helmand*, p. 72. Martin cites Professor Habibullah Rafi, Kabul University, quoted in Tom Coghlan, 'The Taliban in Helmand: An Oral History', in Antonio Giustozzi (ed.), *Decoding the*

Taliban, p. 125, 129; S. Gordon, *Aid and Stabilisation: Helmand Case Study*, Royal Institute of International Affairs, p. 52.

10. This was an idea formally put forward by R. G. Collingwood in *The Idea of History* (1946), although the actual phrase was coined by E. H. Carr, *What is History?* (1960).

11. See for example Jill Lepore, *The Whites of Their Eyes, The Tea Party's Revolution and the Battle over American History* (Princeton: Princeton University Press, 2010).

12. Leo Tolstoy *War and Peace* (1869), trans. Louise Maude, Aylmer Maude (Oxford: Oxford University Press, 2010), Book 3, ch.1, p. 650. Tolstoy's theory of history is fully expounded in the second epilogue of *War and Peace*.

13. Harry S. Truman, 'Inaugural Address', 20 January 1949, *Public Papers of the Presidents* (1949), pp. 114–15.

14. 'Point IV', *Fortune*, February 1950, p. 88.

15. Cullather cites Jawaharlal Nehru, *The Discovery of India* (New York: Doubleday, 1960), p. 393.

16. Nick Cullather, *From New Deal to New Frontier in Afghanistan: Modernization in a Buffer State*, Working Paper #6 (August 2002), 'The Cold War as Global Conflict', International Center for Advanced Studies, New York University, p. 3.

17. See for example Antonio Giustozzi, *War, Politics and Society in Afghanistan 1978–1992* (London: Hurst, 2000), especially ch. 13 on 'National Reconciliation', pp. 154–85.

18. These observations came from discussions with my father, James Simpson, the author of *Burning to Read, English Fundamentalism and its Reformation Opponents* (Cambridge, MA: Harvard Belknap Press, 2007), p. 247.

19. Ibid., p. 247.

20. On the role of rumors in Afghan politics see for example Antonio Giustozzi, 'The "Great Fears" of Afghanistan: How Wild Ideas Shape Politics', *Ideas Today*, issue 04.10, London School of Economics and Political Science (June 2010), pp. 9–13.

21. BBC Radio 4, Political Hour, 28 June 2009.

22. James Simpson, *Burning to Read*, p. 178.

23. This interpretation follows Saint Paul (2 Corinthians 3:3) which might be taken to suppose that the true text of the literal sense is written 'in the fleshly tables of the heart'. There is a much wider theological debate over this which this Book is not concerned with.

24. Lord Denning in *Magor and St Mellon RDC* v. *Newport Corpn* [1950] 2 All ER 1226 at 1236, CA. Cited in Ian Loveland, *Constitutional Law, Admin-*

NOTES pp. [228–242]

istrative Law, and Human Rights: A Critical Introduction, 5ᵗʰ edition (Oxford: Oxford University Press, 2009), p. 69.

25. General Sir Graeme Lamb in House of Commons Defence Committee, Fourth Report, Operations in Afghanistan, 17 July 2011, p. Ev 66, Q 288.

CONCLUSION: CONTEMPORARY STRATEGIC THOUGHT

1. Clausewitz, *On War*, Book 6, ch. 30, Howard and Paret, p. 515.
2. President G. W. Bush, address to a joint session of Congress, 20 September 2001.
3. Ian Traynor, 'Russia accused of unleashing cyberwar to disable Estonia', *Guardian*, 17 May 2007.
4. Although even the practice of capturing people in the Afghan conflict illustrates the differences with conventional war, since detainees are not prisoners of war, and so have to be prosecuted by the Afghan justice system. The notion of routinely gathering 'evidence' against enemy soldiers is alien to conventional war.
5. This doctrine was consciously Clausewitzian. See Hew Strachan, 'Strategy and the Limitation of War', *Survival*, vol. 50, no. 1, Feb.-March 2008, p. 50.
6. Additional Protocol I to the Geneva Conventions 1949, Article 52.2, states that: 'Attacks shall be limited strictly to military objectives. In so far as objects are concerned, military objectives are limited to those objects which by their nature, location, purpose or use make an effective contribution to military action and whose total or partial destruction, capture or neutralization, in the circumstances ruling at the time, offers a definite military advantage'.
7. Jack L. Snyder, *The Soviet Strategic Culture: Implications for Limited Nuclear Operations*, Report for the United States Air Force R-2154-AF (Santa Monica, CA: RAND, 1977).
8. The Network of Concerned Anthropologists, *The Counter-Counterinsurgency Manual* (Chicago: University of Chicago Press, 2009).
9. Clausewitz, *On War*, Book 1, ch. 1, Howard and Paret, p. 77.
10. Ibid., Book 3, ch. 16, p. 217.
11. Ibid., Book 8, ch. 2, p. 579.
12. Ibid., Book 1, ch. 1, p. 76.
13. Ibid., Book 1, ch. 1, p. 89.
14. Ibid., Book 1, ch. 1, p. 86.
15. See Daniel Moran, *Strategic Theory and the History of War*, p. 4. He cites, for example, Jeremy Bentham, *A Plan for Universal and Perpetual Peace* (London, 1789).

271

16. Daniel Moran, *Strategic Theory and the History of War*, p. 4.

17. Clausewitz, *On War*, Book 1, ch. 1, p. 80.

18. HM Government, 'A Strong Britain in an Age of Uncertainty: The National Security Strategy' (London: Stationery Office, October 2010), p. 15.

19. Nicholas Watt, 'Senior military figures tell Liam Fox: "rescrub" your defence review', *Guardian Online*, 13 June 2011.

20. The report is clear that the UK had at that point strategically lost its way: 'this leads us to the profoundly disturbing conclusion that an understanding of National Strategy and an appreciation of why it is important has indeed largely been lost'. Public Administration Committee, 'First Report: Who does UK National Strategy?' Published 12 October 2010, ch. 4, paragraphs 32, 39, 40.

INDEX

INDEX

First World War (1914–18): 33–4, 58–9, 138, 198, 211; Battle of Verdun (1916), 199; belligerents of, 127, 137; Nivelle Offensive (1917), 199; US Declaration of War on Germany (1917), 208

France: 127; Châlons, 64; École spéciale militaire de Saint-Cyr, 113; military of, 195, 199, 202; Paris Commune, 227; Revolution, 64, 74, 193, 228

franchise movement, concept of enemy as: see 'enemy'

Franco-Prussian War (1870–1): 59; Siege of Paris (1870–1), 112

Franks, General Tommy: 141

Frieser, Karl-Heinz: 186–7; *The Blitzkrieg Legend: The 1940 Campaign in the West* (2005), 137

Geneva Conference (1955): 158

Gentile, Colonel Gian P.: 144–6, 148, 155

Germany: 32, 58–9, 172; colonies of, 33; military of, 137, 145, 186, 197–8, 202

Ghimire, Rifleman Man Bahadur: 189–90

Giustozzi, Antonio: 'Armed Politics and Political Competition in Afghanistan' (2011), 80; concept of 'armed politics', 102; *Koran, Kalashnikov and Laptop: The New-Taliban Insurgency in Afghanistan 2002–2007* (2008), 48

Glatzer, Bernt: 78

globalisation/role of information: 6–7, 12, 67–75, 88–9, 126, 173–74, 177, 205–6, 208, 218–226, 228, 232, 236, 243

Gurkhas: see 'United Kingdom'

Gurung, Sergeant Bel: 19–20, 216

Gurung, Rifleman Bom Bahadur: 190

Gurung, Sergeant Govinda: 212

Haddick, Robert: 9

Hadrian: 59

Halutz, General Dan: Israeli Defence Force Chief, 71

Hannibal: defeat at Battle of Zama (202 BCE), 132

Haqqani Network: 52, 75

Harold, King: defeat of (1066), 27

Healey, Denis: British Secretary of State for Defence, 158, 169, 176

Hekmatyar, Gulbudin: 52, 80

Helmand Valley Development Project: aims of, 217

Herberg-Rothe, Andreas: 133

Hezbollah: 69–71

Hizb-i-Islami Gulbuddin (HiG): 52, 75 80, 82

Ho Chi Minh: 103

Holloway, Adam MP: 79, 125

Huntington, Samuel: conception of civil-military relations, 121; *The Soldier and the State* (1957), 112–15, 121

Hussein, Saddam: 71–2, 211

Hybrid war: 10

Imperialism: Japanese, 33

India: military of, 166

Indonesia: 158, 162, 170, 175; Bali, 173; government of, 163; Jakarta, 159–60; military of, 159, 163, 165, 168–70, 176; Sumatra, 173; War of Independence (1945–9), 161

Indonesian Confrontation: see 'Borneo Confrontation'

Office, 43, 172–3; government of, 42, 125, 158, 161, 163–4, 167, 174, 221; Gurkha Welfare Scheme, 221; House of Commons, 158; House of Commons Defence Select Committee, 101; House of Commons Foreign Affairs Committee Report (2011), 51–2; Labour Party, 242; London, 182, 208; military of, 2, 41–2, 46, 48–9, 52–3, 71, 108, 122, 126, 136–7, 143, 148, 153, 159, 162, 165, 167, 175, 225; Mercian Regiment, 76; Ministry of Defence, 171; National Security Strategy (2010), 241–2; navy of, 173; Parachute Regiment, 43, 169; Parliament, 43, 51, 122, 225, 242; parliamentary expenses scandal (2009), 222–3; Royal Air Force (RAF), 173; Sandhurst Military Academy, 17, 136–7; Special Air Service (SAS), 151; Strategic Defence Review, 242
United Nations (UN): 38, 159, 162–3; Charter, 173; Security Council, 173
United States Army War College: faculty of, 140
United States of America (USA): 10, 99, 145, 159–60, 163–4, 181; 9/11 attacks, 229, 242; Air Force, 199; Civil War (1861–5), 59; Congress, 229; Democratic Party, 100; Federal Reserve, 213; government of, 146, 213; Marine Corps, 103, 125, 138, 181; Military Academy at West Point, 113; military of, 15, 36–7, 47, 63, 113–14, 144, 146, 200, 234; National Security Council, 123;

navy of, 94, 181; Pentagon, 141; Republican Party, 100; Tea Party, 214; *US Army and Marine Corps Counter-Insurgency Field Manual*, 144; use of drone strikes by, 3; War Department, 114
use of force: absolute/total war, in relation to limited war, 12, 36, 39, 54–56, 64–66, 133, 176–77, 231; armed political activity/politicisation of conflict, 1, 4–10–13, 23, 42, 66–75, 77–79, 84–89, 91–129, 107, 134, 137, 144, 147, 213, 229–32, 236–38, 243–44; a-symmetry in conflict, 37–39; decisiveness in conflict, 2–4, 10–11, 14, 23–24, 34–39, 41, 54–75, 84–89, 92–7, 99–101, 113–15, 132–34, 138, 140, 207, 210, 213, 218–19, 232, 235–38; domestic politics, analogy with, 4, 75, 97–101, 214, 232–33; grammar/explosive expansion of war, 126–29, 238; interpretive concept of war/mechanism of war, 9, 14, 15–39, 54–66, 68–75, 84–89, 99–102, 177, 189–197, 207, 210–13, 220, 229–32; kinetic (violent) and non-kinetic (non-violent) means, 2, 6–8, 28, 71–73, 102, 153–55, 231; measures of effect, 139–40; military domain, 1, 3–4, 8–9, 12, 15, 21, 23, 31–39, 55–56, 63–66, 68–75, 84, 91–7, 99–101, 111–15, 131–32, 134–44, 160–61, 190, 200, 228–32, 235; polarity, see 'enemy'; sequential/cumulative campaigns, 2, 94, 98, 113–15, 128, 233; 'sides', concept of, see 'enemy';